Understanding The Rescue Dog

All you need to know about rehoming a dog with a past

Carol Price

Illustrations by Drew Marland

© 2001 Carol Price

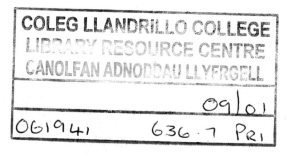

Published by
Broadcast Books
4 Cotham Vale
Bristol BS6 6HR
Catherine@broadcast books.demon.co.uk
0117 9732010 fax 9044830

Illustrations © 2001 Drew Marland
6 Belvedere Rd Bristol BS6 7JG

Cover Photograph by Warren Photographic

Cover Design by Sally Mundy and David Gould
Book Design David Gould

Printed in the U.K. by Bath Press Limited, Bath

Dedication

This book is dedicated to all the unique people involved in canine rescue and to everyone who strives to make the world a better place for dogs. It is also dedicated to my beloved Border collie, Ilona, who would only sulk otherwise.

Biography

Carol Price is a canine behaviourist specialising in rescue dogs and the Border Collie breed and is also a well-known journalist writing regularly on animal subjects for, among others, **The Times**, **Dogs Today** and **Your Dog**. She is, additionally, a member of the UK Registry of Canine Behaviourists and author of the best-seller, **Understanding the Border Collie**, also published by Broadcast Books.

Carol's main professional aim, she says, "has always been to explain dogs better to people, in a practical, accessible and 'non-psychobabbly' way. Because only once owners can really understand why dogs are what they are and behave as they do, will you start to see their relationships start to improve with them no end."

Carol Price with Ilona
(Reproduced with kind permission of **Your Dog Magazine**)

Acknowledgments

In writing this book I would particularly like to thank Clarissa Baldwin, Erik Mitchell and Tony Brenton of the National Canine Defence League for their support and also Pat White of the UK Registry of Canine Behaviourists for going over it, at proof stage, with such an expert eye. I would also like to thank all the rescue dogs and their owners, over the years, who have taught me so much of value, and of help to others. Most of all I would like to thank every person who has ever taken the step to give an unwanted dog a new and better life. Dogs can't tell you what a difference you make to so many of their otherwise uncertain destinies, every day of every week of every year. But I can.

CONTENTS

Introduction

*The World of Rescue Dogs - And The Realities of
Living With A Dog With A Past*

In an ideal world, there would be no such thing as a 'rescue dog'. People would not get dogs and then discard them, for whatever reason, just as they would not abuse them, neglect them, nor allow them to breed indiscriminately, with no thought given to the welfare of any future offspring. They would see dog ownership as a life-long commitment.

If you are reading this book, then the chances are you know already that real life is very different. You'll know that because people can't, or won't, always do what they should do for dogs, many of them will suffer or will be seeking new homes each year. And those put up for rehoming are actually the 'luckier' ones. This is because as many as 50,000 stray or unwanted dogs in the UK now can be annually destroyed, either because they are working animals - e.g. sheepdogs, greyhounds - who have outlived their usefulness for owners, or because new homes or rescue places cannot be found for them. Either way, they never get the opportunity to start a new or better life.

Maybe you have decided that you want to give a rescue dog a 'second chance' and a better future, and will possibly have visited centres or shelters run by any one of the numerous canine rescue agencies nationwide, big or small. Or perhaps you have taken on a stray, or a dog passed on by former owners, and want to know how best to 'rehabilitate' it within your home. Whatever the circumstances of your rescue dog's past, this book aims to help you every inch of the way.

From choosing your rescue dog, dealing with - or anticipating - any 'problems' that might arise with it, to building up a rewarding and successful long-term relationship with it, we will give you the best possible advice and highlight the most common mistakes. This is because it can be easy for people not to know what they should know about rescue dogs when it matters. There can be a lot to learn in a short period of time, and when you most need advice, there isn't always the correct person around to give it.

The truth about rescue dogs

The media, and others, can often portray rescuing dogs in a rather sentimental or 'rose-tinted' light. It's understandable. Dogs can and do arouse strong emotional reactions in us all, especially when they have suffered and then found salvation in new loving homes.

Similarly, we constantly hear today about the 'popularity' of rescue dogs as a 'first choice' of pet, and how the large numbers of them now being rehomed annually represents the growth of a new, more 'caring' culture towards dogs within society. In truth, it can equally represent a 'culture' of canine abandonment that has remained much the same. This is because you only have thousands of new dogs to rehome each year because thousands of former owners didn't want them.

So more practically we could ask ourselves, who *are* all these 'former owners', and why did so many of them take the step to discard or ill-treat their dogs? These are the people who have forced the whole animal rescue 'business' to exist and yet our curiosity about them, or inclination to more seriously challenge their attitudes, seems to remain so low.

Undoubtedly there are many people who will only relinquish their dogs with great reluctance, or because their circumstances - or the nature of the dog itself - have given them little other choice. In other cases, however, it appears that people truly believe they have a 'right' to acquire and dispose of such dependent animals with little sense of responsibility or commitment. And as long as attitudes like this are allowed to prevail, we cannot make the world a better place for dogs.

Dogs with a past

People will routinely wonder why rescue dogs, during early days in new homes, can have 'problems' or will simply not behave like their idea of an 'ordinary' dog. And this is because very often they will not have had 'ordinary' pasts, of a kind destined to give them a secure and trusting view of the world. Or because no one had the inclination, the time or the knowledge to teach them more 'acceptable' ways to behave. Or maybe because they simply are highly challenging or 'testing' dogs by nature, and 'difficult' personalities can exist in the canine world as readily as they can in the human one. When we take on a dog with a past, we do something very special. We decide to make a difference to an animal's life and have the power to change its future forever. But we cannot always know in advance what 'psychological baggage' it might bring with it from a former life, or how its past could affect its future - at least initially - with us.

When looking for, or living with, a rescue dog, it also has to be realised that **no two rescue dogs will ever be the same**. Dogs, like us, will vary in character or behaviour as much as in looks, due to a wealth of different factors - both genetic and environmental - which have 'shaped' them individually, and made them what they are.

Greater understanding

Because all these considerations are so vital for new owners to understand, this book is going to look in depth at how the mind of a rescue dog often works; the influences or background that can make it think or act the way it does, and why so often its behaviour might be at odds with your own expectations, especially during your earliest weeks or months with it in a new home.

Hopefully it will also make you realise how much dogs, like us, get mentally affected by what they have been exposed to in early life, as well as outline how often a dog perceived to be 'bad', 'mad' or 'difficult' can simply be showing symptoms of stress, anxiety, insecurity or fear.

So often when 'problems' do arise with dogs - be they rescued or otherwise - then it's because we cannot accurately read or interpret what is going on in their minds. We can easily see what makes them like us, as social animals, but find it harder to grasp what also makes them so very different. When we understand more about the way dogs think, what motivates them, pleases them, makes them happy or unhappy, well-balanced or insecure, then we have the insights and 'tools' for a vastly improved relationship with them - as I hope this book will show in later chapters.

About the book

In writing this book, I am assuming that you are someone who cares deeply about dogs but would like to know or learn far more about canine behaviour, in terms of how you should generally handle, train - or in the case of puppies - raise your rescue dog most successfully. And, as well as knowing how to best approach or deal with any problems that might arise, you might also want advice on what dogs might demand or require during different stages, or phases, of their lives. So whole chapters are dedicated to all these subjects.

Throughout this book, the aim is to give advice to you in the most straightforward and realistic way. And if regularly dog behaviour is compared to human behaviour - which I know many behaviourists, quite rightly, tend to frown upon - it is not because it has been forgotten how different these two species remain from each other in many ways, but because such comparisons can, where applicable, make dog behaviour that much easier for most people to understand, or relate to.

Similarly, it is understood that people, just like dogs, cannot always be expected to do the right thing a hundred per cent of the time and there may be occasions when you could feel worried, stressed or anxious yourself about the demands of the new responsibility you have taken on. You should know that this is normal, certainly during the early weeks or months of rehoming a dog. At such times you may be needing additional advice, help or reassurance, and this book will tell you how to find it.

Expectations and rewards

Too often, as previously touched on, the impression can get conveyed that rescuing and successfully rehoming any dog will be a relatively easy or 'pain-free' process. And while many rescue dogs may settle in immediately, and never give you a day's grief in their lives, others can be a lot more challenging, for a variety of different reasons.

As also already highlighted, not all dogs are up for rescue simply because they are unwanted, or suddenly rendered homeless, but also because their behaviour or character might have been too demanding for previous owners to deal with. This book will explain what might be involved in taking on such dogs, in order for you to realistically assess whether or not you could be up to the task.

Through a lengthy interest in rescue dogs, and through experiencing personally what it can be like to rehabilitate a dog with a very troubled past within a new home, I have learned many things. And mostly what I have learned is that rescuing dogs is never all a one-way process. It can be as much about what dogs can do for people as what people can do for dogs.

Many people become better people through rescuing dogs. Not only are their lives richer for the companionship a dog brings, but the efforts they can often put into regaining a troubled animal's trust teaches them many valuable lessons about patience, persistence and compassion. Rarely do such efforts go unrewarded, and the bonds people form with their rescue dogs as a result can be quite exceptional.

The world may still be full of rescue dogs, but it is also full of a lot of people who care enough to want to make a difference to their lives, and do. Every day in life, dogs stripped of much hope or trust in humankind will find owners prepared to give these things back to them. Usually, in terms of what such owners do for dogs, and can achieve, they are very special people without realising it. Maybe you are going to be one of them, or already are.

An honest picture

From the start, my objective in writing this book was to give people as truthful and honest a picture possible of what rescuing and rehoming a dog, successfully, might involve. In other words, I wanted to cover all the possible 'lows' as well as well as 'highs'. In aiming to cover potential 'problems' with rescue dogs in such explicit detail, however, I did hear fears expressed that this could 'put too many people off the idea'.

While respecting such fears, my own feelings are that most new rescue dog owners, if given the chance, would prefer to be better informed about what could lie ahead and how to deal with it. And certainly, you cannot easily deal with problems that you are unequipped to either predict or understand.

I also know of so many people who thought that their rescue dogs were 'abnormal', or felt 'failures' themselves, simply as a result of what they did not know, or could not foresee. And I have often wondered how much easier, or less traumatic, early days for new owners and dogs alike might have been with the benefits of better insights, and knowledge.

At the end of the day, none of us is born knowing the best way to handle dogs or live with them successfully. These are things we have to learn. And as we learn, as I hope this book illustrates, we can discover that dogs aren't really as big a 'mystery' as we might have previously thought. If we frighten them, threaten them, make them anxious or insecure, there will be some fairly predictable negative results - just as there will be more positive ones once we have re-established a sense of trust, security and order in their lives.

Ultimately if this book gives just one owner the opportunity to have a far richer and happier relationship with their rescue dog, due to greater enlightenment and understanding, it will have been worth it.

Chapter One

Why Do You Want A Rescue Dog? Important
Things To Ask Yourself Before You Get One

Before you even start the trek to rehoming centres or organisations, it's best to get some practical considerations about rescue dogs sorted out in your mind. This is because the emotionally charged atmosphere of many rescue places can make it hard to think clearly or realistically. Faced with all those needy faces and wagging tails, it can be very easy to act on impulse and choose a dog that, while incredibly appealing, could be completely wrong for you or your family. Long-term this does nobody any favours - least of all the dog who might later have to be returned.

Many good rescue centres today are aware that visitors can be over-impulsive or unrealistic in their initial choice of dog, even if with the best of intentions, and for this reason do their best to engineer a more suitable match. You, however, can help them greatly in this task by weighing up the following questions and considerations in advance. Starting with:

1. Why do I want a rescue dog?

- **You might think that this is an incredibly straightforward question,** but it is not. The truth is, people want rescue dogs for a wide variety of reasons, but not all of them are the right ones. 'Feeling sorry' for a dog, for instance, is not a good enough reason for taking it on unless your sympathy can be backed up with the practical day-to-day care it will require.

- **It's also a bad idea to get any dog as a 'present'** to keep a partner or 'the children' happy, without full thought given to the realities of its future needs. Dogs require levels of consistent care, responsibility and commitment which not all partners or children are ready for, long-term - however much they might like the initial 'idea' of dog ownership. Everybody within a household has to be happy about taking on the commitment of a new dog. This apart, dogs were not put on this earth to be 'presents' or 'playthings' for the human race, and have a right to be treated with far greater dignity and respect.

• **All animals require us to make sacrifices in some way,** adapting our time, and often lifestyles, to properly meet their needs. If we cannot give dogs what they need then we cannot make them happy. If we cannot make them happy then we will have achieved nothing in 'rescuing' them.

• **Over and above general day-to-day care,** some rescue dogs might take additional effort, time and patience to properly settle into their new life with you. If you already have a lot of existing stresses, pressures or demands in your life, such dogs might prove to be one burden too many. And one you certainly aren't ready for yet.

• **Some people might want a rescue dog to keep another existing dog at home 'company'.** This can work out well, but greatly depends on the choice of dog you make (see next chapter, **'Why dogs do and don't get on'**). Not all dogs - as highlighted later - can be guaranteed to 'get on', and by choosing the wrong 'new' dog you could end up creating no small amount of friction and / or upset.

• **Maybe you want a rescue dog to replace another beloved rescue one who has died.** Often, when people lose a dog, they want to get another that reminds them of it, then get disappointed when it turns out to be very different - in terms of character and behaviour, if not looks. It is normal for all dogs to be different, whether rescued or not. If you find it hard to accept how different a new dog might be from the one you have lost, then it might be better to wait a while longer before getting it. Also remember how long it took before your past dog settled into your general routines and ways. It took time before it could become so 'special' to you - and your new dog will be the same.

• **Perhaps you think a rescue dog will be 'less work' than a puppy** (and note - are covered puppies in Chapter four). Puppies can certainly be very demanding and lots of older rescue dogs, in particular, could give you a quieter life. Rescue dogs, however, come with no guarantees as to how easy or difficult they might be during their early weeks or months with you. Some may be highly stressed or traumatised from their past background, leading to other problems with toilet training, say, or destructiveness, which will require some patience and / or good 'forward planning'. Others may never have had the benefit of any proper training, from puppyhood, to teach them right from wrong, or basic commands and manners around the home. So you may need to start such training, and the laying down of 'house rules' from scratch. The bottom line is that all dogs - whether puppies or adults - don't come into your home knowing what they should or shouldn't do or how they should behave. They have to be taught. For those who may be harder work to teach than others, you will need a lot of patience and perseverance.

2. Can I Manage A Rescue Dog's Needs?

• **A dog's needs will vary according to its age, background, breed and individual character.**

Some dogs will require more grooming or exercise than others, for instance, and younger dogs will obviously need more physical and mental stimulation than older ones. For far more details on all these considerations, see Chapters four and nine.

• **Additionally, the way a dog needs to be trained and handled** to get the best out of it, and keep it relatively problem-free, has to be tailored to its individual personality / character. Timid or nervous dogs, for instance, will benefit most from gentle and patient handling, designed to boost their confidence, whereas 'pushier' dogs with more forceful characters will need a much firmer approach. If you are not a fairly strong personality yourself, or find it hard to sustain endless patience without getting aggravated or frustrated, this will naturally influence how well, or not, you might get on with these different types of dog. There will be much more on this whole subject later in the book.

• **On a basic level, most dogs will need the following:** First, regular daily walks. Some owners can view these as a 'chore', but the point of daily walking your dog is not just to give it exercise and keep it healthy, physically. Daily outings will also help to improve its 'social skills', and its ability to happily adapt to a wide range of other people / dogs or novel experiences without fear or aggression. The stimulating variety of new sights, sounds, smells etc. a dog experiences when out on a walk contributes greatly to its mental well-being, and the fun you share with it strengthens its bond with you. Is it going to be practical for you to give your dog - ideally - two good walks every day (obviously tailored to age and breed), even when you're tired or it's belting down with rain outside? If not, would this really be fair to any dog you took on? Walks are usually the greatest highlights of any dog's day, and they do owners a lot of good, too.

• **Your dog will also need practical things like - as a legal requirement - some proper form of identification.** This can be in the form of a collar tag or a microchip inserted by your vet. Additionally it will require its own bed or 'den' area, a healthy balanced diet (more details later), access to good local veterinary care - as well as health insurance, if required - and regular episodes of 'quality time'. By 'quality time', I mean routine periods set aside when you will train your dog - either in a local class or, at least initially, at home - groom it, play with it and generally give it some enjoyable attention. Gradually, this will establish its trust and confidence in you - which in turn will pay great dividends later on when you want its cooperation (see Chapter six on building relationships and training). Be aware, too, of the duty you have to always clean up after your dog when out - especially in public places.

• **If you decide to take on any dog, and especially one with a tendency to 'wander',** then your garden will have to be as near escape - proof as you can make it. And if you don't have a garden then you might just find this limiting your choice of dog pretty drastically. Many centres / organisations might not let their dogs go to homes without gardens as a point of policy.

- **Nobody can be with a dog every hour of the day, seven days a week.** If there's ever a family crisis, or you need to go away - either on holiday or in an emergency - you'll need to arrange for other people or another person, preferably nearby, to look after your dog during this time. Do you know of such a person, or - if not - some reputable local kennels where your dog could stay for a short while if necessary? Good kennels never mind if you turn up one day for a 'tour' and ask lots of questions.

- **If you have never owned a dog before, or not owned a young one for a long time,** it can be easy to overlook their potential for mess-making and general mayhem, if only because they know no better. Dogs can't exactly grasp the principle of being 'house-proud', or which items - including mud and sticks - are best left outdoors. When they wag their tails because they are pleased to see you, they tend not to predict that this is going to clear half the ornaments off the coffee table behind them as a result. Most dogs shed hair, and some dogs shed lots of hair very often. Or chew the furniture or dig holes in the garden until taught otherwise. This is all just what dogs do because they are dogs. There are many ways - outlined later - to minimise the mayhem they can cause, if so inclined. I know countless people who thought their most important priority in life was an immaculate house and garden. Then suddenly they got a home with a dog in it - and decided they would rather have that instead.

- **If you're still not sure about what a rescue dog might involve, in terms of time, effort and expense,** as well as possible alterations to your daily lifestyle, talk to other people who have successfully rehomed dogs and ask them as many useful questions as you can. Most rescue centres / agencies could put you in touch with past clients - with their permission - who could tell you what the realities of taking on a rescue dog really are. Though still remember that no two rescue dogs will ever be exactly the same.

3. If Things Don't Work Out With My Rescue Dog Can I Take It Back?

- **Most people - hopefully - don't see rescue dogs as little more than goods in shops;** in other words, items you can always take back the moment they strike you as 'faulty' or do not immediately meet your expectations. They appreciate that an insecure or frightened animal arrives in a new home with needs of its own. It will require time and patience to readjust to different owners and a completely new lifestyle and living environment, and while this adjustment is occurring its behaviour can't always be expected to be 'perfect'.

- **The more thought, consideration and research you put into getting and choosing a rescue dog,** before you actually get it, then obviously the fewer the ' surprises' occurring later, once you get it home.

- **Taking a rescue dog back to a centre because things haven't 'worked out' can be very**

traumatic for owners and dogs alike. It is not something you would want to do, or would want to put a dog through, if you could possibly avoid it. This is why good rescue centres work so hard, initially, to match the right dogs to the right owners, or why you'll hear so many people saying that it's harder to get a rescue dog than a puppy. It needs to be. You'd only think otherwise if you didn't appreciate how many puppies that were too easily acquired later ended up in rescue centres. Dogs do not fare well as 'recyclable goods'. There's a limit to how often they can be shoved back and forth between short-lived homes before incurring psychological harm.

• **This being said, however, a fair percentage of rescue dog rehomings fail for reasons that can't always be foreseen.** It isn't necessarily the fault of new owners, or dogs. It's just that they can prove, in time, to be ill-suited to each other, even with much work put in by owners. Or maybe an owner's circumstances suddenly change, affecting his or her new dog, or the new dog doesn't get on with existing pets. Good rescue centres will always take dogs back, whatever the reason for their return.

This chapter has covered a lot of considerations you may need to think about, or discuss with a partner or your family, prior to getting a rescue dog. The purpose of this is to prepare you for what might be involved when you take on a dog with a past - or even a dog, full stop, if you have never had one before. If you have thought about them all fully, and still feel ready to take on a rescue dog, then read on. The next chapter will look at finding and choosing one.

Bit by bit, as you go through this book, you will see that taking on a rescue dog, and successfully rehoming it, involves one long journey. A journey of enlightenment, discovery and readjustment for all concerned - and with its fair share of 'fallings-out' and 'makings-up' along the way. Just like any growing relationship, in fact.

The day usually comes, however, when you can look back on that journey together and barely recognise the dog you first took home. This is because it is **no longer** the dog you first took home. It's a dog that has proved to be all the better for being yours.

Chapter Two

Finding And Choosing A Rescue Dog; Pedigree Or Crossbreed?
Where to Go And What To Ask; Understanding The Impact
Of 'Kennel Life' And The Truth About 'Bad Dogs'

LUCKY
DIP

Most people harbour their 'ideal image' of the rescue dog they want. Typically, it will be young, good-looking, friendly, great with children / other pets or dogs, well-trained, obedient, healthy, easy to look after, a good guard dog - but love the postman, milkman etc. - and have no 'bad' or 'annoying' habits. And maybe, when it's got a moment, it might also tackle the washing-up and do a bit of light dusting round the lounge.

Unfortunately there aren't many dogs as perfect as this anywhere in the world. And in rescue centres, particularly, 'perfection' is not a usual requirement for entry. 'Sorry, I couldn't cope with my dog anymore because it's perfect. Sounds a bit unlikely, doesn't it? It's also important to remember that dogs aren't born knowing what you expect them to be. They have to be **taught**. This in turn requires levels of patience, effort and commitment which previous owners might have lacked.

There are lots and lots of really good dogs in rescue centres, dogs with great potential in the right hands, dogs who could positively bloom with more attention and care and dogs with tremendous character and intelligence. One of the most rewarding things about rescuing a dog is that you tend to start off with something a little short of perfect, something which perhaps no one else wanted or could see the true potential of, and then you turn it into something special, with unique value to you.

Planning your search

There is nothing straightforward, however, about choosing a rescue dog. This is because often you won't know what you really want until you see it, or because the dog you might most like the look of - at least at first - will not necessarily be right for you.

As already touched upon earlier, different people - as well as different circumstances - will suit different dogs. Some dogs, for instance, may not get on well with young children. Prospective owners could, and sometimes do, view this as some sort of 'character defect' but the reality is, sadly, that such dogs can often come from former homes where children were allowed to torment or frighten them in some way, or were generally not taught to respect them. Or the dogs were never taught to respect children.

In similar vein, dogs who were not properly socialised with other dogs early enough, or in the right way, or have had bad experiences with other dogs in the past, could be more fearful or aggressive towards their peers as a result. You may feel you have the patience or determination to significantly improve such dogs. On the other hand, they may need more work, time and expert 'remedial training' than is either practical or possible for you to manage, especially if you already have another dog - or other dogs - at home.

Some breeds or breed 'types' - e.g. terriers, lurchers - may, as outlined a bit later, have stronger 'predatory instincts' than others. This means it could be more risky to rehome them with other 'prey-sized' pets like cats, rabbits, rodents or other small mammals. Although many individual dogs within these breed types can learn to live in harmony with other smaller pets be aware, when considering such a dog, that this state of affairs cannot be guaranteed.

In searching for your dog, it might help to narrow down a limited set of desired factors which are of utmost importance to you - e.g. it is male / female, isn't too big or small, won't need too much exercise, has a pretty friendly nature. The diagram below will give you a rough idea of how to list these out.

My new rescue dog

Qualities	Very Important	Quite Important	Preferable	Don't Mind
Looks / breed type				√
Sex (dog or bitch)			bitch	
Age			under 5 years	
Size			medium	
Good with Children	√			
Good with cats / other pets			√	
Easy to groom				√
Exercise needs		√		
Training needs				√
Friendly nature	√			
Good guard dog				√
Lively				√
Can be left alone a few hours		√		

Obviously different people will have different priorities, when it comes to what they are looking for in a dog. Plus, as outlined later, some things you might need to know about a dog won't necessarily be discovered until you take it home. But if you head off on a search with too lengthy, or idealistic, a list of preferred qualities you could end up being consistently disappointed. Your over-strict requirements could also make you rule out dogs that might have been ideal for you, given better consideration and study.

Also, never rule out the possibility of taking on an **older dog**, rather than being stuck on the idea of a youngster. Not only do many rescue centres / organisations now offer help with any possible veterinary bills for older dogs - should this be a chief concern - but an older dog can also be a far less demanding pet, especially if you are older or less active yourself. There are so many wonderful, yet frequently overlooked, older dogs in rescue centres who could be fabulous companions if given the chance. More on older dogs in Chapter four.

In the meantime, for what it's worth, I rescued my last dog - a Border collie - at the age of 13. She lived another three-and-a-half blissfully happy years, and turned out to be the most rewarding and exceptional canine companion I have ever owned.

Pedigree or crossbreed?

Dogs, like people, have an unfortunate tendency to be judged / desired not just according to their age, but also according to their looks. So naturally young, good-looking dogs in rescue centres will tend to be more in demand than older and / or less attractive ones. Pedigree dogs, rather than crossbreeds, may also be more in demand, simply because there tend to be far fewer of them in most general (rather than breed-specific) rescue centres. This in turn can give them the appearance of having greater 'status' or 'value'.

The way a dog looks, however, or the age it happens to be, shouldn't make you blind to other considerations that will be far more important in the long term. Not every young or good-looking dog has the kind of temperament that would best suit you or your family, for instance. And if you see a fabulous-looking dog who appears to have been brought back by new owners to a rescue centre at least twice, you'd have to ask yourself why.

In life, most of us eventually discover that people who have the best looks don't necessarily also have the best character, personality, intelligence - or just general qualities we find easiest and most pleasant to live with, long term. And it's much the same with dogs. So never rule out a dog's potential suitability for you simply on the basis of its looks Many people decide they want to rescue a certain type of pedigree dog because they've had one from the same breed before. They seem to imagine that they 'know what they will be getting'. In reality, no two dogs from the same breed will necessarily be the same in any way apart from looks.

Pedigree dogs, additionally, can be no less immune from the effects of a troubled or mismanaged past background than crossbred ones. Pedigree dogs, rather than crossbreeds, are also far more likely to have come from commercial breeding establishments, some of which have scant regard for the welfare - either short or long term - of the animals they produce for profit. We will cover the impact of these appalling places on dogs in the next chapter, but for now bear these realities in mind.

Increasingly today, there seems to be an argument put forward that crossbred dogs, in the main, tend to be healthier (see **Understanding 'genetic disorders'**, Chapter nine) more intelligent and live longer than many pedigree ones. Both types of dog will always have their fans, for different reasons. In the end, all that matters is that you end up with a dog you like, whichever type it happens to be. **If you do have a certain pedigree breed in mind, however, ensure that you research / read up all you can on its general needs and characteristics before you get it.**

Where to go

At the end of this book we will give you an extensive list of places where you might find your new rescue dog - providing you haven't found it already! Let us also not forget that many people will not get rescue dogs from the centres of specific organisations. They may find them themselves, wandering the streets, for instance - though note all stray dogs found should first be reported to the police or local dog warden - or they may inherit them from other people in any manner of ways. In such cases it can really seem that fate has 'lent a hand' or that it was the rescue dog who really 'found' its new owners, rather than the other way around.

If you have not found your rescue dog yet, then there are several options. You can visit rescue or 'adoption' centres run by big charities like the National Canine Defence League, Battersea Dogs' Home, the RSPCA, Blue Cross and others (see end of book). Or you can visit smaller local individual shelters or sanctuaries.

It might help you to know that many reputable rescue centres, charities or organisations - whether national or local - now belong to the Association of British Dogs' (& Cats') Homes, which in turn commits them to a set code of practice as to how they should be managed and run. As this code lays down high standards for the welfare of animals within their care, any member organisation of the ABDCH might be a good place to start your search.

Words of caution

If a smaller shelter, organisation or sanctuary does not belong to the ABDCH, this does not necessarily mean it is badly run. Many smaller rescue organisations, in fact, can be extremely well run. But what it does mean is that you may have to approach them with a little more

caution if you do not know enough about them or their reputation, or do not feel suitably qualified to judge how good, or not, they happen to be.

There can be rescue places dotted about which have plenty of good intentions and fine sentiments towards animals, but not necessarily the proper resources, or expertise, to manage their welfare, or subsequent rehoming, to a sufficiently high standard. So if you go to any place where:

- General standards in animal welfare, say, or hygiene, don't seem impressive - e.g. water bowls are empty / mucky, pens dirty or very few dogs seemed to have been groomed recently

- There are lots of different animals all cramped up together in somewhat ramshackle quarters

- No-one asks you many questions before offering you a dog

- There appears to be no access to anyone suitably qualified to correctly assess a dog's character for you, or offer suitable back-up behavioural advice if needed

- No one can tell you much else of importance about the dog - like when it was last vaccinated or wormed (and if it has been vaccinated, then it should have a relevant 'record card' to prove it)

Then be aware that these are **not promising signs**. If in doubt about any rescue centre, always do a bit more research about them. Ask a local vet or anyone else (e.g. local dog warden) with likely knowledge about the place whether it has a good enough reputation. Or whether you should go elsewhere.

This could be very hard to do if you have already seen a dog in such a place that you really like, or feel sorry for. You might want to take the risk in rehoming it and it might just pay off. But equally, you could find that this dog subsequently falls ill, as a result of the conditions it was kept in, perhaps, or because its vaccinations weren't kept up to date. Or you might be faced with a dog displaying behavioural problems you were never made aware of before you took it home and don't know how to deal with. Such scenarios can cause immense amounts of heartache for all concerned, which is why you should be **forewarned**.

Other options

Not all rescue agencies have 'centres' as such. Many will take on unwanted dogs and then foster them out to suitable volunteers, with whom they will live until new homes can be found for them. This happens a lot in '**breed rescue**' - i.e., among agencies that specifically cater for one type of pedigree breed.

In many ways, this system can work very well. First, because dogs will be spared the unnecessary stresses of kennel life and second because both agencies and volunteers, over time, build up considerable experience of the breed they are dealing with. They will thus know the most important things about the breed to tell new owners, and which individual dogs might suit different people or homes, according to their characters or specific needs.

If your sights are determinedly set on a pedigree dog, be aware again, however, that the quality of breed rescue agencies can still vary. Some will be a lot better run, have better facilities or resources, and have far more skilled or experienced personnel to 'assess' individual dogs correctly, than others.

In the very worst scenario, there can be a few unscrupulous individuals who will actually call themselves a 'breed rescue' organisation, when they keep dogs in very poor conditions, or will actually function just to make money out of pedigree dogs through selling them on. So you may still find it helpful to ask around about them first. Many, if not most, of our bigger canine rescue organisations will have some contacts within breed rescue, and could maybe give you advice on this front if desired.

The Kennel Club also publishes an **annual directory** of rescue organisations catering for different pedigree breeds. More details on breed rescue at the end of this book.

Where you live may naturally govern where you go initially to find your rescue dog. It seems easiest, and most sensible, to go to a centre closest to your home. Being a little bit more adventurous, however - presuming you have a car - and travelling a little wider around the country to different places can pay dividends, in that your choice of dog will be that much wider, and you will have seen far more other dogs to make comparisons with.

Wherever you go to begin your search for a rescue dog, remember one golden rule - and that is, **don't make any decisions in a hurry**. You are choosing a very special companion to share your life and home with you, perhaps for the next ten or more years, and for whose welfare you will be totally responsible. You owe it to your future dog, as well as yourself, to take the time to get things right.

What to ask and find out

We have already mentioned how hard it can be to be practical and clear-headed when you enter a rescue centre. You may be faced with a sea of needy and appealing faces and instantly wish you could take every dog home. Or just the one that looks the most miserable, beguiling or helpless. Even the most strong-minded individual, in such circumstances, can be hit by a sudden wave of 'Saviour Syndrome'; the urge to make a troubled or unwanted dog feel 'loved' again. It is a natural, and perfectly understandable, reaction.

If you have done your 'homework', however, as previously outlined in this book, then you will already be aware that successfully rehoming a dog revolves more around day-to-day practicalities than spontaneous waves of emotion. A dog's 'appeal factor' apart, there are lots of other things you will need to know about it to establish whether or not it really would be right for you.

Absolute priorities

As touched upon earlier, it is important that anyone seeking a rescue dog has in mind **a few requirements that have to be met, come what may.** If you have very small children, for instance, you simply **cannot** afford the risk of taking on a dog which might not get on with them.

Similarly, if you already have a dog, or other dogs, at home, you will have to choose another which is likely to be compatible with them. If you have other pets, like cats or rabbits, then obviously it would be sensible to avoid a breed with high predatory or chase instincts. More advice on these subjects now.

Why dogs do or don't get on

Dogs always have their reasons for why they don't 'get on', even if they aren't always obvious to us. We can't always explain why we dislike some people on sight, but we can appreciate that it seems to work on a 'gut' or 'instinctive' level. If we thought about it more rationally, we'd maybe realise that the reason we don't like them is because we sense they represent a 'threat' to us, or our own personal standing, in some way - which in turn can make us feel 'defensive' or 'edgy', or more tempted to 'have a go' at them.

Dogs experience similar 'gut' feelings about other dogs, usually backed up by subtleties of canine posture and 'body language'. **If they get on,** then it's usually because they either do not view each other as particularly 'threatening', or because they are able to quickly resolve who is the more 'superior' or 'inferior' dog with minimum conflict.

If they continually cannot get on, however, then it's often because the issue of who is 'superior/ inferior' remains - to their eyes - unresolved. Or because one, or both dogs, resents the other's ambitions to be more 'superior' than they should be. This in turn can lead to frequent bouts of 'needling' or - at times all-out aggression, which can be very difficult for owners to live with in the confines of the average home.

Should it be of additional help to you, Chapter six will cover issues concerning the **canine 'rank' system** in more detail, and how disputes between dogs (**Rescue dogs and other pets**) might need to be handled. For now though, be aware that potential 'conflicts' between an existing dog - or dogs - and a newer rescue one could be minimised by appreciating the following points:

Most good rescue centres encourage owners to introduce their existing dog - or dogs - to a **potential new one on some fairly neutral territory** within their grounds. And if they are totally incompatible, it is usually immediately obvious. But as this initial sort of introduction can't always be a foolproof test of how dogs might get on once they all live together under the same roof, it might help to know which combinations are likely to be 'trickier', or better suited, than others in the long term.

In the main, dogs of different sexes - i.e. a bitch and a dog - are more likely to get on than those of the same sex. This isn't a hard and fast rule, but two bitches, or two dogs - particularly if they are of similar age, or size or both pretty strong characters - are more likely to see each other as obvious 'threats' or 'rivals' than dogs of the opposite sex. Neutering one of two dogs of the same sex can reduce levels of strife between them, providing the dog you choose to neuter is the less naturally 'dominant' of the pair (again, see **Rescue dogs and other pets**, Chapter six).

Also be aware of the implications of upsetting the 'gender applecart'. You may, for instance, have two or more bitches that get on fairly well together until you suddenly bring a male dog home to stir up sexual rivalry in the ranks. Or two or more dogs that fall out as soon as you bring a bitch back to live with them. This might be less of a problem if the relevant dogs are spayed / neutered, but even if they are, it can still happen.

If your existing dog is a rather timid / submissive character, then do be aware that a more dominant / pushy individual - especially of the same sex - could end up ' bullying' it and making its life rather miserable. And while the new dog is simply establishing its 'natural rank', many owners can find this state of affairs very upsetting.

By the same token, it's often said that a puppy or much younger dog could give any existing older dog you have a 'new lease of life'. This can be true, particularly if the younger dog is of a different sex. However, do be aware that not all 'oldies', who have previously had your home, and attention, entirely to themselves will necessarily welcome the sudden imposition of a 'new upstart' upon their territory. It could make them, at least initially, either openly resentful, or quite withdrawn and depressed. This can also be quite upsetting for owners, who feel a first loyalty to their old dog even if, in time, the two dogs might get on much better together.

Some rescue centres may be aiming to rehome two dogs together, perhaps because they have lived together so long in a former home that separation would cause them much distress. If you are interested in such a 'pair', it might not be wise, again, to house them with an existing single dog you might have at home. This is because the pair will have bonded so strongly with each other, over time, that they could only view your other dog as an 'outsider'.

It's also strongly inadvisable ever to take on two dogs who are littermates, whether of the same sex or not and even if they are puppies or quite young. Again, these dogs will bond - or will already have bonded - incredibly strongly with each other, to the extent where any other dog - or indeed, person - can be viewed as 'redundant' to their needs as a 'pack'. This can cause problems both in training and in all-over management of the dogs concerned. Even very experienced dog people can have an awful lot of trouble with littermates, and this is why a lot of rescue centres will rehome them separately.

If you have any doubts as to how well, or not, a new dog might get on with others, then do seek the best advice you can first - from the rescue centre, your vet, a dog trainer, or anyone else with suitable knowledge - **before** bringing it home. Or take longer at a rescue centre, assessing how the different canine parties get on, and looking for signs of potential conflict - e.g. over toys, treats or owner attention. In the long run, this could save a fair bit of strife for dogs and owners alike.

Predatory instincts in dogs

If you have cats, rabbits or other small animals at home, then naturally you might be worried about getting a dog who might chase, attack or generally 'worry' them. Some breeds or breed types - e.g. lurchers, terriers - are renowned for the strength of their predatory instincts. But then again, not all individual dogs run true to their 'stereotypical image'.

It is popularly imagined, for instance, that a greyhound represents a lethal threat to anything small and fluffy, or feline. And often it does. Yet plenty of other greyhound owners will tell you that their dogs live in perfect harmony with their cats. When dogs are crossbreeds, you also can't always know which behavioural traits or instincts they might have inherited in the genetic mix - until, of course, they suddenly get set off by the right 'trigger'.

Chapter six will outline how to best manage rescue dogs and existing pets, but for the moment I think it is wise to look at this whole issue in a practical light.

If you have a cat, or other small animals at home, then your first basic loyalty is to them. And it would be foolhardy, if not unkind, to inflict on them a dog that has even the remotest potential to cause them real distress or harm. A lot of good rescue centres do have cats or other small animals around the premises, and will often try to judge how well - or not - individual dogs in their care react to them. If they have even the vaguest suspicion that a dog might be 'tricky' with smaller or 'prey-sized' animals, don't get it. If **you** have even the vaguest suspicion that a dog might mean trouble for existing pets, **don't get it.**

Also be aware that there are cases where a dog's predatory instincts can be focused on to other dogs. Any dog with instincts like these should always be muzzled when it is taken out.

Other questions

Let us suppose that you have now got your eyes on a dog that meets all your 'absolute priorities', whatever they happen to be personally for you. Additionally it would be wise to try to establish:

- **Any possible details about its background** - e.g. whether it arrived as a stray, formerly lived with a family or one person, was brought in for a particular reason. The more you can know about a dog's past, the more this will help to explain much about its future behaviour

- **If the centre / organisation has a resident or visiting behaviour expert** or someone suitably qualified to make some overall professional assessment of the dog's character - and if so, what is it?

- **Could they also tell you how much training / 'rehabilitation' work it might need?**

- **Does the same expert - or do experienced centre staff - believe this dog would be truly right for your lifestyle and circumstances, and if so why?**

- **Does the dog have any existing health problems** which might need ongoing treatment?

- **Has the dog, as yet, displayed any recognisable 'behaviour problems',** or any fear / phobias about specific things - e.g. certain people, sights, sounds, experiences?

- **Does it generally get on well with other dogs?**

- **Are the dog's vaccinations up to date - and has it been spayed / neutered?**

- **If the dog has been kept in kennels, how long for** - and is its behaviour outside of kennels much different to that within them (the relevance of this will become clear in a moment)

Naturally there will be lots of other things you might really like to know about the dog's potential behaviour in your home. Like whether it is suitably 'toilet trained', is likely to chew your furniture, or whether it is likely to suffer from 'separation anxiety' when you leave it alone. If the dog has been living in a temporary 'foster home' prior to you getting it, or if former owners have given honest answers to rescue centre staff about their dog's domestic 'quirks', then you might be correctly informed one way or another.

But if not, or if dogs have arrived at kennels as strays, imagine how hard finding totally reliable answers to such questions is going to be. **This is because the answers are usually only discovered once a dog is living in a home, rather than in kennels.**

The set-up, and general environment, of average kennel life can sometimes play a part in 'distorting' or 'masking' many aspects of a dog's 'true' behaviour or character. This is such an important factor for you to know about, when choosing a dog for rehoming, that we shall cover it fully now.

The Effects of kennel life on dogs

Kennel life is often judged to be a 'necessary evil' of the rescue dog world. By this it is meant that, although kennels are designed to most efficiently meet the daily hygiene / basic welfare requirements of large numbers of very different dogs, under one roof, many dogs can find them pretty stressful and upsetting.

For most dogs - other than those who were raised in them from puppyhood - kennels are not a 'normal' place, or environment, to live in. This is because prior to residing in rescue centre kennels they were either living in a domestic home or else running loose on the streets.

Today, rescue professionals are increasingly aware that some dogs fare a lot worse than others in kennels, and that kennel life can - in some cases - have some pretty adverse effects on the canine psyche. And the more sensitive the nature of the confined dog, or the longer it is confined, the more adverse these effects are likely to be.

The trouble is, **we** know that dogs are in rescue kennels 'for their own good', or until such time that they can be found new homes, but unfortunately dogs don't. They don't know why they are confined in a small space or when - if ever - they are likely to get out of it. Additionally, they can be highly distressed by the noise of other anxious dogs, or the possibility that any of the strange people or dogs approaching their kennel might wish them harm.

When we view their situation through their eyes, it is far easier to understand why some dogs in rescue centre kennels can display forms of behaviour which we might find 'off-putting' (see below). But they do not necessarily do it because they are 'bad' or 'mad'. They do it because they are stressed or frightened, or because they are struggling to make sense of what is happening to them.

'Kennel stress'

If dogs in rescue centres ever had an inkling that by leaping around in their kennels, constantly barking, chasing their tails, looking aggressive or sitting in a zombie-like state in a corner, they would greatly be reducing their chances of finding freedom and the comfort of a new home, it's highly unlikely that they would do it. They would all sit there quietly instead with the sweetest, most winsome doggie grin they could find. And indeed, a lot of smart dogs in kennels quickly work out the sort of 'charm offensive' postures or looks that will secure them most attention from visitors or staff.

Other dogs, however, simply cannot look beyond the anxieties caused by their immediate situation. Being unable to know anything about the future, they can only try to deal with the stresses they feel **now**. With some dogs, this can mean mentally 'shutting off' from the worrying world around them, and becoming noticeably despondent and depressed. Others will choose to 'externalise' their stress in varying forms of 'manic' or 'defensively aggressive' behaviour - just like many people, under pressure, in fact.

The most important thing for you to realise is that dogs displaying these different forms of 'stress behaviour' aren't all necessarily 'worse' dogs, intrinsically, than others you might see looking more relaxed. Many of them are just dogs who don't cope well with kennel life, and who could improve considerably, given more favourable surroundings and individual attention.

Rehabilitation

It can be very frustrating for a lot of rescue centre staff to know that they have potentially great dogs in their care who 'let themselves down', and ruin their rehoming chances, due to the way they behave in kennels.

Fortunately, however, not only are more and more good rescue centres today doing what they can to reduce 'kennel stress' in dogs, through giving them greater attention and stimulation, and in some cases redesigning living environments to look more like homes, but increasing numbers of visitors to rescue centres are also now more aware of this phenomenon. They are thus more likely to give a stressed dog a second look and - hopefully - to appreciate that, long-term, maybe the best 'therapy' it could have would be a new and loving home.

If you see a dog you are interested in, which appears to be showing symptoms of 'kennel stress', do make sure, however, that you get someone suitably qualified to tell you how serious, or not, its overall problems happen to be, beyond a basic intolerance to its current environment. They should also be able to judge whether or not you would be the right person, or have sufficient experience, to turn its life around in a new home.

Other factors about kennel life

We have just looked at how the pressures or anxieties of kennel life can lead to a misrepresentation of a dog's 'normal' behaviour or character. In similar vein, sometimes dogs who can seem very quiet and subdued individuals in kennels will prove to be anything but once they start to regain confidence in a new home. Equally, dogs who looked pretty 'hostile' or 'manic' in kennels can quieten down considerably once they feel more settled and secure.

As knowledge of dog behaviour increases, and more and more rescue organisations employ professionals suitably qualified to make proper assessments of individual canine characters or problems, this in turn can produce two main benefits. First, it can increase the chances of the right dogs going to the right homes and second, the earlier a dog's 'problems' can be diagnosed, the quicker they can be suitably addressed, or stopped from getting worse

This being said, however, it is still important to accept that an 'element of the unknown' is frequently going to be part of the rescue dog package. With the best will in the world, you cannot expect rescue centres, particularly those with high numbers of inmates, to know every conceivable detail about the behaviour of all the dogs in their care before they are taken home. Which means there are likely to be a few 'surprises' about many dogs when you start living with them, though the surprises won't always be unpleasant.

Most people who take on rescue dogs understand this basic reality.

There is an awful lot we will not, and cannot, know about people until we actually live with them. Why should it be so different with dogs? Similarly, few of us are faultless in all aspects of our behaviour, but this doesn't mean we can't still learn to change or modify our faults, given the right motivation or encouragement. Dogs can do the same, and often a lot quicker, and better, than us.

What is a 'truly bad dog' or 'hopeless cause'?

Many people - quite understandably - can be worried about the prospect of taking on a rescue dog that will prove to be a 'nightmare'. And in this context their greatest fears - though there can be others - usually revolve around a dog that will either be excessively destructive around the home or aggressive towards them or other people; perhaps two of the greatest 'canine crimes'.

As **destructiveness** in dogs tends to be a symptom of other underlying problems, which will cover later in this book (in Chapters five and seven), I will not dwell on it in too much detail now. If you have other real fears about behaviour in a dog, hopefully they will also be covered in the same chapters.

What does need to be said in advance about potentially destructive dogs, however, is that they will generally require not only patient and persistent owners, but also owners prepared to work through, and understand, all the anxieties / inner energies that might be causing destructiveness in the first place. If people are prepared to do this, rather than just dismiss or condemn a dog outright for its actions, then vast improvements - or total cures - can be brought about. And frequently destructiveness in dogs will only last for as long as it takes to allay, or find a way around, the actual reasons causing it.

Dangerous dogs

Aggression, naturally, is a far bigger problem. Aggression in dogs can come in many different forms for many different reasons which which again, again, will be covered later in this book (Chapters five and seven). This being said, however, a dog whose aggression is totally unpredictable, and who could turn on and bite anyone at any time, is a **very dangerous dog to own**. Such dogs have a fundamentally 'unstable' temperament and any reputable rescue centre, with access to good behavioural advice, would never let you take one on, because they would already have recognised its dangerous potential. Which is yet another argument for picking a rescue organisation with access to good behavioural advice or assessment.

You might wonder what then happens to these 'truly bad dogs', as it were, or 'hopeless causes', if they cannot be rehomed. It will depend on the policies of different rescue agencies or charities. Some rescue organisations feel an obligation to 'euthanase' such dogs, as they not only represent a danger to the public, but also cannot be guaranteed any satisfactory future life with people. Other organisations, with a policy never to destroy healthy dogs, may prefer to keep them in their care instead.

Dogs like these can cause an awful lot of soul-searching and upset for many rescue staff, especially when it is suspected that human cruelty lies at the heart of their shattered or fearful psyches. The bleaker decisions made about their futures, however, are rarely taken lightly or without good cause. We can understand all the reasons why dogs 'turn bad' - e.g. poor genetics or a damaging upbringing - because they are not so different from the reasons why people do the same. But this still doesn't mean we can always 'cure' them.

Most highly experienced rescue organisations tend to know when they have got a dog too risky to rehome. Just as they know how many people in the past have broken their hearts over dogs they couldn't 'cure'. If they say a dog is too dangerous or unpredictable for you to own, and especially if you are in no way a canine expert, then I'd take their word for it.

Last points

Hopefully, this chapter will have given you an awful lot more to think about, and weigh up, before making your final choice of rescue dog.

Remember, too, that any good rescue organisation will need to be assured that their dogs are going to the most suitable new homes. If they appear to make you 'jump through hoops' to get a dog, then this is actually a good sign, indicating how much they care about their animals' welfare and long-term happiness, as well as their compatibility with you. Conversely, if they seem to be in a noticeable hurry to offload dogs, with few questions asked, this might seem less hassle, but won't necessarily be in the best long-term interests of either you or the new dog.

Ultimately, the most important thing about a rescue dog is that you have got to feel that you can cope with it. If you have any doubts or misgivings at all about a dog, or you feel that a rescue centre might not be giving you as accurate a picture possible of its potential - in terms of character or future problems - then get someone else with suitable experience / qualifications in dog behaviour to look it over. Maybe a good local dog trainer, or a behaviourist recommended by your vet, or anyone you know who has considerable knowledge / experience of dealing with a wide number and variety of dogs.

Remember, once more, that former owners aren't always truthful about the reasons why they are giving up their dogs - so more careful consideration and assessment on your part is always sensible, and could prevent a lot of avoidable grief later on.

As already stated, no two rescue dogs will ever be the same, but often people are highly curious about why dogs vary so much from each other in so many ways, or wonder how different their needs might be at different ages, or stages, in their lives. As knowing more about these subjects may help you even more with your rescue dog, we shall cover them in the next couple of chapters.

Chapter Three

Why All Dogs Are Not The Same: Understanding All The Factors Which Make A Dog What It Is And The Requirements of Different Breeds or 'Types'

Chapter Three

When looking at the physical differences between a Bulldog, say, and a Greyhound, or a Great Dane and a Chihuahua, it can be hard to believe that they are animals belonging to the same species, or that they have all evolved in some way from one common ancestor - the wolf.

Many people, indeed, can struggle to see a link between this original keen, cunning and tireless predator and the mutt snoring on their living room sofa. But rest assured that it is there, and precisely what your dog has inherited, genetically, from its oldest ancestors - as well as its parents! - will govern a lot about its instincts and behaviour, as well as looks.

If owners of new dogs often feel that they have got more, or less, than they bargained for with a particular breed or individual, then the chances are it is because they have not understood enough about its basic genetic heritage, or how other factors in its early life might have shaped its overall 'character'. So let us look at these important issues now.

Looks, function and genes

The fact that dogs can come in so many shapes, sizes and overall varieties today is not just an 'accident' of evolution. It's purely down to us. Over thousands of years man has relentlessly manipulated canine genes to produce not just the 'domestic dog', but also dogs that could be of use to him in many different ways - e.g. in terms of hunting, tracking, guarding, or herding livestock.

To do this, he would naturally have chosen only to breed from specimens whose instincts in these areas were strongest or most superior, as he would have developed dogs with qualities or characteristics best suited to their roles.

The function for which a dog was originally bred can still dictate the way it looks today. Many terriers, for instance, will be smaller than other dogs because this better enabled them to pursue rats, mice and other prey into restricted spaces. Lurchers and other lean and long-legged 'sight hounds' will be so designed to pursue prey at immense speed over distance; the sort of canine equivalent of racehorses. If a classic sheepdog, or Border collie, is black and white, then logically this is because the black would have enabled a shepherd to easily distinguish his dog from sheep at a distance, whereas the distinctive white markings would not have confused it with an approaching predator of similar shape or size.

How should all these considerations affect you, as an ordinary 'pet dog' owner? Well hopefully, they will help you to realise that all dogs, fundamentally - and whether pedigree or not - *can only be what their genes dictate they can be*. And this relates to temperament, and basic instincts, as much as it does to the way they look.

Not all of us were born with the bodies to be supermodels, the brains to be rocket scientists or the physical superiority to be world-class athletes. Some of us are far more confident, or ambitious, personalities than others, more short-tempered or easy-going characters than others, or more natural 'followers' than 'leaders'.

Generally, we are able to accept how much about us - from looks, shape and character, to general strengths and weaknesses in personality or performance - will be governed by individual genes, plus the effect of formative influences in our early lives. We just find it harder to appreciate the same factors at work in dogs. As a result we can end up making lots of quite unfair comparisons between our own dog and others.

If we did understand more about all the elements that contribute to making a dog what it is, in all departments, it could not only help us to appreciate our own dog's limitations better, but also aid us a great deal with our handling of different dogs in general.

Understanding dog character

If we were trying to work out why a certain person, or a certain dog, had a particular character, the chances are we'd be looking at three basic factors to give us the answers - namely, genes, upbringing and other early influences or experiences that had a marked impact on their developing psyches.

The difficulty, however, would lie in establishing which, out of all these three factors, made the **most** difference to that individual person's, or dog's, eventual personality or 'nature'.

Some experts believe than *genes* are the most important factor in determining individual character. Logically, they must play a substantial part, yet we know that even identical twins can have very different personalities, with one often being a more dominant character than the other.

Others might believe that *upbringing* and other *early influences* had the most impact on shaping future character. Yet we know how often adopted children will run true to the strengths or weaknesses of their real parents, character-wise - as in many other regards - come what may.

In similar vein, it is clear that some dogs can endure enormous suffering and / or abuse in their lives, yet still retain essentially 'docile' or 'trusting' natures. Others, however, seem to be born so 'fearful' or wary of the world around them that just one particularly frightening or 'threatening' experience, or even just inadequate early 'socialisation' when they were puppies, can have long-lasting effects on their character and subsequent behaviour.

The point is, with dogs - as with people - and with rescue dogs in particular, we cannot always know which one factor, or **subtle balance of factors, interacting with each other**, most definitively shaped their characters. **But what we can do is predict which type of background factors are likely to have had a more positive, or negative, effect on the way a dog turns out.** We'll look at these factors now and begin with:

Genes and temperament

One of the first things anyone gets advised about, when choosing a puppy, is to '**make sure you see the mother**' - **or, even more ideally, both parents.** The point of this is obvious in that, if one or either of the puppy's parents seems nervous, shy or 'snappy', then there's a high chance that their offspring will have inherited similar temperaments, or the genetic capacity to have similar temperaments given appropriate ' triggers', or the wrong sort of early upbringing and handling (of which more later). **It can, as well, be incredibly easy for dogs to pass on their own particular fears or 'phobias' to their offspring via example.** Much in the way a mother who is terrified of spiders, for instance, or the dentist, can end up with children who are similarly inclined.

We tend to take it for granted, thanks to generations of selective breeding, that dogs - and most specifically pet dogs - are going to have 'trusting' or 'even-tempered' natures, but in doing so can forget dogs' real roots as a species. This means that often, what we will see as 'faults' or 'defects' in a dog's temperament are merely the genetic re-emergence of original, and pretty strong, canine instincts which we do not like or find disturbing.

We might regard **nervousness**, for instance, or **aggression towards other dogs** or animals, as somewhat inappropriate or unpleasant traits in a 'social companion'. For our dogs' earliest ancestors, however, such cautious, defensive, or predatory instincts would have been **basic tools of survival**, and there can be many modern dogs who still feel highly driven by them.

This being said, however, a dog with a basically 'sound' or 'easy-going' temperament is not only easiest for most people to handle and live with, but can also be guaranteed a far happier and better quality of life within human society. For these reasons alone, you would expect that anyone in the business of producing dogs destined to be pets would always make a 'sound temperament' their most urgent priority when picking breeding stock. But sadly they don't, and in the process of not doing so, can cause an awful lot of grief for future owners of their dogs and the dogs alike.

Some debate can rage over how much can be done to 'improve' or 'remedy' the behaviour of dogs whose temperaments are fundamentally 'flawed', genetically. In other words their behaviour is more inborn / instinctive than **learned**, and thus often more difficult to fundamentally change or reverse. The most common serious problem with such dogs is inappropriate / uncontrollable aggression. My own feelings are that dogs so inclined are only for the most dedicated and experienced handlers.

Very often less experienced owners do not, and cannot, know how much of their dog's behaviour stems predominantly from genetic factors. As a result they may unfairly blame themselves for not being able to sufficiently control or change what their dogs do.

Although, as outlined previously, it's unlikely that any good rescue organisation would ever give such a potentially dangerous dog to a novice handler, a few could 'slip through the net' of less experienced places, or be obtained in other ways. Should you ever suspect that this could have happened in your case, it is **vital** that you get the dog properly assessed by someone sufficiently experienced in your dog's breed, or in dog behaviour in general should the dog in question be a crossbreed. They should not only be able to tell you how much of your dog's behaviour/ overall temperament has genetic triggers, but also realistically evaluate what - if any - improvement could be made and how.

If necessary, get at least two or three different opinions until the answers make sense and match your own instinctive feelings about the dog.

Upbringing and early influences

If dogs are commonly such 'different personalities' - e.g. dominant or submissive, outgoing or shy - then upbringing and early influences, as well as genes, can play a part.

In any natural dog pack you will see a hierarchy of different 'characters' or 'personalities' best suited to different roles. These 'characters' can vary to quite an extent but, typically, there will be the outright 'dominant' ones, destined to be leaders, and on whom the pack's overall security generally depends. There will be more nervous individuals whose sensitivity to possible outside threat can make them useful 'watchdogs'. There will be 'middle-ranking' dogs whose ability to get on with all others, or play 'peacemaker' in disputes between ranks, acts as a sort of 'social glue' for pack cohesion. And then somewhere there always tends to be a classic 'underdog' destined to get picked on by most of the others.

You'll see many of the same roles being rehearsed within any litter of puppies. Puppies soon learn from their littermates the extent of their own 'social standing', and which sort of behaviour will be most - or least effective or rewarding among their peers and other adult dogs. This in turn seems to give them the outline of distinctly different 'personalities'.

Sometimes dogs with dominant tendencies learn that through being 'over-pushy' with littermates, they can miss out on a lot of enjoyable joint-interaction and play, and will thus learn to modify their behaviour to secure such a reward. Equally, more submissive dogs can learn to 'play the clown' to get more favourable attention, or use a range of other manipulative tricks and ingratiating postures to get what they want from others.

If puppies are born without littermates, or have to be hand-reared, they can miss out on these vital early lessons in canine social skills. As a result, although they might have 'bonded' extremely successfully with people, they can have problems relating to other dogs, without fear or conflict, when they are older. This problem can often be minimised if owners go out of their way to get such puppies adequately socialised with other dogs as soon as they can after vaccination is complete.

Puppies who have been raised with plenty of other puppies / dogs, but with very little human contact, can have this problem in reverse. They might interact pretty successfully with their own kind, but can find the presence of people - particularly strangers - quite worrying or threatening.

As I am going to cover this whole vital subject of puppy socialisation, and the part it can play in 'shaping' the adult dog, in Chapter four, I will avoid too much more on it for now.

Already, however, you should be starting to see how much about your current, or future, rescue dog's character, personality and temperament can be explained once you're more aware of the different factors that could have contributed towards its development.

Other points about background

It is often imagined that if a rescue dog has a 'problem temperament', then this must be due to its 'bad past'. This isn't always true, as often 'genetics' could play a larger part, or the dog would be better behaved with more experienced handling.

However, it is a sad fact of life that some rescue dogs can come from very troubled backgrounds. And if any dog gets subjected to lengthy abuse - whether physical, psychological, or both - or is forced to live in an atmosphere of perpetual anxiety and insecurity, then it is bound to have some impact on its future behaviour and the character it subsequently presents to the world.

Throughout this part of the book, we might seem to have dwelt heavily on factors that can affect a dog's future character negatively. If so, then this is purely to underline how much of a dog's less favourable character 'influences' - from the way it was bred onwards - can lie beyond its own control. It does not mean that given the right home, the right time and the right care, the impact of such disadvantages on rescue dogs cannot be overcome, as so frequently they can - and are.

Puppy farms

Earlier in this book, when discussing pedigree dogs, we looked at the dangers of getting them from 'puppy farms'. Although much campaigning has gone into getting the worst of these kind of establishments banned, too many are still around. Puppy farm operations can vary considerably in terms of size and turnover, but what characterises them generally is that they mass-breed dogs purely for profit, and with scant regard to any other welfare concerns. Because of the endless chains of misery they can cause for the dogs they breed from, their offspring and their offspring's future owners alike, they are important places to know about.

In a nutshell, dogs originating from such establishments often do so with three distinct disadvantages. **One**, they won't necessarily have been chosen for a 'sound' temperament or the healthiest of constitutions; **two**, they will have been raised in a highly stressful environment, and **three**, they will not have been adequately socialised with the world outside their kennel blocks while they were young enough to view it without fear.

Lasting problems

Sometimes, just one of these unfavourable factors is enough to give a dog lasting problems in later life. Imagine the possible impact of imposing all three together on one dog, and you will better understand why some canine victims of 'puppy farms' find it near impossible to lead a happy or 'normal' existence as a pet, no matter how caring or dedicated their future owners.

Puppy farm-bred dogs usually find their way into rescue from owners who originally got them through small ads in local papers or other journals, or from a petshop, in the mistaken belief that they were getting a 'quality' animal on the cheap. Most experienced rescue staff have a 'nose' for a dog that is likely to have come from a puppy farm, as such dogs can often have developed 'weird' behaviour patterns, unlike those found in other dogs (e.g. walking backwards or licking walls), as a result of the early stresses in their lives. They may appear to have unpredictable 'mood swings', or they could be unnaturally wary or fearful of people.

It would be wrong to think that every dog coming from a puppy farm is 'doomed' as a future pet, because many can be - and are - 'rehabilitated' into domestic life by new owners with considerable success, depending on the extent of their individual problems or disadvantages. Both people, and dogs, can be extraordinarily resilient when they are motivated enough to make something work.

But if a puppy farm-bred dog can never be a hundred per cent like any other 'ordinary' pet dog, at least you can now better understand why. Basically it's because someone, somewhere, didn't care enough to give it that advantage in life.

Different breeds or 'types' of dog and their needs

We have just looked at some of the general reasons, to do with genes, upbringing and early influences, why dogs are often so different from each other. But naturally individual breeds or 'breed types' are also going to vary from each other - in terms of character, and overall daily needs, as well as looks - because we've bred them to be that way.

Different 'functions' in dogs can require specific traits of temperament or character. Dogs from guarding breeds, for instance - e.g. Dobermanns, Rottweilers, German shepherds - wouldn't have originally been chosen for their ability to adore strangers or lick their faces like old friends. Similarly, dogs originally bred to be keen, tireless and highly motivated workers - e.g. Springer spaniels, Border collies - are far more likely to have low boredom / frustration thresholds when under-stimulated or confined.

And when many people condemn certain types of terriers or hounds for having 'wilful' or 'independent' streaks, they might be forgetting how often such dogs, in their original hunting/ tracking roles, were successful through working on their own initiative. Similarly, many terriers needed to have levels of personal courage - when tackling or 'worrying' prey larger than themselves - which compensated for their lack of size. This in turn would call for a character that was pretty defiant and strong.

As owners, we can so easily 'fall out' with a dog when our expectations of it exceed its own genetic capabilities; imagining, in effect, that a 'square peg' of a dog can be rammed into a 'round hole' of our preferred needs without conflict or disappointment.

If we want to know why a breed, or individual dog, acts in a certain way, but not in other ways we might prefer, **then the answer is frequently because it has set genes determining set instincts, characteristics or behaviour which it cannot change.**

Realistic expectations

If we had two parents who were brilliant mathematicians but appalling athletes, this rather increases our chances of being similarly inclined. People might have urged, or preferred, us to be a brilliant athlete instead, but we found we couldn't meet this expectation no matter how hard we tried.

Dogs face similar problems and pressures every day when they go to homes that have not taken their basic genetic origins or needs into account. In turn, it can be highly distressing for owners to live with dogs whose expectations they cannot meet, either physically or mentally.

If you're an incredibly tidy person forced to live with a very untidy person, then you know you are going to get stressed about this 'failing' in a way that another untidy person would not. Equally, what people can, or can't, tolerate in dogs varies considerably and what one person might see as a 'failing' - e.g. high energy levels or strong guarding instincts - another might see as an asset.

In the main, a tremendous amount of dog behaviour can be modified, more positively re-channelled or altered for the better, given sufficient work and patience. But if a dog has certain inborn qualities or demands that you know you have neither the time nor inclination to deal with, it is fairest for both of you not to get it.

Dogs for 'lifestyles'

Frequently people looking for dogs will hear the stock phrase, 'choose an individual / breed best-suited to your 'lifestyle'. But this pre-supposes that everyone **knows** the breed or type of dog that would best suit their lifestyle before they get it, when they don't. Equally it may give the impression that a dog can come 'ready-made', like a bathroom suite, to slot effortlessly into your home and domestic requirements, when it can't, and the process of adaptation and adjustment always has to go both ways between owner and dog.

In the case of **crossbreeds**, it can also be harder to prejudge their general suitability, making you more dependent on a reliable 'assessment' of future needs / character from a rescue organisation. Even with pedigree dogs, however, there can be individuals who do not conform to their standard breed 'image'. Not all Retrievers, for instance, will be friendly and outgoing characters, some dogs from working breeds can be bone idle and others from guarding breeds can be utter 'wimps'. So you should bear this capacity for variation in mind, especially when it comes to temperament.

Breed origins

As a rule though, you can still predict a fair amount about your dog's future character qualities and needs by looking at its origins as a breed or type. This is because dogs bred for different functions - e.g. herding, hunting, guarding or tracking - will often have inherited characters or instincts in keeping with their original roles.

Some of these might suit you more than others:

Dogs with strong herding instincts - e.g. Collies - for example, aren't always the best choice if you've got very young children. They can also be highly sensitive and reactive dogs that will need ample training and stimulation to get the best out of them.

Large and assertive guarding or hunting breeds - e.g. German shepherds, Rottweilers, Dobermanns, Akitas, Weimaraners, - are not for the less powerful of frame or character.

Some Lurcher or terrier types, as previously mentioned, may have hunting instincts that could put other small pets or wild animals at risk.

Dogs designed for both distance and stamina - e.g. Dalmatians, Pointers, Setters, some spaniels and other gundogs, Boxers and Collies again - are never going to be happy, exercise-wise, with a 'spin round the block'.

Size can also be deceptive in terms of exercise needs. Many big dogs, for example - like Greyhounds or larger Mastiff types - do not need hours and hours of walking, as might be imagined, to keep them happy. Some smaller terriers however, like Jack Russells, seem to thrive on high mileage.

Ex-racing Greyhounds can often be found in great numbers in rescue centres, once their working lives are finished on the track. Although predatory instincts towards smaller animals, in some individuals, might have to be anticipated, it is often overlooked what brilliant pets they can otherwise make for families or older people. Generally they are very gentle and placid-natured dogs and sprinters rather than 'marathon runners' - meaning that, unlike some other breeds, they not so likely to wear you out round the house with boundless excitement and energy. They are also quite happy to put their paws up in their beds, or on a sofa, in-between walks.

The above can only be a rough guide to the attributes of different breed types - bearing in mind that the British Kennel Club alone now recognises 195 pedigree varieties, before one even moves on to the additional, almost infinite, permutations that can arise with crossbreeds!

Even if your dog is a crossbreed, as many rescue ones are, there should be something about its appearance to give you clues about its genetic heritage. This in turn might give you more ideas about its possible instincts or personality. You can't always predict which features, out of two breeds, will predominate when they're crossed, but if you're lucky you could get only the virtues - rather than the vices! - of both. If your dog is a cross of a cross classically known as the 'Heinz 57' or 'Bitsa' (as in, bitsa this and bitsa that) - you, in common with countless other owners might be in for a lot of guesswork.

Such dogs can be one big genetic lucky dip. A few owners could find this daunting, but most seem to think that this constitutes half the joy of owning them. Some of the brightest, healthiest dogs I have ever known have been crossbreeds. It also has to be said how often rescue dogs which, initially, might not have been someone's 'first choice' - e.g. they had other breeds or types in mind - turn out, in time, to be ideal for them. In the end it is their sheer, irresistible personality, rather than mere looks or 'image', which has won an owner round.

Size

If your sights are set on a big dog, and you live in a small house or flat with an equally small garden, then obviously your preference is neither practical nor kind.

Big dogs - as already mentioned - don't always require enormous amounts of exercise, but they do need space, and generally have higher food bills than dogs from smaller breeds. If you are not a particularly strong person physically, the prospect of over 100lbs of dog tugging on the other end of a lead - and not necessarily heading where you want it to - is also bound to cause problems. The same would be true if younger children were expected to walk the dog, which certainly wouldn't be sensible near busy roads, or anywhere else where they could all get into trouble. This being said, however, lots of big dogs really can be 'gentle giants'. With adequate space and responsible handling, many have the capacity to make excellent pets, and they will always have their fans.

Many **medium-sized** dogs can seem ideal because they are not too big to manage physically, but at the same time are not too small to get 'under your feet' or sustain potential harm in more boisterous families with young children. Very often a medium-sized dog will also be a compromise for a couple who originally wanted different things. The wife or female partner might have wanted a 'cute' and small dog, perhaps, but her other half wanted something bigger and more in keeping with his 'masculine image'. Yes, such factors often do seem to matter - but if they're both happy, this is what counts.

Smaller dogs are generally the choice of older or less active people. Some smaller breeds, however - particularly terriers - can still have pretty high exercise requirements, so look into this possibility first if you think it could cause problems for you. As previously mentioned, some terriers and smaller hounds can also be quite challenging characters, so if you wouldn't find it easy to live with a strong-willed dog, or reliable 'recall' / obedience is a priority for you, you may have to consider other varieties.

Grooming needs

Much is often made of the amount of grooming different dogs need and how this might affect your choice. Naturally dogs with thicker or longer coats are going need more detailed and regular combing and brushing and some might need routine trips to the grooming parlour to deal with more unruly growths of hair. Smooth-coated dogs, on the other hand, will be more low-maintenance, but many may need to wear coats in very cold weather.

Of all the reasons I have heard why people have, or have not, picked their rescue dogs, however - asthma sufferers apart - I cannot recall one which was based exclusively on the length, texture or combing demands of its coat, particularly if it had so many other things going for it.

From time to time I have heard rescue centres say that someone brought a dog back 'because it shed hair all over the place'. But I think this is an issue hinging more on human commitment than anything else. Most people expect dogs to grow hair, shed hair and need it tending to fairly regularly in between. And as far as I know, they don't think any the worse of them for it.

In fact, for many owners, the way in which they can nurture a rescue dog's formerly 'unkempt' or 'tricky' coat back to full glory is often a matter of pride. When a dog is moulting, or shedding hair excessively, it's also commonsense to put covers over any furniture it uses, or temporarily restrict its access to rooms you'd rather not have knee-deep in fluff.

There will be more on dog grooming - and general health - in Chapter nine. For the moment, though, assuming that you now know more about different dog breeds and characters and what has made them that way, let us move on - in the next chapter - to what dogs might need at different ages or stages in their lives.

Chapter Four

The Five Ages of Dog. From Puppies to Pensioners - What Dogs Might Need, And Demand, At Different Stages of Their Lives

Chapter Four

Dogs can be rescued at any age, even during puppyhood, but what they might need from you - and what you can expect from them - will vary throughout their lives. Although dogs can differ considerably in how fast, or slowly, they will mature and 'age', with larger breeds usually having shorter life expectancies than smaller ones, there are roughly five stages in a dog's life - namely, **Puppy, Juvenile, Adult, Middle Age and Old Age.** You might see a dog through all these phases, or have just rescued it at one phase in particular, and would like more relevant guidance.

Please note that advice on exercise and diet for dogs of different ages appears in Chapter nine. So now let us look at other important issues governing the Five Ages of Dog - beginning with:

Puppyhood

Very few rescue organisations have difficulty rehoming puppies - they are so incredibly cute and appealing. Additionally, people can imagine that in a puppy they are taking on a 'blank canvas' - e.g. a dog too young to have been 'damaged' psychologically by past experiences, and one they can more easily 'shape' to the demands of their households or lifestyles.

In a lot of cases this may well be true, but not always. As outlined in the last chapter, genetic factors governing character or behaviour may still need to be taken into account. A rescue puppy of seven or eight months could also be quite a different prospect from one of seven or eight weeks, in terms of the less favourable things it might have already learned about life.

Early frights

Puppies who were originally acquired as 'playthings' for children, for example, and who were subsequently teased or tormented by them, might have been left with a lingering fear of youngsters. If they were ill treated by other adults, or attacked by a certain-looking breed or type of dog, this could also have an impact on how they later relate to similar-looking people or dogs in the future.

Puppies who were raised in relative isolation from the outside world during their early formative months might be fearful about a whole range of unfamiliar new sights, sounds or people, if only because their 'strangeness' can be perceived as threatening.

Though much can often be done, with caring and patient handling, to reverse or modify 'fear reactions' in such puppies, be aware that progress cannot happen overnight. Neither can you 'bully' any dog out of fears or anxieties it regards as 'real' or 'legitimate', even if you do not.

A dog, given sufficient gentle encouragement, **has got to come to the conclusion that something or someone is 'safe' by itself.** This can take weeks or months, or even longer, depending on the individual and the original strength of its fears. For more advice on preventing 'fearful' responses in dogs, see later section in this chapter on '**Socialisation**'. For dealing with them once they has occurred, see '**Fearfulness**' in Chapter seven.

Genetics and 'maternal example'

Even if a puppy has not had the disadvantage of an 'early fright', or is too young to have completed its crucial 'socialisation period' - i.e. it is well under 14 weeks old - its individual genetic make-up, as previously mentioned, might make it more prone towards nervousness or fear. If you have any suspicions on this front - e.g. a puppy seems very timid, or wants to hide at the back of its kennel, or doesn't seem very 'outgoing' - discuss it with rescue centre staff. There could be other, temporary reasons for its behaviour, such as a bout of illness. If, however, the puppy - in their opinion - is a naturally shy or more nervous type, it might not be suited to a more boisterous or noisy household.

Be aware too that some bitches who give birth in rescue centres might have had quite traumatic pasts. When one adds the responsibilities of motherhood, plus the unnerving atmosphere of kennel life to their list of anxieties, it is little wonder that they will feel stressed or insecure, no matter how hard staff might have tried to put them at ease. Such levels of maternal anxiety could, in turn, affect the state of mind of their puppies, even if this is only short term, until they can settle into a new home where they feel more secure.

Rearing your puppy

Let us suppose that the rescue puppy you get has none of the above-mentioned disadvantages. It is happy, healthy, bouncing with life and on its way to your home.

Hopefully, before you left the rescue centre, you will have been given details about **vaccination and worming programmes**. Most puppies begin a **vaccination** programme at around eight weeks, although this can vary, with some vets now recommending that an earlier completion of crucial 'jabs' will enable a puppy to begin 'socialising' with the outside world / other dogs that much sooner, and thus to most successful effect.

Puppies are usually first **wormed** at around three weeks of age, and will then have to be wormed again first at **fortnightly**, then **monthly** intervals, up to the age of six months. Thereafter they should be wormed **every six months**. Your vet can advise you about correct doses for the puppy's weight.

The puppy crate or 'indoor kennel'

Very few people can supervise a boisterous, and inquisitive, young dog 24 hours a day - which is why modern 'puppy crates' or 'indoor kennels' are such a boon. The point of these strong metal crates or pens, however, is to give puppies or dogs their own 'den' or place of safety - typically overnight, or at regular intervals when they need to rest.

They are **not** supposed to be **prisons**. Unfortunately, some owners really do seem to have the idea that the crate was developed purely for their own convenience, as sort of 'sin bin' or 'escape-proof' cell they can stick their dogs or puppies into when they are remotely tiresome, or until they feel inclined to spare them some time.

As a result, dogs can be left to languish in cramped and stressful misery in these devices for vast numbers of hours every day. In some cases the crates are not even big enough for them to properly stand upright in. This is not only cruel but, psychologically, it can also **be highly damaging**. Dogs and puppies so treated will soon learn to dread the opening of a crate door - or even confined spaces in general - and may also be baffled as to why you torment them in this way. This in turn can lead to the destruction of the very vital trust a dog needs to have in its owner.

Any human would view enforced confinement in a cramped space as a form of punishment or torture, and also something destined, if continued long-term, to inflict psychological harm. Why should it be any different for dogs?

Commonsense should also tell you that if you want a well-socialised, happy and outgoing adult dog then clearly it is not going to become this way through spending most of its puppyhood in a crate.

How to use a crate

If you do decide to get one of these crate devices for your puppy, then get one as large as possible, and certainly big enough for a dog to easily stand in, and move around in, when it is fully-grown, should you still be wanting to use it at times then. You may also want to get a type that can be fitted into your car later to keep the dog safe while travelling.

Next, make the crate as cosy as possible, with warm bedding and cuddly toys and chew items installed. In colder weather, a hot water bottle under a blanket may also help. The puppy should be encouraged to have only 'good associations' with the crate - i.e. it is fed or played with inside, or is given treats there. It should be gently persuaded into the crate at regular intervals, but should **never be physically forced into it against its will**. It also helps, at the beginning, to keep the crate door open until the puppy is happy to go inside its 'den' and stay there of its own free will. Make a great fuss of the puppy when it does this. Also stay in the same room with the puppy while it is in the crate, at regular intervals, and only distance yourself further away from it into other rooms gradually, as it settles down.

Patience over this issue will really pay off in the long run, whereas any suggestion to the puppy that its crate is a form of 'punishment' can affect it adversely, or reverse any previous progress towards its happy acceptance of its 'new den'.

Once your puppy is happy about going into its crate, you will find this device can help in the following ways:

- **It can aid toilet training**. Few dogs like to 'foul' near their sleeping quarters, and many may hang on longer in their crates overnight until they can go out to 'perform'. But still do not expect them to wait too long for this opportunity in the morning, and puppies will always have 'accidents', so leave some thick newspaper in their crates for this purpose. Also note that if you have an over-large kennel, your puppy could mentally divide it up into two distinct 'zones' - i.e. one 'end' for sleeping in and the other, more distant one marked out as its en suite 'lavatory'!

- **It can help with chewing problems.** If your puppy is chewing something it should not, gently encourage it into its crate with its own chew item / toy instead, ideally with the door left open. It should hopefully soon learn not just that its crate is where it chews, but also what it is, and is not, supposed to chew

- **It will keep the puppy out of danger** - e.g., when workmen are coming constantly in and out the front door into the street, or you are decorating or using potentially harmful chemicals. Likewise, in moments when you can't supervise it, it could chew poisonous plants, or through electric cables

- **It will give the puppy the comfort of its own secure 'retreat' when it wants it**

- **It will help the puppy learn to cope with periods on its own**

As a rule, the puppy should **not be left more than two hours at a time in its crate - three at absolute maximum** during the daytime. Most puppies will settle into them best when tired - e.g. after a meal, or an energetic play session. Ideally, with correct anticipation of when it is likely to be most tired, your puppy will soon begin to associate 'crate time' with rest or sleep time.

Once a puppy has got older and learnt the basics about toilet training, being on its own and not destroying things either in or out of your presence, many owners - myself included - will prefer to abandon the routine use of the indoor crate. By that stage your young dog should have earned your trust and its 'freedom' through its good behaviour - plus the right to be treated more like an 'adult'!

First nights

Where should a puppy sleep during its first nights with you? This is usually up to owner preference. Sometimes keeping a puppy in its crate in your bedroom for the first couple of nights can make the transition into a new home a bit less traumatic - even if you later then move its crate further and further away from your room, in gradual stages, until it is where you want it to be permanently.

Other owners might prefer to 'start as they mean to go on' and leave the puppy in a crate downstairs from day one. Wherever you put your puppy to sleep overnight however, do make sure it is as warm and comfortable as possible, with cosy bedding - plus a hot water bottle under this if it is cold - and maybe a soft toy or two for company. A ticking clock - mimicking the heartbeat of its mother or littermate - might also bring comfort, as will a radio left on low nearby if the puppy is left on its own downstairs.

First nights alone somewhere strange, and away from mother and / or littermates, can be very traumatic for young puppies. Appreciate this, but also understand how **vital it is that you do not go to your puppy the moment it cries or whines in protest to get your attention.** Pitiful little shrieks echoing round the house can be very hard to resist, but if you do not resist them you will have a puppy that will then continue to howl longer and longer, and louder and louder, just through knowing that in the past this tactic was once effective in getting your attention.

You can always go and talk to your puppy and reassure it as soon as it has been quiet for a few minutes. This way your puppy will learn that being quiet always gets more of your attention than being noisy.

Toilet training

Large quantities of grief seem sometimes to be shed by owners on the subject of toilet training puppies, when it should really be easier at this stage of a dog's life to plant the 'right ideas' into its head than at any other.

To my mind there is only one sure - and proven - way to 'toilet train' puppies, and that is through '**correct association**'. In other words, the puppy has to be as frequently as possible in the 'right place' - outside - when it 'performs'. There will always be 'accidents' along the way, but eventually it will only be a matter of time before 'outside', within the puppy's mind, equals toilet opportunity.

To bring this state of affairs about, younger puppies in particular may need to be taken outside every hour, or sooner if they have just eaten, woken up or had a frantic bout of play. **And yes, even if it is cold or raining,** they still need to go out, as sadly puppy bladders and bowels are no respecters of climatic conditions.

To speed up the 'association' process, owners can accompany a 'performance' with a treat and specific word command - though don't make it something you'd find excruciating to repeat in public. Some puppies will take longer to be 'clean' around the house than others. Not because they are 'bad' or 'naughty', but because they are still perfecting a reliable association between location and action, or because they are not being taken out often enough and therefore cannot 'hold on'. Do also be aware that puppies who have previously been in kennels - where no discrimination was made between areas where they should, or should not, relieve themselves - may need longer to grasp that this is now no longer acceptable.

Do not punish or chastise your dog when it has had an accident. The chances are you will only discover the 'accident' too late for the dog to understand the connection between its deed and your sudden angry reprimand. It will therefore just get upset, frightened or bewildered. **You will also simply teach it not to relieve itself when you are anywhere around, for fear of punishment.** If you do catch it 'in the act', then quickly encourage it, or carry it, outside to complete its business. And for goodness sake **do not rub your dog's nose in it.** Unkindness apart, all you simply have then is a dog to clean up as well as a carpet made somewhat messier through your actions.

Should your puppy foul anywhere indoors, then it's best to thoroughly wash over the affected area with **biological washing powder.** Once the area has dried out, then go over it again with dabs of surgical spirit. Many other household cleaners will not sufficiently remove the lingering smell - to a dog - of its previous 'accidents', or could contain chemicals reminiscent of urine, like ammonia. Either way, this makes it more likely that the puppy will return to relieve itself on areas it has previously used before.

Adult rescue dogs with 'toilet' problems may have them for a variety of different reasons, which we will cover later in Chapter seven.

Puppies and sanity

Do be aware that puppies at some time, during their early energetic lives, are going to drive you **mad.** They may make messes, dig up the garden, devastate bits of laundry or furnishing and have an almost supernatural capacity to be at their most active when you are most tired.

This is all an incredibly normal state of affairs for healthy young animals exploring their world. Equally normal is the tendency for new puppy owners to look permanently shattered. Puppies, like young children, have a hungry need to be occupied, and if you do not give them something to occupy them, then unfortunately they will find other things for themselves. **They** might think that these things are great fun but you may not.

Because it can be near impossible to always keep a puppy occupied or adequately supervised, but you don't want it in its crate too long, expect to spend early months trailing in its wake with a mop, broom, dustpan and weary grimace on your face. This again is normal. If things get really bad you can try - as I know some owners have - getting into your pup's crate with a stiff drink and shutting the door on the mayhem outside. Or going into another room or the garden and counting to ten, or 1055. Whatever helps you to cool off, and to remember that puppies just do what they do because they are young and know no better, and not specifically to instigate nervous breakdowns, even though they've such a skill for it.

In time, however, and particularly with patient handling and proper training (see Chapter six), puppies do improve and go on improving, and owners gradually find themselves recovering their sanity. Honest.

Meanwhile, for more advice on dealing with **chewing / digging** in any rescue dog see Chapter seven. For more advice on **destructiveness** see Chapters five and seven.

Socialisation

Often people will take the credit for assets in their dogs - e.g. a naturally placid, friendly or 'obedient' nature - that were actually down to a random, if fortunate, input of genes. (Weirdly though, this never seems to work in reverse, with a dog's 'faults' invariably being due to 'its breeding' or 'former owners'!)

Puppy socialisation, however, really is one of those areas where owners can make a significant difference to how an adult dog turns out, depending on how well - or badly - it is handled.

As previously outlined, a puppy's most crucially 'formative' period for socialisation is thought to be within its first 14 weeks. The full 'science' of how growing dogs relate psychologically to their outside world can be complex, but in a nutshell, if a puppy is exposed to a wide variety of new sights, sounds, experiences, animals or people while it is well under four months of age, it is most likely to accept them as 'unfazing' parts of normal life. If, however, this process is left until a lot later particularly in the case of more nervous breeds or individuals - then the puppy has more chance of perceiving that **strange** equals **threatening**, and will be more fearful in its response.

The fear principle

If you wanted a classic example of how this same principle applies to young humans, take a common 'fear of water'. Several studies have shown that many young babies, when put into water, will not only have little fear of it, but will also be able to swim. If they are not introduced to the experience of water and swimming until they are much older, or adults, however, they are far more likely to be afraid or panic at the prospect of going 'out of their depth', and it could take considerable encouragement and time to reverse this state of mind. Some humans will retain their fears about water for life, regardless of what is done to persuade them out of them.

Much the same happens with dogs who have not absorbed a sufficient range of novel experiences in the right way at the right time - only with one major difference. We cannot **explain** to dogs, as we can to humans, why something that might look, or sound, threatening is really safe. Dogs cannot possibly **know**, for instance, that a pneumatic drill is a noisy but harmless human tool, or that most strangers they see won't carry any risk of danger.

This lack of 'rationalising insight' throws a dog back on its own instincts to assess threat. Instincts which, in turn, give it two basic choices - it can either **trust that something is safe**, giving stranger sights or noises the 'benefit of the doubt', **or it can believe that something is unsafe** and react accordingly - i.e. by running away or attempting to defend itself.

In the main, dogs who have been **poorly socialised as puppies,** and / or who **lack sufficient trust in their owner's ability to 'safeguard' their welfare** in the face of threat, are more inclined to react negatively to something more unsettling or unfamiliar - though individual genetics, as ever, will also play a part.

A socialisation programme

When dogs are young puppies, they are more amenable to the view that new things are 'normal'. They are also more inclined, however, to accept that things are safe - or, for that matter, unsafe - through example. Thus, if you take your young puppy in your arms - until it has finished its vaccination programme - to a busy road, or up to strangers, and you appear quite happy or nonchalant about the experience, it will be inclined - in terms of a suitable reaction - to take its cue from you.

Here are just some things it is really valuable to get a puppy used to in its early months:

- **Travelling in a car** - or just being in a car, not just with you, but also on its own

- **Meeting a host of different people and children** - plus dogs when it has finished its vaccinations. This should include strangers and other dogs coming into the home

- **Meeting a whole range of other animals** - e.g. cats, rabbits, horses, cows, sheep, pigs

- **People in stranger headgear** - e.g. motorcycle helmets - and pushing things like prams, wheelchairs or noisy carts or trolleys

- **Trains, motorbikes, loud traffic**

- **Everyday household objects** - e.g. TVs, washing-machines, tumble-driers, vacuum cleaners

- **Loud noises.** Obviously you cannot 'manufacture' things like a thunderstorm or firework display for this purpose, but you can now get tapes of them from many suppliers of dog accessories or training aids. Other noisy venues - e.g. building sites, airports, fields where there are 'bird scarers' - might be useful to visit

All these things need to be introduced **very gradually**, at a pace your puppy can cope with. Remember you are trying to **socialise** your puppy, **not scare it out of its wits**. Trying to introduce too much too soon will both bewilder and frighten a young dog. In the case of 'noise tapes' (above), should you decide to get them, the volume should only be increased slowly, as long as the puppy remains unafraid.

Minimising fear

If your puppy seems afraid at any point during the socialisation process, **do not soothe and comfort it**. Inadvertently, you will simply be giving it the message that it is right to be fearful. Instead, ignore it and appear nonchalant - eat a snack or start running about with one of its favourite toys. Eating and playing are two things dogs normally find hard to do when they are anxious, so you will be giving your pup the cue that there is really nothing to worry about. If your puppy has an excessive fear response to anything or anyone during socialisation, and cannot be persuaded out of it, **do not prolong exposure to whatever is making it terrified**. In the long-term, this will be entirely counter-productive

If your puppy is at home when it gets frightened and dashes under a table or behind the sofa, leave it there until it is ready to come out. **Do not talk to it or try to forcibly drag it out.** Instead, wait for it to eventually come out by itself, then reward it with a treat, game, toy or praise - whichever proves most effective. Over time your puppy should learn that its fearful reactions are both unnecessary and inappropriate, whereas being more confident gets rewards.

When out, and not yet fully socialised, your puppy should be kept on a lead, or long line, to stop it 'bolting' away in fright. If your puppy is severely frightened when out on a lead, don't let it drag you away in the direction of home. Instead, sit down somewhere, and take your time. Look nonchalant, maybe eat a few sweets, read the paper or get out a ball or toy to play with (items worth taking with you). Focus on these, ignore the puppy's agitation and look completely unbothered and relaxed. Your puppy should register your total lack of worry and gradually calm down. When it does so, continue your walk in a similarly nonchalant manner - not home, but also not in the direction of the puppy's original 'terror trigger'. Try reintroducing it to that another day or time, initially from a greater distance. Repeat the whole above process, as required, until its fear over a noise or object subsides entirely.

Last points on socialisation

Yes, socialisation must look like quite a bit of effort. But if someone were to show you how tragically different a badly-socialised dog can be from a well-socialised one, in adulthood, you would know, without any further explanation, why the effort is worth it - both for you, and for your dog.

Despite all this, however, it is important to be aware that not all dogs who missed out on the above sort of 'socialisation programme' when young will have 'irredeemable' problems as adults. With time and patience, much can be done with many dogs to 'recover lost ground' when they are older. Success, however, can often hinge on a dog's 'innate character' - i.e. whether it is naturally more trusting / docile or naturally more sensitive / fearful.

It does seem to be the case that individual dogs, or breeds of dog, with more sensitive temperaments - e.g. Collies, German shepherds - need to begin a good socialisation programme as early as conceivably possible to acquire future benefits, in terms of improved levels of trust and confidence. Not only that, but they can also find it harder than others to 'recover' such benefits once this vital early 'window of opportunity' has been lost, or mishandled.

Early training

Chapter six is going to cover dog training in greater detail. In puppies, however, remember that you will always have the best possible chance to get the 'right' ideas into a dog's head - as regards behaviour - before it has had time to learn 'bad' ones - or even worse, to find bad ones more fun, or more rewarding!

One of the commonest mistakes people can make with puppies is to start their basic training, or 'behaviour modification' too late for most successful results. For some reason, they'll imagine that around six or seven months, or even later, is a suitable time to begin teaching puppies basic commands or the difference between acceptable, and unacceptable behaviour.

In truth, puppies need to get into the 'habit' of good behaviour far earlier. From about seven to eight weeks old, they should be quite capable of mastering basic commands like 'sit' or to come when called. The 'recall' command, in particular, is a vital one to teach a puppy when it is still very young and dependent and thus most likely to respond to you.

What also needs to be appreciated - as further outlined in Chapter six - is that all dogs, however young or old, **need to have a reason why they should want to do as you ask.** If your puppy has been allowed to do exactly what its likes for the first seven or eight months of its life, without any 'bad behaviour' being consistently corrected or challenged by you, then it has no reason to want to change this satisfactory state of affairs when it is an older and more confident dog - and thus even more of a mind to defy you. So you are going to have far more of an uphill struggle to gain its cooperation and generally overturn this state of affairs (for more advice on this issue, again, see Chapter six).

Letting puppies get to seven months or older without regular training or 'behavioural guidance' and then suddenly expecting obedience is somewhat similar to letting a child run riot from toddler-hood to adolescence without ever facing discipline, or learning respect for authority, and then imagining it can still turn into a 'model citizen' when desired. If you rarely see this miraculous transformation happen all by itself then it's because it rarely does - with children, or with dogs.

Jumping up and biting

Puppies, from as early an age as possible, need to be deterred from habits like excessive jumping up or 'play-biting'. One way to deter the former is to turn your back on the puppy and ignore it completely when it's about to leap up upon you, and to get everyone else to do the same. If eventually the puppy comes up to you but stays on the ground, praise it effusively. The object of both exercises is to make only n**ot** jumping up - rather than jumping up - rewarding. Also see '**Jumping Up**' and '**Biting**' in Chapter seven.

One of the best solutions to puppies biting is to give a loud theatrical yell or cry - like OUCH! - when the puppy nips, much as dogs or other littermates would do to warn the puppy that it has 'gone too far'. Puppies will explore the world with their mouths much as toddlers will do so with their hands. In nipping you they are actually testing the force of their own bite, and need to be taught to 'inhibit' it during interactions with others. If you yell loudly enough every time the puppy nips, then walk away ignoring it, or looking suitably offended, most puppies soon learn that such behaviour is neither appropriate nor acceptable. It will also help to always keep your hands still when the puppy is around. As long as you tolerate the nipping, the puppy will believe that it is acceptable, and will carry on doing it. If you physically punish the puppy for its actions, however, it might get frightened, or could become more aggressive to defend itself.

On the lead

Pulling on the lead can be one of the most annoying - and exhausting! - habits a dog can have. In Chapter six we will look at why the problem arises and how to stop it. But for now remember that dogs who pull on the lead as adults might never have done so had they been better trained as puppies to walk at your side, or at your pace.

Puppies and children

If you have young children, and a puppy, then they **must all learn to respect each other** to make the relationship work. In terms of how they should generally be approached and treated, children do not always understand puppies and puppies do not always understand children, and out of the confusion can arise the potential for considerable **upset** or **conflict**. In Chapter six, again, we are going to look in detail at how puppies, or dogs, and children should be taught to respect each other, and what to do should any conflict between them arise.

Emerging adolescence

As most owners know, puppyhood often seems to pass in a flash. One moment you are watching a pot-bellied, stumpy-legged bundle of fluff career across your kitchen floor, and the next it appears to have shot up into a gangling great teenager. Generally this all appears to start happening around six to seven months, depending on breed, and brings us to our next major phase of canine development which is:

The Juvenile Period

A very high number of dogs, particularly males, end up in rescue centres, or need rehoming when they become adolescents, or young adults - roughly between the ages of eight months to two or three years. It is sad, but not so surprising. Sometimes you have to wonder how many parents of human teenagers might have yearned to offload them elsewhere during this 'difficult phase' if they could, and if they could, would they ever have found a space in the rush?

Teenage dogs are often 'difficult' or 'exasperating' for much the same reasons that human ones are. Hormones are exploding, urging them to roam and test their individual strengths and identities. They don't want to be 'cuddly' and 'dependent' anymore, they want to be respected by their peers, assert their independence and, inevitably, find a mate.

Often owners can be quite shocked when their well-trained and superbly behaved little puppy suddenly turns deaf to their wishes when reaching adolescence, or appears to have forgotten all it was formerly taught. Or they will take on a teenage dog from a rescue centre and find that it can have the manners, and manageability, of an unruly delinquent.

Keeping your cool

If your puppy becomes this way, or you take your dog on at this stage, **the most important thing is to keep your cool and not panic.** The worst symptoms of 'teenager hood' in dogs, as in humans, do subside - only the good news is that with dogs it tends to happen a lot quicker, especially - as outlined later - if you handle it right. Better still, very few of them like to play loud music in their rooms, run up terrifying phone bills or experiment with drugs.

In a juvenile dog, what you will often see is an animal attempting to test your authority and will, in order to assert its 'independence' or give itself a better picture of its own status. It may be an incredibly maddening or frustrating instinct, but it is also an entirely natural one, essential to a dog discovering its own 'position' or 'role' in life. The more personally 'ambitious' the dog about its standing, the more it will 'push' to establish a 'superior' status, not just with owners but with other dogs.

In a rescue teenage dog, the problem can be worsened by a variety of other insecurities stemming from its past. In a new home with strangers, it could try that much harder to 'test' you simply out of a desire to establish your true levels of authority and commitment - both things on which its own future security will hinge. In troubled dogs or troubled children, this is a self-protective quirk of psychology known to foster parents, as well as canine rescue centres, the world over.

Sometimes castration in male dogs - as can be routine policy with many rescue centres - is thought to reduce the more aggressive or anti-social aspects of adolescent behaviour. But be aware that this operation isn't always a 'cure-all' measure by any means. Sometimes it can take months after the 'op' before results - in terms of improvement - can be seen, and sometimes it is a dog's natural character, or its own individually 'learned' behaviour, rather than its hormones, which are governing many of the ways it chooses to act / react. So the operation has to be coupled with re-training the dog to behave in a more 'acceptable way' (see Chapter six). Meanwhile, much more on **neutering / spaying** in Chapter nine.

What to do

Having established the reasons for your dog behaving as it does, the next thing is to know what to do about it. Here are some basic guidelines.

- **First, if you have a 'teenage' rescue dog, be patient.** On top of the insecurities this dog may have brought from its past life, it is also being challenged by the additional stresses of a strange new home, growing in general and - if still entire surges of powerful hormones. Give it time to feel more secure before you start adding any more demands and pressure of your own. You can be understanding without being over-indulgent, and your perseverance will pay off

- **Second, do not enter into 'battles of will' that you can never win** - e.g. you ask your dog to do something, and it won't, so you shout at it and it still won't etc...etc. And never, **ever**, plead or resort to wheedling little voices to try to persuade it to do what you want. This way you will rapidly lose your authority. You could also soon fall into the trap of giving your dog far more attention for not doing what you ask. If your dog won't do as you ask on first or second command - presuming, that is, that it **knows** what you want it to do - then starve it of attention. Walk out of the room without a word, or put it into another room or the garden, and ignore it for five or ten minutes. Then try again, repeating the exercise until you get a better response - then praise the dog and reward it. Remember the last thing any teenager can stand is to be **ignored**.

•**Third, do not let anyone persuade you that aggressive treatment or harsh physical punishments are 'the best way to deal with such a dog'.** They aren't, and you could just make matters worse through forcing the dog into a retaliatory confrontation - especially if it has come from a former home where such treatment was routinely inflicted on it, making it feel threatened and scared.

•**Fourth, whether or not your dog continues to defy your authority, on top of ignoring it, or 'banishing' it for disobedience (as above) when it does, make it 'earn' any privilege it gets** - e.g., food, treats, a game or walk - by first doing something that you ask, like a 'sit' or 'down' for 30 seconds (no longer) till you 'release' it. In other words, no 'obedience', no fun and no resources. **Do not let your dog have *anything* it wants, or would like, before it has first done something that you ask, and until its obedience or 'co-operation' significantly improves.** This way your dog will learn that nothing is for free, and if it wants things from you, it needs to show respect in order to get them. **It is important, however, not to over-oppress or attempt to humiliate your dog during these exercises.** Do not shout - keep things calm but firm. The aim is to show your natural authority over your dog, not to build up its resentment towards you through bullying it.

Through following all these steps, **you are minimising the chances of overt confrontation, but still showing your dog that you are fundamentally 'in charge'.** From this stage you can then consider more formal training if required (see Chapter six). Your dog, in time, should learn that defying your authority is essentially futile, because you are the key to everything it needs. It should also eventually learn that, because you have never frightened or threatened it, you ultimately must have its best interests at heart.

It should be said that not all teenage or juvenile dogs will pose problems as covered above, and many can sail from puppyhood to adulthood with barely a hitch. Sometimes, in fact, the only reason why adolescent dogs get abandoned or discarded is for the 'crime' of growing up and not being cute little puppies any more. Just through becoming real animals, with accompanying needs and demands, rather than cuddly playthings, they can outlive their 'novelty value' for previous owners. Assuming that we now know a lot more about canine teenagers, let us move on to:

Adulthood

If you put a lot of hard work and time into your dog when it was a puppy - in terms of training and 'behavioural guidance' - and / or persevered valiantly on through its teenage excesses, then adulthood is generally where you should see these efforts providing dividends.

Adulthood represents a dog's prime. Physically it will be at the height of its powers and mentally it should be growing calmer and more 'amenable' as it settles into its natural role or position in life, with less desire or inclination for rebellion - though there are always exceptions! Different breeds and individuals 'mature' physically at different rates, with many bigger breeds taking longer to complete their full skeletal development - i.e. up to two years, or even a bit beyond this.

Two to three years is also around the time most people judge that a dog has reached 'mental maturity'. Others, looking at the infantile antics of their so-called 'adult' dogs, might reckon that it never happens at all!

Adults in rescue

The most popular dogs in rescue centres, or for new owners in general, tend to be the younger ones. A preference for youth may be understandable but, as we have already seen, youth is not necessarily without its problems - or hard work - in any dog, whether rescued or not.

Prejudices people can harbour about older rescue dogs include the notion that they will have a considerable 'unknown past' whose effects might never be reversed. Psychological damage, however, has no set timescale determining 'minimum' or 'maximum' effect on individual dogs and their future behaviour. **It is as easy to 'mentally scar' a dog during its earliest months, or even weeks, of life, as it is over three or four years,** and be faced with similar problems, or insecurities, to be overcome later as a result.

Adult dogs may have different reasons for being in rescue centres than younger ones. The latter, as we know, can often be discarded when they become trickier or more labour-intensive adolescents, or because they have developed 'behaviour problems' which former owners could not deal with, or did not have the time or inclination to correctly tackle.

Adult dogs, like younger dogs, could have spent some - or most - of their lives as strays. With older dogs, however, there can be a high chance that a change in former owners' circumstances, rather than the dog itself, was most to blame for its homelessness. A relationship might have split up, for instance, with both halves of the partnership then moving into accommodation unsuitable for a dog. Or children might have come along, causing problems with the dog or leaving little time for it. Or an owner could have died, been evicted, or had to move to a place or job which made keeping a dog near impossible.

Most of us can find the apparent 'abandonment' of any dog tragic or 'irresponsible', but at the same time it has to be remembered that not all dogs are disposed of easily by their former owners. Sometimes the decision to get a dog rehomed can involve incredible heartbreak, and will have been made only because former owners really felt they had no other choice, or because they genuinely thought it would be in the animal's best interests, long-term.

Past lives, new lives

When you take on an adult dog, at least you know what size it is going to be when it is fully grown. If it came from a former home where it was loved, and encouraged to get on with children or other pets, then these could well be inherited advantages for you - similarly, if it has already had the benefit of some basic training.

Trickier dogs in early adulthood can be **those who have spent most of their lives on the streets as strays.** This is either because they were homeless, or because they were 'latchkey dogs' let out to roam at will, all day or night by previous owners, and probably knew the local dog warden like an old friend (or enemy!) Often such dogs can find it very hard to have their customary 'freedom' curtailed by the confines of a domestic home, and may regularly try to escape - at least initially - to recover their old way of life.

Dogs who had less happy, or successful, lives on the streets, however, might be glad of a far more 'cushier' and secure existence. At the end of the day, not that many dogs lack the brains to know when they are on to 'a good thing' worth sticking to.

Some rescue centres can have 'rebound' dogs. Dogs who might have had four, five or more homes by the time they were three or less. It isn't always entirely the dog's fault. It might not have got on with some owners' pets, could have been too energetic for many people, or it simply **never found a person or family prepared to persevere long enough with its anxieties or stresses in a new home.**

Unfortunately, the more homes such dogs get taken into and out of again, the more insecure they can get, and the cumulative anxiety can adversely affect their behaviour. Only when they find someone who fully understands this, and is prepared to stick with them through their troubles until they feel secure again, will you see a very different dog. This, however, can take a very special and dedicated sort of person. These can only be some rough guidelines as to why adult dogs might have ended up in rescue. Unfortunately, as with younger dogs, there can still be the possibility that former owners simply tired of them, or created problems in them - even if unwittingly - that they then neither wanted to cope with, nor take responsibility for.

This is why, as ever, it's best to only get your adult dog from a reputable rescue organisation, who will make proper assessments of an animal's 'real' character or possible problems themselves, rather than merely accept what they were told by former owners.

Training

Your success in training a dog rescued in adulthood can depend on how much work, on this front, has been put into it before, and also on the dog's general character and state of mind. A dog of any age that has just been rescued is not normally in the right state of mind to begin formal training.

This is because a) **it might still be feeling rather anxious or stressed,** and therefore cannot concentrate and b) **it does not know you well enough.** If it does not know you well enough it cannot trust you, or know whether it should respect your authority - it will thus be far less motivated to do what you ask. Much more about all this in Chapter six.

Meanwhile, we shall move on to:

Middle Age

What constitutes middle age in a dog? It can depend entirely on the individual or the breed. What is typical middle age for smaller or middle-sized breeds - e.g. age seven or eight - can be positively geriatric for bigger ones. **Some dogs will always act younger than their chronological age, and others will act older.** Most of us know people who are the same.

The rate at which dogs age, and the way they behave at different ages, is thought - much as in humans - to be down to individual genetic 'biological clocks'. But overall fitness and suitable levels of daily stimulation can also play a big part.

Time and again I've known owners rescue fat, inactive and under-stimulated middle-aged dogs, dogs who truly seemed 'old before their time' due to their former 'couch potato' lifestyles, and utterly transform them. The fitter they got, through better diet and increased exercise, the more active they wanted to be, and the increased mental stimulation they got from going out far more, experiencing new sights and smells and other people and dogs, made them take on a much more 'youthful' personality.

Sedentary lives

Unfortunately people who lead pretty sedentary lives, with too little exercise and unhealthy dietary habits, tend to have dogs who do the same, if only because they have little other choice. Dogs, however, do not really have lives long enough to waste being couch potatoes and hastening the arrival of many different illnesses / conditions related to obesity and the over-consumption of unsuitable food.

Owners who have given their dogs such lives, into middle age, probably did so with the best of intentions, reckoning that what was good enough for them was good enough for their dogs, or imagining that an over-abundance of treats was 'a way of showing their love'. In truth, it is a form of **cruelty** to impose on a dog a lifestyle so detrimental to its long-term health, and general well being, purely to suit one's own convenience or desires. So if you take on a middle-aged dog with such a background, one of the best gifts you can give it is the chance to lead a more active, healthier and longer life. For more on this whole subject, see **The perils of obesity,** Chapter nine.

Brood bitches

Some middle-aged female dogs - pedigree ones in particular - will be handed over to rescue centres purely because they have 'outlived their usefulness' for a breeder. Having spent their lives as 'brood bitches', providing numerous puppies merely as 'income' for their former owners, they are now no longer wanted because they are 'past their prime'. Either that, or because they have already had the maximum amount of litters that The Kennel Club will register from one bitch.

It is a callous practice that does not reflect well on pedigree breeders, even if others might be far more caring and responsible. It also shows how common it can still be for people to view dogs as nothing more than 'commodities', put on this earth to be exploited entirely for their own financial gain.

You cannot always tell how 'damaged', mentally, a bitch with this sort of past might be. If the dog was badly reared or treated, or kept in a very isolated or confined environment, she could be quite nervous or fearful, at least initially. Other bitches from a similar background, however, might retain a miraculously good temperament, and can go on to make very loving and rewarding pets.

Health checks

Many older people might choose to rescue a middle-aged dog, or an elderly one, feeling that younger ones could be too much for them. And not all middle-aged dogs will be 'crocks' - a lot of them can be in extremely good health, if they were previously well looked after, or they may just have the benefit of good genes.

Even if they appear in great health, however, it might be a good idea once you've taken them home to get a general veterinary check-up. This could not only improve your peace of mind about the dog, but also be an opportunity pick up any small problems that might be brewing - e.g. a sore tooth or any strange lump or bump.

If you take on a middle-aged dog who is fairly obese, or previously had a rather inactive life, **then do not suddenly give it lots of exercise.** This could put an intolerable strain on its heart or joints. Instead, build up a new 'fitness regime' gradually, changing its diet and increasing its exercise in small stages, so that its body can adequately adjust. Most good vets would be happy to give you additional advice about this, and also give your dog's heart a checking over. More details on all health matters in Chapter nine.

Expectations

By and large, owners taking on middle-aged dogs do not have excessively ambitious expectations of them. Often they have chosen a dog of this age in the hope that it will be a fairly undemanding companion, or will perhaps keep another dog company, or they will simply have an urge to make the rest of its days peaceful and happy.

This is perfectly understandable. If, however, the dog is still incredibly fit for its years, and amenable to learning new things - and you are the same! - it would be shame not to give it a chance to maximise such potential in activities like Obedience and yes, even Agility. You don't have to do such things competitively. You can do them at any level you like, at a local training club, and simply for fun. Chapter ten will outline all the different activities you can get both yourself, and your dog, involved in. You and your dog will not only have an enjoyable time - you will also make lots of new friends, both human and canine.

For what it's worth, the Collie I rescued at 13 was still doing Obedience competitions, and whirling round veterans' classes in the show ring, at the age of 15½ - and loving every minute of it. Which neatly brings us on to:

Old Age

There is always something particularly tragic about an elderly dog languishing in a rescue centre, at a phase of its life when it is most vulnerable and can least afford to waste time being unhappy. Many rescue staff will have particular soft spots for the 'oldies' in their care, but the time they can give them may be limited, and they still cannot be a substitute for the comfort and security of a loving home.

It's an obvious reality that many older people will own older dogs. And when an elderly dog's previous owner dies, becomes ill, or has to go into accommodation where pets are not allowed, then its own life is turned upside down. If a friend or relative of its owner cannot take the dog on, then it often ends up in a rescue centre. As unbelievably unkind and callous as it might appear - and is - some younger owners will discard elderly dogs into rescue centres purely to make way for a puppy or more 'youthful model'. A dog has given it loyalty and devotion all its life to such people, and this is the way they choose to repay it.

Concerns about 'oldies'

It is easy to get distressed by the fate of oldies, and the bewilderment which often accompanies the loss of all the security they might have previously known. Mostly what they need is some sense of security back as quick as possible, but this won't always happen as a lot of people do not want to take on an old dog. They worry that it might not be able to adapt to new circumstances, that it might require expensive veterinary treatment, or that it will die just as they have become very attached to it.

Answers to all these fears will depend on the individual dog. Some old dogs, for instance, might take on a new lease on life when rehomed with younger dogs, or with lots going on in the household. Others, and particularly those who have always led a quiet life, with perhaps just one owner who wasn't highly sociable, could find the same circumstances distressing.

It's inevitable that as dogs get older, their health will decline. They could have problems with their hearts or joints, their organs and bodily systems won't be quite so efficient and likewise their sight and hearing. But this is going to happen to any dog ultimately, even if you first got it as a puppy. You should also bear in mind that there are rescue centres and organisations - such as the NCDL, see back of book - who now offer many back-up schemes to owners taking on or fostering older dogs, in some cases even paying veterinary bills if necessary.

If you take on an old dog and worry about it dying, then this too is inevitable at some stage. But just as I have known many older dogs who had long, active, and pretty healthy runs before a sudden decline, I've known younger ones who died tragically early, through accident, illness or a heart defect. Either that or they wrestled with debilitating conditions like epilepsy or joint disorders throughout their lives (more details on these in Chapter nine). So nothing about a dog's health at any age can be guaranteed.

Twilight years

The reason why I have so much admiration and respect for people prepared to take on old dogs, and see them through their 'twilight years', is because ultimately they are putting the needs of the dog first and their own concerns second.

They appreciate the possibilities of the dog getting ill, or not being around too long, but it still doesn't matter as long as the time the dog still has left is full of happiness, security and tender loving care. And what such people will, and can, do for old dogs when they are in their most vulnerable and final phase of life can even be regarded by them as a 'privilege'.

It also has to be remembered that dogs do not **know** that they are irreversibly ageing - just that other dogs, perhaps, are beginning to run a bit faster - or that eventually they are going to die. This 'happy ignorance' frees them from the burden of an awful lot of philosophising and agonising about decline and death, all the better to get on with the business of enjoying each day as it comes.

As they get older, with perhaps a few more aches and pains and failing faculties, dogs can get more 'clingy' more 'crotchety' and more obsessed with the security of routine. Much like old people, in fact, and it is entirely natural. Let them have their peace and quiet when they need it, and a deep, warm bed in a draught-free spot in which to enjoy it. They are dogs who have seen a lot of life, perhaps not all of it good, and who throughout their lives have probably given a lot to other people. You now have the chance to acknowledge and, in some part, repay this - and it's unlikely that you will ever regret it.

The Cinnamon Trust

Should you be an older person taking on a rescue dog and are worried about the possibility of getting ill, or that your animal might outlive you, then you might want to know about a unique charity called **The Cinnamon Trust**. Although based in Cornwall, it has a nationwide network of volunteers to help out in such circumstances, either through visiting daily to see to pets' needs, or else placing them in temporary and loving foster homes when required.

They also have two special sanctuaries for pets who have lost their owners, where they can spend the rest of their days being loved and cared for, in surroundings that are as much like an ordinary domestic home as possible - including comfy sofas and TVs! They also take cats. For more details, see advice section at the end of this book.

Meanwhile, having completed our look at 'the five ages of dog', we will now move on to typical problems that can arise when you first bring a rescue dog home.

Chapter Five

Help! Early Days With A Rescue Dog. Understanding How The Mind Of A Rescue Dog Works. What's Normal /Abnormal Behaviour For A Rescue Dog Adjusting To A New Home? How To Get Things Right - And Keep Your Sanity!

Anyone in the habit of reading up on canine behaviour will know that there's a massive amount of technical advice to consult when your new dog comes home and is a little short of perfectly - behaved. During early days, when things are getting a bit worrying, say, on the toilet training, cushion-shredding or general won't-do-as-told front, it's very easy to get neurotic or stressed, so here's another bit of excellent advice that I always recommend first:

1. Stop panicking
2. Shut door on canine chaos scenario
3. Plug in kettle or get wine bottle
4. Walk into other room or garden and scream
5. Sit down, drink, consider blood pressure
6. Play soothing music or keep counting until blood pressure appears to return to normal
7. Return to baffled-looking dog
8. Consider more technical advice

If you are already feeling better for this, and have completed all eight stages, then it's clearly time to read on.

Early days with a rescue dog

Lots of people are fortunate enough not to have that much trouble 'settling in' a new rescue dog. And maybe, as they go on about how 'quiet and easy it was from day one' or 'it immediately seemed at home and never gave us a moment's bother', you'll sense a prickly feeling going up the back of your neck.

Your dog isn't like this. Your dog races round and round rooms. It barks and whines. It chews doors and won't listen to, or do what you say. It seems to have forgotten its 'toilet training', won't eat, won't go into the car or out into the garden, or goes shuddery with fear or aggression when it sees strange new people - most commonly, male - in the house.

At which point you are going to be thinking, what's wrong with **my** dog, or me, or us, or our house? And the answer, fundamentally, is probably not a lot. You have simply inherited a dog with a past and - potentially - an existing burden of worries and insecurities. **It can be quite normal for dogs who are highly stressed and / or who have a troubled past to react in this way when suddenly put into a strange new home.**

Later on we shall be looking in more detail at why rescue dogs can behave in any of the above-mentioned ways when you first get them, the part stress can play in it and what can be done about it. For now, though, it might help to understand far more about the basic psychology of a rescue dog, and the impact this can have on its overall behaviour.

Understanding how the mind of a rescue dog works

Sometimes, the best way to view the minds of many rescue dogs going into new homes is much like foster children, or children who have been 'in care', doing the same.

We do not always know the full story of these dogs', or children's, backgrounds, but we can predict that they have not - to date - been 'normal' ones, in terms of what we perceive 'normal' to be. Life has not been one steady, uninterrupted line of cosy routine and security, affording them the luxury of an easy-going, calm and 'hang-up free' personality.

Somewhere along the line there could have been a history of broken trust, shattered confidence, upheaval and terrifying uncertainty. And sometimes, there might also have been additional cruelty or abuse. **Such experiences will leave 'scars' on their victims and possibly alter the way they will later view the world and their own level of personal security.**

Few foster care professionals, or foster parents with much experience, would expect a child with a troubled, or insecure past, to settle into a new home without a few initial problems. There may be rages or tantrums, bouts of destructiveness or blatant rebellion as the child externalises its inner anxieties, furies or fears. Either that, or the child may turn such stressful feelings more 'inward', becoming depressed or despondent, having nightmares or developing 'compulsive disorders' - like constantly washing its hands - to calm itself down.

Such children may desperately want to trust someone, and feel secure, but at the same time are wary or frightened of doing so in case they are 'let down' again. This means they could push longer and harder to 'test' the strength of your commitment to them - often without even realising it - simply to gauge how 'safe' they really are. **And only when they do feel really** safe and secure can they begin a transformation for the better.

Dogs are consistently judged to be far less 'psychologically complex' or sophisticated than humans, yet no one who has successfully rehabilitated a rescue dog with a particularly insecure or troubled past could look at the above and not see a distinctly familiar story.

Conflicting expectations

If there are major differences between rehoming troubled children and dogs, they include the simple fact that troubled children generally go to places deemed to have sufficient knowledge or previous experience of their potential problems, even if they aren't all ideal. Quite a lot about an individual child's background will also tend to be known.

The same often isn't the case with rescue dogs, and - except in the case of particularly difficult or dangerous dogs - no one can really be blamed for it, as everyone's experience of rescue dogs has got to start somewhere.

What it does mean, however, is that less experienced owners can be less prepared for more troublesome or challenging behaviour because of what they **do not know**. They will not, or genuinely **can't** see why a rescue dog might act or behave in the way it does when it first comes into to their homes, and will instead get understandably distressed or despairing about it. Or they will blame themselves for doing something 'wrong'.

Less experienced owners of rescue dogs can also start their relationship with their new charge on the basis of conflicting expectations or needs. Even without necessarily admitting it or acknowledging it, there will be a part of them expecting their new dog to be 'grateful' for the wonderful new life they have given it. Equally, they can imagine that a dog must 'instantly know' that it is 'safe' with them, or at last in a permanent home, and should thus behave with relevant respect, co-operation and 'gratitude'.

Unfortunately dogs, especially those with previous histories of 'abandonment', **can know no such thing** - at least, not until a suitable amount of time with you, and experience of your treatment of them, has proved otherwise. During early days or weeks, all they'll know is that they are with strange people in a strange place. Maybe previously they were with strange people in a strange place and bad things happened, and could therefore happen again.

Additionally, they're not sure yet where they stand in this household or 'pack', or who is really in charge, or whether they will necessarily be 'safe' within this set-up. All these factors, especially on top of existing anxieties from a former life, or time in kennels, can lead to them feeling pretty stressed.

Stress-related behaviour

Dogs get stressed for the same reasons that we do. Because they feel vulnerable and threatened, uneasy or insecure, or because they feel unable to escape or control what is happening to them.

As with us, also, stress causes physical and psychological changes in dogs due to alterations in various hormonal and chemical levels within the body. The following symptoms can be signs of stress in a dog:

- Lack of appetite
- Less reliable 'toilet training'
- 'Manic' energy levels or general over-excitement / restlessness
- Barking, panting, whining with seemingly little reason
- 'Compulsive behaviour' patterns - e.g. tail chasing, rolling over and over, excessive licking or gnawing of paws or other parts of the body
- General over-reactiveness / defensiveness
- Shaking or shivering
- Inability to concentrate
- Poor coat, diarrhoea, excessively itchy skin

It is not unusual (See **Anxiety** Chapter seven) to see any of these symptoms in a newly rehomed dog. The longer a dog is stressed, or exposed to stressful things, the longer the 'symptoms' can prevail, and the longer it will take to bring it down from its state of anxiety.

Dealing with stress during early days

It cannot be denied that a stressed dog suddenly arriving in a new household can be pretty stressful for its owners. There will be times when you might regret taking this new responsibility on, and others when you might resent its behaviour, feel angry with it, or just not like it very much at all, especially if it has just destroyed something of real value to you, or is 'playing up' when you feel particularly stressed and / or exhausted yourself.

Again, all these feelings are quite normal, and sometimes it does more good to accept them as a natural early part of the 'rehabilitation' process than to feel guilty about their existence. When you do feel angry or offended by your new dog's behaviour, your first immediate, instinctive urge might be to shout at it or, worse still, hit it. **And if so, you must fight this urge as hard as you can.**

Remember:

- This dog could have been shouted at, or hit, every day of its life in a previous home

- You need to show it different reactions or behaviour to increase its sense of safety and regain its trust

- It is very unlikely to have known that it's behaviour was bad or offensive, and therefore your punishment will only upset it or frighten it more

- The more 'attention' you give your dog for less 'preferable' behaviour in early days - even if this is just shouting - the more it might feel tempted to repeat it simply to gain this distinct 'reward'

When dogs feel free of the risk of any personal harm or threat within a new home, they begin to relax more. When some firm sense of 'order' and 'comforting daily routine' is established, or re-established, in their lives, they relax more. When they're kept suitably occupied, physically and mentally, but not perpetually over-stimulated or over-excited, they relax more. And finally when you relax more, they tend to relax more.

Often owners will say that they had just got to the stage of accepting, with little more grief or neurosis, that their rescue dog was always going to be crazy or hideously behaved **when it suddenly began to improve.** It's one of those strange quirks of dogs the world over. When you're tense, they're tense, and when you start to relax and feel happier, they start to do the same. Much more on stress and anxiety in dogs in Chapter eight.

Neurosis versus neurosis

Having looked at how stressful having a new dog in the family can sometimes be for owners, during early days, this might be a good stage to warn why some owners might find it more stressful than others.

If you are an exceptionally house proud person, the sort of person who might develop a nervous tic if a mat isn't straight or an ornament is 0.5 cm off its rightful place on the mantelpiece, all but the most mild-mannered rescue dog could be quite a challenge to your 'values system'. Unless of course, you subsequently feel able to relax your standards because you find a dog worth relaxing them for - as can often happen.

Additionally, if you live in a rather volatile or neurotic household, this also might not be the best environment in which to settle a stressed new dog - especially one with a distinctly sensitive, reactive or neurotic temperament itself. Dog and owners could continually 'wind each other up' and both parties could find it hard - if not near impossible - to change enough about what they fundamentally are to make it work.

A lot of neurotic households never actually view themselves as neurotic. So here's a quick test. **Is it ever possible, at any given time in your household, for two days to elapse without:**

- A major drama over something pretty basic

- Lots of shouting

- Someone of any age having tantrums, crying, screaming

- People constantly tearing up and down stairs / out of rooms and slamming doors

- People getting resentful, sulky, tense

- People deploring the smallest levels of imperfection / mess / untidiness

'No' to more than three of these would seem pretty neurotic to a dog, even if lots of people might thrive in households like this, and even regard them as quite 'normal'. For a highly stressed and sensitive dog in particular, who will mostly crave tranquillity and order in its life, this sort of set-up can be the equivalent of living in a permanent psychological war zone.

Dogs cannot understand, or rationalise, human neurosis in quite the way that we can. For them, particularly if they are already stressed, human neurosis has no sense or function other than to generate a constant atmosphere of unease and tension. This in turn can give them the notion that they are living in a pretty unstable 'pack', and can lead to them feeling even more anxious or insecure.

Temporary household neurosis and dogs

Sometimes 'neurosis' within a household will only be temporary, due to transient traumatic events or upheavals within a family. Most households cannot avoid such events and upheavals, or the stressful feelings they subsequently generate, at some time. When they do occur, however, be aware that although your dog can never know what has made you so suddenly tense, upset or irritable, it can still be adversely affected by the general atmosphere of unease and instability that such feelings will create. If dogs always seem to 'play up' or 'behave at their worst' when you are most stressed or preoccupied with other concerns, it's because they are stressed by your stress, or disturbing change in behaviour. And when you return to more 'normal' behaviour, it's highly likely that they will do so, too.

All in all, dealing with, or having to tolerate, human neurosis seems to be the price modern dogs have to pay for living so intimately with us 'as family', and some will always be able to deal with it better than others. It can, of course, also be argued that dogs have quite a few little foibles of their own which, at close quarters, can test our tolerance to the limit.

The myth of dog 'guilt'

Another important point to be aware of, during early days with a rescue dog, is that when they do something bad and you tell them off, or look like you are going to tell them off, they are not looking / feeling or are, in any way, **guilty** about it.

Dogs do not understand the concept of guilt - you just *think* they do. What they do understand, however, is when you are looking distinctly hostile, or angry towards them. They will rapidly read this in your more aggressive body language and fixed stare and will react to it with suitably apprehensive / submissive postures or behaviour. **Not guilt.**

If they are in the middle of doing something 'bad' when you get angry with them, they might well make a connection between the 'bad thing' and your anger or disapproval. But otherwise they won't.

If you take them up to a door even just five or ten seconds after they've been chewing it to tell them off, **they will not understand why you are telling them off.** If you come home and find that they have had an 'accident' on the floor, you can point at it and jump up and down in indignation for five minutes and they **still won't understand why you're telling them off.** But they could get fairly worried and upset, especially if you get angry with them, often, for reasons they don't understand.

Further, if you get into the habit of coming home and being angry with your dog, it will just start to associate your return with hostile / unpleasant behaviour, rather than anything 'bad' - e.g., fouling, destructiveness - that it had done before this point. This in turn can fill it with great anxiety, making it more, rather than less, likely when you are out to repeat the 'bad' behaviour that is making you so cross.

With dogs who do 'bad' things like fouling or chewing you have these options. One, catch it in the act, and give it a brief word of rebuke - e.g. 'no!' - to make it understand that it has done something 'wrong'. Two, resolve to make it easier for the dog to do the 'right thing' in future (more advice, Chapters six and seven). Anything else isn't too effective. Do not waste your time - and emotional energy - trying to make a dog feel guilty.

What's 'normal' for dogs adjusting to a new home?

When rescue dogs arrive in new homes there are two common possibilities, other than the one that they will not give you many problems. The first is that, during earliest weeks or months, they will behave not that well - e.g. they'll be exceptionally restless or destructive - and then gradually get better. The second is that they will start off fairly well behaved, or appear quite biddable and quiet, and then suddenly get worse, after what is commonly known as 'the honeymoon period'.

There are perfectly good reasons for both situations. In the first case, a dog is immediately externalising existing or current anxieties within a new environment - or even just the excitement triggered by novel surroundings and / or its escape from the confines and restrictions of kennel life, should it have come from such a background.

These 'excesses', however, can just be transient reactions within new surroundings, rather than a true indication of the dog's 'normal character'. If the dog's normal character is far less volatile or over-confident, then it should quieten down considerably once it feels more settled and secure, even if this could take a few months.

In the second scenario, it is likely that the dog came into your home in a more subdued or withdrawn state - almost, if you like, in a state of 'shock' - as a result of successive knocks to its confidence, either in a former home - or homes - or within kennels. This is what gave it the appearance of being so 'quiet' and undemanding during early days.

However, again, this behaviour might not be a true representation of its normal character. It might by nature be a more boisterous or challenging personality, and it is this 'real' personality that can begin to re-emerge once the dog feels more confident, and less 'oppressed' within a new home.

What to do

In the first case scenario, it is often merely time and patience that will see the dog through its initial phase of readjustment. This is a dog who may have lost all 'security anchors' in its life and is therefore cast adrift on one big churning tide of anxiety and uncertainty. You have got to gradually give it some anchors back, and here are some ways to do it.

First, however your dog behaves, keep it to the same set **routine**. Make sure it gets walked, fed, groomed, played with, has toilet opportunities and goes to bed at roughly the same time every day - certainly for the first weeks or months. This will be the dog's first 'security anchor'. Second, give it its own 'den' or cosy sleeping quarters well away from the main bustle of the household where it can go, undisturbed, whenever it likes - another 'anchor'.

Third, do **not** inflict any additional stress on the dog by shouting at it harshly or using any form of physical punishment. However hard this can be when it severely tests your patience, through doing so you can rapidly reverse any progress.

Remember, as previously outlined, that for many rescue dogs being shouted at or hit is frequently nothing new, and can merely reactivate old anxieties - the sort of anxieties, in fact, that you are hopefully aiming to overcome. This apart, for some dogs maybe the only form of real 'attention' they ever got from previous owners was shouting - a state of affairs that quickly teaches them to repeat any behaviour that seems to bring about this distinct 'reward'. And you don't want to fall into this trap.

Your clear intention never to harm or threaten your dog will eventually give it yet another 'anchor'. Your dog will also greatly benefit from knowing that it has the protection of a convincing 'pack leader', and a consistent set of rules governing its behaviour. For more details and advice on these 'relationship building' issues, see the next chapter

In the second scenario - the dog who appears to 'get worse'. No one can deny that some naturally unruly dogs, like naturally unruly children, will exist - especially if never suitably discouraged, or taught more acceptable behaviour, at an early stage in their lives.

If your dog, from a fairly quiet or subdued start, then begins to get either more destructive, rebellious or even aggressive, let us look at some possible reasons why.

Early destructiveness

There are two common early 'destructiveness scenarios' with rescue dogs. The first will usually happen on the night they arrive in a new home or soon after. On its arrival at a new home, the dog will generally have had a huge fuss made of it - or certainly more fuss and attention than it was previously used to - over several hours, if not a whole day. It would also have been intensely stimulated by a wide array of new sights, smells, people and perhaps other animals.

Later on, when the new owners decide to turn in for bed, they will often relegate the dog to one particular room - usually the kitchen - and shut it in there for the night. In doing so, they will have visions of a pleasantly exhausted dog sleeping sweet doggie dreams in the comfort and security of its new home.

The next morning or even hours later, however, their kitchen might look like it has been in the eye of a very bad hurricane. And the dog who **was** the hurricane can appear in a pretty agitated state. What went wrong?

First, although owners may have been exhausted when they went to bed, the dog was still 'buzzing' from all the earlier excitement and stimulation. Second, it was also confined and left on its own, which could have made it additionally anxious - why has its great new 'pack' suddenly abandoned it again? Finally, it had the most fantastic array of new and interesting objects to explore and unleash its energies and anxieties upon for as long as it took to feel better.

However much it might go against the grain, or your general principles about 'a dog's place', a way to avoid an early scenario like this is to keep the dog with you, in your room, on the first night or two, or even more until it winds down and gets more settled. Make it keep in its own bed - within a good-sized dog crate if necessary, unless it has a phobia about cages - and later on, if, desired, you can then move this and the dog further and further away from your room in gradual stages, until the dog is finally situated where you want it at night.

This way you can keep the dog under supervision and it has the comfort - if not inhibiting influence - of your presence. **It is not a good idea to let your dog sleep on your bed** until you have a better idea of its character - see **'Early rebellion'** / **'Early aggressiveness'** sections later.

Also avoid the dog getting too 'wound up' or over-stimulated before bedtime with lots of excited play or rushing around. Keep it very active if you like, during the day, but then wind things down a good hour, if not two, before bedtime, even if this means consistently ignoring the dog's 'play overtures', or general 'attention-seeking behaviour' during this time until it gets the message to settle.

The second early destructiveness scenario can often occur a little longer after the dog has first come to your home. You may come home from work, or a trip out to the shops or friends, and find that the dog has chewed and clawed the front door, or the door of the room it was confined in, plus anything else it could find - and most particularly items or objects with the strongest concentration of your scent - e.g. shoes, bedclothes, or chairs or sofas you use a lot.

It is highly likely, in such scenarios, that you have not left the dog on its own very long before. Maybe you wanted to give it time to 'properly settle in' before you returned to work after time off, or you didn't leave it on its own until you imagined it was 'ready to cope'. Maybe you also found, during early days or weeks with the dog, that it thrived on all the concentrated attention you gave it and that it insisted on following you from room to room - yes, even to the toilet - and wouldn't let you out of its sight.

Naturally, there are a lot of people who might find such early devotion quite flattering or endearing, when in fact it is quite **unhealthy** for a dog to be so over-attached to its owner that it later finds any separation from him or her traumatic. Out of this trauma can come quite despairing anxiety, and the nervous energies responsible for destroying objects with your scent on as the dog attempts to comfort and calm itself. Either that or it will focus on chewing doors or door frames in an effort to get to you, or even just to free itself from its immediate worries about solitude or abandonment. Such dogs, clearly, are not 'ready to cope'.

Rescue dogs will often have a greater tendency towards 'over-attachment' because their backgrounds have left them fundamentally more insecure, and more fearful about 'abandonment'. But when you do not teach, or allow, a dog to keep some 'natural distance' from you, or accept periods on its own as a temporary but normal state of affairs, you are denying it the ability to be adequately equipped, psychologically, for your absence.

In Chapter seven, we are going to look at **Separation Anxiety** and **Destructiveness** in far more detail, and outline how you can teach a dog to cope better with your absence. For now though, here are the most important things to keep in mind about destructiveness in rescue dogs:

1. Do everything you can, as early on as possible, to get to the root of what might be causing your dog to be destructive - preferably with the aid of some sound professional advice.

2. Stop destructiveness in your dog becoming a **habit** through constant repetition and regular access to things it can destroy. Sometimes the original roots of a dog's destructiveness will be anxiety, then it can soon escalate into something it also does anytime it feels bored or frustrated because it has discovered it can get a distinct 'high' or 'feelgood factor' from it. There's a chance that your dog's former owners let its destructiveness get to the 'habit' stage, and this may even be why they subsequently got rid of it, even if they gave its rescuers a different story.

3. Often a dog's destructive frame of mind will subside when other issues at the heart of it - e.g. insecurity, stress, lack of adequate mental stimulation - are properly addressed. But this can take time. If you cannot immediately stop your dog having 'destructive urges', what you can do is minimise its potential to unleash them and have them sufficiently rewarded. Dogs will only destroy what is available to them to destroy, as often as they are given opportunity to do it unchallenged. Do not leave them alone with access to any items or objects you do not want destroyed.

4. Initially, you may have to put a rescue dog in a good-sized crate when you go out, to avoid it chewing doors / flooring etc. Until the dog is properly settled in, this should **not be for more than half an hour or an hour at most, at a time.** It will also help greatly if the dog has previously been allowed to get used to the crate gradually (see **How to use a crate**, last chapter, under **'Puppyhood'**), so it will not see it as a 'punishment'.

Fill the crate up with plenty of toys, chew items, and 'activity cubes' full of food to keep it occupied. **The exception to the above might be a dog who had been kept over-lengthily, and with frightening associations, in a dog crate in its former home.** If your rescue dog is clearly terrified by the prospect of going into a crate, **do not force the issue.** It could do more harm than good.

Instead, you could try getting it used to being in a certain room or area of the house in which it can do minimum damage. Again, before you leave the dog alone here, try to get the dog used to it while you are still around, for five or ten minutes at a time, maybe three of four times a day. The use of **child or baby gates** to separate a dog from you in another room / area, while it can still see you, should help. Build up good associations with its separate room or area - e.g. it is always fed there, or you come up and make a fuss with it and play with it for five minutes while it is there, and give it treats. Again, leave the dog in the room or area with things to chew and play with, and at regular intervals while you are still in the house. Also give it some old blankets rather than fancy or expensive new bedding you wouldn't want it to rip up. A radio playing in the background when you leave it - out of its reach - may also help. **Do not just put the dog in a room or confined space for the first time and then go out and leave it alone**, as it may well be terrified or highly anxious

In time, as your dog gradually settles down and relaxes within its new home, learns that your absences are only going to be temporary, and is always left plenty to do, the use of either crate or confined area may prove unnecessary whenever you go out. **As ever it is unadvisable, if not plain unkind, to leave a dog alone, restrained or confined, for regular long periods of time**

If all the above can seem a bit like hard work, remember that what is at stake here is not only your dog's gradual adjustment to your home without learning - or rediscovering - the 'habit' of destructiveness, but also your own psychological well-being. Even if dogs may not know that they have destroyed things of value to you, just by doing so they can cause you tremendous distress, resentment or anger. These feelings, in turn, can so easily be projected on to your dog, undermining your developing relationship with it, and also perhaps weakening your motivation to want to get to the heart of deeper-rooted problems likely to be causing its destructiveness in the first place.

If dogs don't, or can't, destroy things, then you can't get upset or angry with them about it, or additionally stressed. And ultimately everybody's better off for an outcome like that.

Early rebellion

Juvenile dogs, as we saw in the last chapter, are quite renowned for their capacity to be 'rebellious' once hormones start raging and they begin the quest to test the limits of both their own, and other people's, authority. If, however, you have acquired a rescue dog who becomes progressively 'more of a handful' during early months in your home, then other - or additional - factors may need to be looked at.

First, a dog who tears boisterously round the house, deaf to any command you might hurl its way, could still be in a fairly 'stressed' or over-excited state. This will limit its ability to concentrate on anything other than its immediate anxieties and desires. Chapters seven and eight cover **Anxiety** and **Stress** further.

Second, you may be giving your dog wrong messages about your actual position, or level of authority, in its life. When we first get rescue dogs, particularly if we know them to have had troubled backgrounds, it's incredibly easy to be over-indulgent or over-lenient with them 'to make up for their bad starts'.

Dogs with quite submissive natures can sometimes thrive on a more 'indulgent' approach, but others - particularly those with a 'pushier', or more 'insecure' character - can read our constant humouring of their desires or excessive attentions to their needs as a **sign of weakness.** This can backfire in two ways. **First,** the dog can begin to harbour notions that it must be 'superior' to us, because we hand it so many 'unearned' privileges - e.g. treats on demand, access to our bed, the comfiest chair or sofa in the lounge - or because we seem so reluctant to challenge many aspects of its behaviour. **Second,** the dog will become even more insecure. It has a need for the protection of a strong leader and you don't appear to be it.

Both possibilities could lead to a generally more 'difficult, or unresponsive dog. Of course, this is also likely to happen when owners fondly - but wrongly - imagine that shouting at a dog is any substitute for **proper training.** Until a dog has been taught to make the right association between a clear command and an action, you might as well be shouting 'strawberries!' as 'stay!' for all the sense it will make to its ears.

It is possible to convey authority to a dog without intimidating it or being a bully, as it is possible to be kind and understanding towards a dog without appearing 'weak'. How to get this balance right will be covered in the next chapter, as well as more details on proper training.

Another possibility with your more 'unruly' dog is simply that it has never been taught basic good manners or acceptable behaviour within a home, and will thus have to be taught such things from scratch - again, see next chapter.

Of all the early worries owners can have about behaviour in rescue dogs, however, one of greatest understandable concern is aggression. So let us look at possible reasons for any early displays of aggression now.

Early aggression

Let us suppose that you have brought home a rescue dog that in many ways seems ideal for you. Weeks, or even months pass without incident, and the dog appears to be settling in well. Then one day, quite unpredictably or 'completely out of the blue', it suddenly appears to 'go mad' - either threatening to attack you or someone else, or actually doing so.

Naturally this can be quite terrifying, but what has gone wrong? A common possibility is that something - some object, person or set of circumstances - has suddenly activated a 'fear response', and instinctive defensive reaction, in the dog's mind. **Dogs always remember what it is important to remember, for their own survival, and what they won't forget is the experience of fear or pain,** anymore than they will forget the object or person associated with it.

You may well think that your rescue dog's aggression occurred 'out of the blue' because, not knowing the full story of its past, you could not predict what would frighten it. I've known rescue dogs go berserk when new owners first opened an umbrella, or came into a room with a tray, or took a broom out of a cupboard, most likely because these were objects they had been beaten with by former owners in former homes. In which case **the dog will view its own 'defensive' response as being both logical and necessary,** even if it baffles you.

It is not very likely that former owners of dogs like this, when bringing them to rescue agencies, are going to say, 'by the way, I regularly beat this dog with a spade and a yard of flex, so it might be frightened of these sort of objects', is it? So this means new owners will not only have to deal with the damage they have done to the dog's psyche, but they will also be - at least initially - pretty much in the dark when it comes to reliably predicting what will make their dog afraid.

It is also possible for dogs to acquire 'fear through association'. In other words, if a certain object or person was in their sights when, or just before, they experienced terror or pain, they would later associate them with the original fear or threat scenario. If someone had previously put their house keys down, for instance, or taken off a particular type of coat, prior to beating or severely frightening their dog, then just the sight of these 'fear triggers' again, or similar looking or sounding objects, could immediately put it into defensive mode.

What to do

Should you inherit a dog like this, then here are the options. You can choose to work with professional advice - as many owners do - on its fearfulness towards certain objects or people, once its 'fear triggers' have been discovered (for more advice on dealing with **Fearfulness** and fearful **Aggression**, see Chapter seven). A lot of owners will do this not only because they have become very attached to the dog, but also because, in all other respects, it is a very rewarding companion.

Second, you can decide that this dog is too risky, or too dangerously unreliable, to own, and return it to the rescue agency you got it from. You may feel bad about this. You may feel that you are further betraying a dog that has already been badly let down by mankind. The bottom line, however, is that dogs like these can be hard, if not stressful, to own and not all of them can ever be fully 'cured', especially if there are genetic as well as historical reasons for their problems.

Other reasons for early aggression

'Fear responses' apart, there could be other reasons why your dog suddenly turns 'nasty' during its early days with you. These include the possibilities that it might be in some sort of pain - thus making it feel more vulnerable / defensive - or that is has some medical condition that might be affecting its behaviour, so it might be worth a trip to the vet to get these treated or ruled out.

Sometimes, too many immediate commands / orders / general 'bossing about' inflicted on a rescue dog, during early days, will put it under so much pressure, on top of existing anxieties, that it will feel forced to retaliate in some way, if only to warn you to 'back off'. This can typically amount to a growl, or curling of the lip and possibly the dog baring its teeth.

What to do

At this stage the dog cannot really know if you are to be trusted, and is making this, as well as its own sense of being under pressure, clear. And if the dog is looking pretty 'scary', this is entirely what it intends, in order to stop you pushing it much further. **If a dog ever reacts towards you in this way it is vital not to push it any further into a potentially far more serious confrontation. Do not shout at it, approach it any nearer and do not, under any circumstances, retaliate with any form of aggression or punishment yourself.** Apart from being highly dangerous, this could seriously undermine your relationship with the dog.

If, however, you immediately back down or go away when the dog adopts such threatening behaviour, it could easily get the message that this is all it will ever need to do to get its own way in future. So instead, do not go away. The moment you see the slightest hint of threatening, or seemingly 'defiant' behaviour in your dog, take a few steps back and completely relax your body language. Avoid eye contact with the dog and stand sideways to it. These are the sort of signals dogs will give others to suggest that they do not want conflict.

You have now given your dog an 'escape route'. **Only if your dog was really seriously intending to attack you will it still look dangerous, in which case it would be sensible to leave the room for your own protection, and maybe even reconsider its future with you.** Otherwise, it is much more likely that your dog was really as reluctant as you to have a full confrontation, unless it was given no other choice, and it will be relieved to have avoided it.

Once things have calmed down a little, call the dog to you, and let it come when it is ready. If it does not want to come to you immediately, **do not force the issue.** Leave the room slowly. Keep coming back at regular intervals to pass by the dog and call it to you, ignoring it as before if it does not respond, and going out of the room again. When it does eventually come to you, ask it in a quiet but convincing way to do something simple like 'sit'. If it does this, praise it well and / or reward it with a treat. This way you are keeping your authority without damaging the dog's trust. Until your dog has learned to trust you more, and become more secure, you may need to be less heavy-handed, or over-pressurising, in the way you assert your authority. Equally, though, your dog will have to learn that co-operating with you is not, ultimately, a 'take it or leave it' option.

It could also be that in a former home, any command, order or even routine owner approach to your dog had a threat attached to it. If you take away any sense of threat in your approaches or commands to your dog, then there will be far less reason for it to react so defensively. **As with all aggression problems in dogs, however, do be aware of how risky it can be to attempt 'solve the problem' entirely by yourself without the aid of additional professional advice.**

Canine 'louts'

The above scenario apart, some rescue dogs - unfortunately - can only be described as 'canine louts'. These are dogs who learned early in life that by far the quickest and most effective method of getting their own way was to push their weight around - either with blatant disobedience, or through intimidating other people, dogs, and their own owners into the bargain. And naturally, the bigger and more powerful the dog, the more weight they have to push around and the higher the chances that this would have proved to be a very successful strategy.

Lots of owners will fall in love with the 'image' of a big and powerful dog under their control, and then find that 'control' of any kind, anywhere else but in their most optimistic fantasies, is a quality that pretty permanently eludes them. At which point, the dog can often be discarded in despair.

Invariably, you will hear it said that such dogs will require 'firm handling'. But this can be a term open to any amount of misinterpretation, abuse or underestimation of one's own true competence in this area.

Some owners can actually believe that 'firm' equals continually shouting at, generally bullying the dog or even hitting it 'until it knows who's boss' which, apart from being utterly barbaric, could also mean they run the risk - during the course of this 'training process' - of 100 lbs of dog or more possibly retaliating and taking their throats out. Or at best, giving both owners - and the nearest casualty department - a pretty nasty fright. And if so, do they then have an alternative masterplan? In the main, a 'firm handler' is usually someone who can fulfil the following requirements:

• They will be fairly strong characters themselves

• They will know a fair bit about - or will have gained sufficient knowledge / experience of - dogs and good dog training methods

•They will be utterly consistent in their dealings with the dog and will never - no, not even sometimes - let it gain any unearned privileges

•They will know how to get what they want from such dogs without confrontation or hostility

•They have a natural talent for eliciting a dog's respect and affection, increasing its motivation to do what they ask

My own feeling is that most really good 'firm handlers' are born. If you are not a naturally assertive and determined character, with a strong will, then it can be near impossible to give a convincing impression that you are, or at least one that any dog with half a brain couldn't see through.

Canine louts and firm handlers, all in all, are probably going to be about the only combination with a real chance of long-term success. Bear this in mind should you ever be tempted to rescue a dog with, potentially, an even stronger will than yours - and the physical power to match.

Cars and gardens

Some people could find that their rescue dog shows an early reluctance to go out into their gardens - especially alone - or into a car.

Sadly, this isn't always as 'odd' as it first might appear. There is a possibility that when your dog was put out into the garden at its former home, it wasn't just for a 'toilet opportunity', but to be left there maybe all day, or all night, and it has not forgotten either the fearful isolation or discomfort of the experience. In time, with suitable encouragement, your dog will learn to have far more positive and happy experiences of gardens.

When it comes to a fear of cars, it could just be that the dog has had very little experience of them in its past life, or that it was left in one during particularly frightening circumstances - e.g. a thunderstorm, or firework display was going on at the time. This again, could pass with enough encouragement, and certainly once the dog has made more positive associations between cars and outings to fun and interesting places.

In some rescue dogs with a distinct terror of entering cars, one also cannot overlook the appalling, yet still too frequent reality that a car was the last thing it knew before it was abandoned by its former owners, either on to a motorway or in some isolated place which filled it with panic. Its fear is thus entirely logical. Depending on the individual dog, and the original strength of its fears, it may take some time before this phobia is conquered. Full advice on dealing with cars and **Car travel problems** or phobias in dogs in Chapter seven.

'Abnormal' behaviour

So far I have looked at types of behaviour in rescue dogs that you could previously have considered 'unusual' or 'worrying' but in fact can actually exist quite commonly in many of them during their earliest weeks or months with you. I have given you some reasons why, and what to do about it and hopefully this advice will have been of some help to you.

At this stage, you may well be asking yourself, what then is **abnormal** behaviour in a rescue dog? And the answer is not as straightforward as you might think, because often when dogs come from 'abnormal' backgrounds, they may have had to learn to react or adapt to them with suitably 'abnormal' behaviour, if only to cope psychologically. Or they could have learned to see 'abnormal', as it were, as the 'norm'.

Earlier on - in Chapter three - we looked at dogs who had been raised in **puppy farms,** and how some of them later would be seen to do things like walk backwards or lick walls. Naturally such habits would strike us as distinctly bizarre, but they - along with many other 'weirder' kinds of behaviour - may simply have been 'invented' by the dog through necessity - i.e., in order to counteract the stresses caused by under-stimulation and confinement.

In similar vein, if dogs have been raised from puppyhood in kennels, then kennel life for them represents 'the norm' and a domestic home will be a more alien and potentially frightening environment. And the same can work in reverse for dogs who have only previously known domestic homes, then suddenly find themselves put into kennels.

Sometimes owners will find it strange that a rescue dog arrives in their home not beginning to know what it should do with everyday pet items like a toy or a proper dog bed, when the truth is it may never have seen such items before in its life. Many owners can view aggression of any kind in a dog as 'abnormal', when in fact - as touched on in this chapter and outlined in even further detail in Chapter seven - this is far from the case.

Ultimately if any form of early behaviour in your rescue dog is striking you as particularly 'weird' or disturbing then the most important issues are:

- **Could it have a logical explanation of a kind previously outlined in this chapter?** In other words, would it seem less 'weird' once you knew more about common early behaviour in rescue dogs? If so, then your dog may simply need more time and understanding.

- **Could it have any clinical cause?** In other words, could the dog's behaviour be due to a source of pain, illness or underlying brain condition - e.g. a tumour, or a certain form of **epilepsy**? Either of the latter conditions can display some 'weird-looking' behaviour symptoms - like obsessive (rather than occasional) tail-chasing or catching of 'imaginary' flies in the air, or the dog pressing its head against walls or having moments when it looks mentally 'absent'. It's unlikely that your dog has any such brain condition, but it still might be worth a veterinary check up for your own peace of mind if you are really worried, and also to rule out any other health problems.

• **Is the dog's behaviour either potentially, or actually, *dangerous*?** In other words, does it represent a real threat to anyone, because its aggression is totally unpredictable / unreliable? If so, you might want to back up your concerns with the opinions of one or two experts in dog behaviour (see advice section at the end of the book). Some dogs with problems like this can be helped or 'improved' considerably with the right advice, but others will be less responsive to 'remedial treatment'. **Never, ever, however, keep a dog that you are afraid of.**

• **Can you really see yourself or your family living happily with this dog, long-term?** Do not make a decision about this impulsively. Lots of rescue dogs and new owners have 'hiccups' or bad patches during early weeks or months. This being said, some dogs and some people just really do not 'belong' together and if so, no favours are done to either party through 'prolonging the agony' of not getting on.

How to get things right - and keep your sanity!

So far we have looked at many different challenges a rescue dog could face you with during its earliest weeks or months with you in a new home. Now, let's look at you. How are you coping with the demands of this new responsibility, and how many times have you walked out into the garden to scream?

Maybe your fingers have itched, at times, to ring the number of the rescue agency who gave you your dog, with a view to sending it straight back. And each time this urge arose, your new dog suddenly arrived with the soppiest and most seductive doggie look on its face and rested its head lovingly on your knee. Dogs really aren't that daft.

Often owners can feel 'failures' or 'guilty' because on occasions they have lost their tempers with their rescue dog, or else resented the way it has disrupted their formerly ordered or carefree lives with new responsibilities and concerns. Maybe they really believe that there are people in this world who can successfully rehabilitate a rescue dog - and a rather demanding or challenging one in particular - without occasionally losing their temper with it, or resenting it, or having doubts about the reality of what they have taken on. But there aren't.

In the end, there are only people who are prepared to stick the course with a rescue dog, and people who aren't, for whatever reason. And of the people who stick the course, none of them always does things right a hundred per cent of the time, because nobody is that perfect. Additionally, if new owners aren't always told, or cannot have predicted, how hard the first few months with a rescue dog might be, they can underestimate the real size of the achievement they have made, just through sticking with the dog when it was likely to be at its most challenging or demanding, or most anxious and insecure.

If progress with 'rehabilitation' can at times seem slow, then do remember that early days with different owners, in terms of the new expectations imposed upon them, can also be pretty hard for rescue dogs, too. As humans, we know that regaining trust once it has been broken, or changing fundamental things about our habits or ourselves, can be amongst the most difficult achievements on earth. If they're massive achievements for us, then they can also be massive achievements for dogs asked to do the same thing. This is why it can take time.

I hope you feel that you'd like to give your dog that time, and would also like to work towards making your future relationship with it as rewarding and successful as possible. If so, then the next chapter should be of help to you in this area.

Chapter Six

Training Your Rescue Dog. When Should You Start? How Should You Do It? Building A Healthy 'Working Relationship' And A Dog's 'Place' Within The Family 'Hierarchy'. Teaching Your Dog Some Basic Commands. Rescue Dogs And Children. Rescue Dogs And Other Pets

Few dogs will not benefit from training of some kind. Training not only builds up a dog's essential bond with its owner, or owners, but one day it could also save its life. I know dogs, for instance, who are only around today because they were taught an 'emergency **down**' or 'recall' so efficiently by their owners that it got them out of immediate danger.

Lethal dangers for dogs, when out, can include anything from heading towards cliff edges or a busy road, to chasing livestock or vehicles like tractors. Farmers, as most owners need to be aware, are within their rights to shoot any dog deemed to be a threat to their animals. A well-trained dog also tends to be a well-behaved dog, and a well-behaved dog is not only much more of a pleasure for everyone to have around, it will also itself - as a result - have a far better quality of life. This is because far more people will welcome its company and will always be pleased to see it.

When people get in a muddle about training, and / or frustrated with their dogs, then it's usually because they think it should all be an easy and straightforward matter of them asking their dog to do something, and it obeying. And if not, well, the dog is clearly 'untrainable' or 'disobedient', isn't it? - End of story. They can forget not only that training is something you need to do **with** your dog, rather than **to** it, but also - as with all endeavours in life - the results you get back will reflect the amount of time and effort you put in. Moreover, you can start with small goals, such as a better 'recall' or 'stay' and then, if you like, get progressively more ambitious. Let us now look more fully at what training your rescue dog might involve, and the most common mistakes that could be made along the way.

Training your rescue dog

Dogs come programmed knowing only how to be dogs, and to do what dogs instinctively want to do. The process of 'training', therefore, is the way we 'educate' them to perform behaviour that is more preferable, or acceptable, to us, if not to human society as a whole. If we can make a dog actually enjoy the process of 'education', and even find it rewarding, then two basic advantages arise. First, the dog is much more likely to remember the 'lesson' or 'correct action' it has been taught and second, it will be that much keener to repeat it.

On paper the above can look like very obvious or commonsense principles. Yet they will be forgotten or go unappreciated by dog owners every day. When we bring impatience, frustration, force, anger or punishment into the business of training, then all we will teach a dog is that training, or indeed any approach from us to do something, equals 'persecution' and anxiety. Anxious dogs can't concentrate well and will always make more mistakes.

The most important human qualities needed for successful dog training are **patience, persistence and encouragement.** It is also vital to allow dogs to make mistakes in training without fear of instant, worrying, owner disapproval or punishment. This way you can soon diminish their confidence, overall motivation and the enthusiasm with which they will want to respond to your future commands.

When you get a rescue dog, you do not know how fast or slowly it might learn new things, or what 'bad habits' it might already have learned in a former home. There is also a good chance that it might arrive in your home 'deaf' to anything you ask it to do, or more interested in anything other than your presence and your voice. If so, be aware that this is very common. It does not necessarily mean that you have a 'bad', 'naturally disobedient' or 'untrainable' dog. It's more likely that your dog simply isn't ready for training yet, and I'll now explain why.

When should you start?

When a dog won't do what an owner asks it to do in training, maybe you think there could be masses of different reasons for it. In fact, problems like deafness or poor vision apart, there are only four basic ones - and these are:

1. **It is stressed, suffering from some form of pain / discomfort or highly anxious - and therefore cannot concentrate**

2. **It is not motivated enough to want to please you**

3. **Other more immediate concerns - e.g. loud noises, approaching dogs or other animals, irresistible smells - have temporarily shifted it's focus away from you**

4. **It generally doesn't know, or *understand*, what you want it to do**

Although any one of these reasons, or combinations of them, could explain a dog's apparent 'disobedience' at any time, the most important ones for owners of new rescue dogs to appreciate initially are **1** and **2**. I'll touch on issues surrounding the other reasons later in this chapter.

(Also see **Disobedience** in Chapter seven for more insights into this subject).

1. When a new rescue dog first comes into your home, it is likely to be stressed in some way, which is why it finds it hard to concentrate on anything other than its own immediate anxieties. Owners can also be told that the first thing they should do with their new rescue dog is to take it straight to training classes, or they might imagine that this is the most sensible thing to do.

In truth, it can frequently be a disaster. If you have got an already stressed, or rather bewildered dog, whom you then introduce into an environment full of other strange people, dogs, and noise, it could find this sort of scenario quite threatening or hostile. **Remember, also, that it does not know you well enough yet to be sure you can be trusted to safeguard its welfare.** So it becomes not only more worried and distracted by its immediate surroundings but, potentially, even more stressed. On top of this, you then start pressurising your new dog even further with a string of commands or orders it is in no state of mind to take in. So do not be too surprised if these early attempts at training in a class don't go too well.

You cannot start training a dog until it has first become less stressed, and also built up greater trust in your leadership. For fuller advice on dealing with **Anxiety** and **Stress**, see Chapters seven and eight. When your dog starts to concentrate far more readily on you, and seems to be generally less restless or distracted around the home, or when out, then you will know that it is less stressed and more inclined to trust you.

Next, 2. - motivation, or lack of it. As we have already outlined in this book, it is pointless to assume that any dog will do anything for anyone, just on the basis that it is a dog and we are its owner. **It needs to have a reason why it should want to do what we ask.**

In the training process, both food treats and praise can be very helpful in quickly getting a message across to a dog that it has done, or is doing, the 'right thing'. Ultimately, however, the most powerful reason a dog has for co-operating with you on a day-to-day basis is because **it wants to please you.** Most dogs, like most people, will always try harder to please people they not only trust and respect, but also have developed an amount of affection for.

Clearly, rescue dogs cannot arrive in homes full of trust, respect and affection for new owners, because these are all things that have to be earned by owners over time. A little later on, I will show you how much successful training revolves around **good 'working relationships'** between dogs and owners, and how you can build relationships like this up.

For now though, be aware that **you cannot start getting the best responses in training until you have first earned sufficient trust, respect - and also, ideally, affection - from your dog.** You will know this point has arrived when you see your dog, entirely of its own free will, trying harder and harder to understand - or do - what you want it to do.

How Should You Train?

Once you consider that you have got your dog into a suitable frame of mind to begin training, your next concern will be, how should you do it? You have the option of going to a good local training club, or hiring the services of a personal dog trainer who will work on a one-to-one basis. The first option will be more sociable for both you and your dog, but if you consider that you have a more nervous, or 'difficult' dog to contend with, you might benefit more from individual attention. Either that, or you could share a private lesson with one or more owners whose dogs you know your own dog will get on with. Details on where to find a good training club or personal trainer at the end of this book.

With most rescue dogs, it's best to start from scratch - in other words, to assume that they already know few, if any, formal training 'commands'. Good and experienced dog trainers will normally be very patient with rescue dogs, understanding their possible problems or 'mental blocks' and also, in many cases, not expecting too much in the way of rapid progress initially.

Most dog trainers will also tell you the same story - which is that their profession principally revolves around teaching owners, rather than dogs, what to do. Do not be offended by this. Obviously experienced dog trainers are going to know far more about dogs than you, and which methods of training and approaches to training are likely to be most successful in your case.

From good, experienced and enthusiastic dog trainers, you can learn a lot of real value to both yourself and your dog. Be aware, however, that not all dog trainers, or methods of dog training, are as good as each other.

Good and bad training

Novice dog owners, in particular, can sometimes find it hard to know what is 'good' and what is 'bad' dog training. So here's a simple guide. **A good dog trainer:**

- Will never use harsh, unkind or punishment-based techniques

- Will never have too many dogs - particularly of varying levels of experience - in the same class

- Will have reward-based methods of training that not only work but make sense to owner and dog alike

- Will be primarily concerned about the quality of the owner's relationship with his / her dog rather than mere 'results'

- Won't care how many questions you ask or how slow your progress is

• Will make the whole business of dog training enjoyable and FUN

By contrast, be wary of any trainer who tells you that they can 'quickly' solve problems in your dog like 'dominant' or 'unco-operative behaviour', or aggression. In these circumstances, a 'quick' way of getting 'results' invariably means the **'wrong'** way. Often severe physical punishment can be used on a dog in an attempt to 'frighten' it out of defiance, or out of aggression which could itself be based on fear.

Such brutal treatment can give a dog the appearance of being 'subdued' - when it is actually more likely to be in a state of **shock** - and that's why, in the short-term, it can also seem to 'work'. Long-term, however, as covered more fully under **Aggression** in the next chapter, you could end up with even worse problems in your dog as a result of this 'remedy' than you started out with.

If you are not highly experienced with dogs, then it's very easy to be 'bullied' by bad trainers into using methods on your dog that you would otherwise be averse to - like physical punishment, again, or routinely picking dogs up by the scruffs of their necks and shaking them. Such people may often tell you that they've 'been training dogs all their lives', which means absolutely **nothing** - other than that after all those years they still haven't learned a more compassionate or acceptable way of educating animals.

Once you've closed your mind to any element of self-doubt, or the possibility of ever doing things differently or better, it's remarkably easy to keep doing the 'wrong' thing for an entire lifetime and still think it right. If there is anything about a training class or method that you feel, instinctively, is wrong for your dog, **trust your judgement.** Your instincts are telling you it is 'wrong' most likely because it **is.** Do not stay in classes like this a moment longer. Go somewhere else better instead. Again, to get a good trainer, see end section of this book.

A last word of warning on training. Never, **ever,** send your dog away anywhere on its own to 'be trained' or to 'have its problems sorted out'. If you are not with your dog, you cannot know what 'training' or 'remedial' methods are being used on it. Your dog has got to live with **you,** not the 'remedial' trainer. What your dog will do for the trainer, possibly under duress, will be no indication of what it might later do for you in different circumstances. Appreciate, too, that it takes **no skill at all** to make a dog afraid, and **if any 'training methods' backfire, or cause the dog lasting psychological harm, it will be you, and not the trainer, who will have to deal with the consequences.**

Doing it yourself

Quite a few people like the idea of training their new rescue dogs themselves. If you really know what you are doing - rather than just think that you do! - or have considerable knowledge and experience of dogs, then obviously you should be well-placed to predict or accurately diagnose any particular problems and deal with them.

If you are not so experienced or knowledgeable, however, there's a chance that your progress could be slower, or you could create more problems for yourself and the dog through doing things **wrong**. It is also a fact of life that as owners we can often have too much emotionally invested in our dogs, or our relationships with them, to be 'objective' enough when any problems arise - be these to do with training, or general behaviour.

For this reason, even some real canine 'experts', at times, will seek independent advice when it comes to sorting out problems in, or with, their own dogs. If you are set on training your dog yourself, don't be too proud or stubborn to seek more expert advice should you find you have hit an impasse, or have a problem you cannot seem to get around. It can happen to us all at some time, and a more dispassionate, as well as more experienced, look at the situation can often work wonders.

Whichever way you choose to train your dog, the fact remains - as outlined before - that your overall relationship with it is the key to success. Let's look now at the 'healthiest' sort of relationship you can have with a dog, and how to build it.

A dog's 'place' within the family 'hierarchy'

Our relationships with dogs can be incredibly inconsistent. One moment we can be treating them like children, or fawning over them like babies and the next we're expecting them to do what we say because we're the **'pack leader'**. Similarly one day, when we're in a good mood, we might suddenly let our dog up on the settee with us as 'a treat', or let it have food from our plates on the table. Then the next day, when we suddenly remember what 'a dog's place' should be, we won't.

This is all highly confusing for dogs, but we do it because as human beings, obviously, we will find the parent / child relationship the most 'instinctive' or natural one to enact with our pets. We are genetically programmed to be parents to children, in other words, but not genetically programmed to be 'pack leaders' to dogs, and therefore can have more difficulty conveying this role in their lives with optimum efficiency or conviction.

Role replaying

Equally, many owners can 'replay' with their dogs the sort of 'parental style' they were raised with themselves, or which had greatest impact on them in their early lives, for good or bad. Owners, for instance, who were brought up in a rather hostile or constantly critical family environment will often perpetuate this 'example' in the treatment of their dogs, even without realising it, because it is 'all they know'. Either that, or they will overcompensate for the distress such a background caused them by being over-lenient with dogs, or too inhibited to enforce even the most basic forms of discipline, for fear of being 'disliked'.

Dogs are not human psychologists, able to analyse or understand why we should treat them in one way or another. They just understand forms or 'styles' of leadership which make sense to them, or make them feel more secure, and other kinds which don't, and will react accordingly.

Many problems with dogs arise out of the confusion, or insecurity, they feel when we are inconsistent in our treatment of them, or fail to read their behaviour along the lines of canine, rather than human, logic. Additionally, we can often be so driven by our own demands of dogs that we can forget that they have certain expectations of us, too, which need to be considered in order to minimise distress or conflict.

It stands to reason that the more we can grasp about what dogs expect of us, and the better we can relate to them in a way they will understand, the happier and less stressful the whole human / canine relationship can be. With rescue dogs, let's look at this relationship from the very beginning.

Early foundations

It can be hard to get any relationship with a dog exactly right, all the time. Not only because of the above mentioned reasons, but also - obviously - because dogs and people are two different species, and thus will tend to have different expectations, priorities and general 'value systems' in life.

With a rescue dog, this relationship can be further complicated by its past. It may, for instance, already have had unpleasant or worrying experiences with people, which will hamper its ability to readily trust you at the start. As already outlined, it is also possible that certain objects or circumstances - e.g. confinement, or getting into a car - might trigger frightening memories from a previous life.

After a rescue dog has got over the initial stress or inhibiting 'shock' of being in a new and unfamiliar home, its next step is usually to work out the household 'hierarchy', and where it might stand in the general 'pack pecking order'.

Many new owners can find it hard to grasp that a dog has no sense of 'equality' in relationships. It is an animal programmed to conform to a hierarchical set-up. For this reason it has a need to know whether other 'pack members' that it shares its life with - human or canine - are actually **superior**, or **inferior** to itself. Sometimes a person can give clear 'signals' to a dog that he or she is inferior or superior (more on this later). At other times these signals can seem more 'ambiguous' or less clear-cut to the dog, and it may feel a need to put the true status of such people to some sort of 'test' or 'challenge', to see who will really come out 'on top'.

There is a good chance that your new rescue dog will never be this way inclined. In other words, that it is a naturally fairly submissive or easy-going character whom you can indulge, or occasionally be 'weak-willed' with, without it ever having an urge to 'take advantage' of the situation in any way. But you will only discover this facet of its nature over **time**.

'Trickier' characters

You could, on the other hand, have a new rescue dog that is a naturally more 'forceful' or 'ambitious' character. The danger of being immediately too indulgent, or 'over-lenient' with dogs like this is that you can easily afford them too high a notion of their own status. This in turn can lead to them being generally more 'disobedient' or 'defiant, or rapidly developing manipulative forms of behaviour, such as barking / whining / or general 'pestering' to get what they want from you - from walks, meals and treats to simple 'attention'. Worse still, they could later resort to displays of aggression to keep their sense of 'higher status' preserved (see **Aggression** in the next chapter for fuller details on this).

Unfortunately this tendency, again, is only something you are likely to see happening over time. And because you cannot know, for sure, how 'ambitious' a dog will later prove to be when you first bring it into your home, it's safest to assume that it will be a fairly strong / manipulative character until experience proves otherwise, and thus you should behave towards it in a suitably 'superior' way. To do this, as we show later, you will need to stick to some fairly firm early rules - either individually as a single owner, or collectively as a household.

Later on, if the dog proves to be a naturally rather biddable or non-pushy character, you can have the option of modifying - if desired - or relaxing some of your stricter 'early rules' a bit, but **it will always be harder to get tougher, convincingly, with a dog you have formerly been lenient with rather than the other way around.**

It is important to understand that strong hierarchical 'ambitions' in dogs are no more a sign of essential 'bad character' than they are in humans. Indeed, powerful drives to succeed, or generally be 'competitive' in life, are rarely seen as 'faults' or 'defects' in people. Society, however, normally decrees that people should be in charge of their dogs' behaviour, rather than the other way around. And if this is to happen with maximum reliability then your dog's position, in any household, has to be kept at the **bottom** of the 'pack'.

Living with new 'pack members'

The way you and other household members 'represent' yourselves to your new rescue dog can govern much of its subsequent reactions or behaviour towards you. Remember, your dog is evaluating you all as a 'pack' and looking to see where it stands in relation to other 'members'.

During early days with your dog, the most important priority will be to start establishing a 'bond' with it. Because your dog may have had unpleasant or unsettling past experiences with people, you'll need to try and reverse such negative associations in its mind. Your dog needs to find your company pleasurable, reassuring, rewarding and essentially non-threatening, and you'll begin to get this message across by sharing plenty of enjoyable experiences together (e.g. games, interesting walks), through caring for its general welfare on a day-to-day basis and through resisting any temptation to shout at the dog, physically punish it, or over-burden it with too many immediate commands and demands.

At this stage, however, it is also very important **not to inadvertently** 'overdo' the amounts of general fuss and attention your dog gets from household members, to the extent where it could feel you are all fascinated by its every action or move. Dogs so treated can soon turn into highly manipulative **'attention junkies'**, unable to cope with owner interest being removed from them, and therefore devising all manner of irritating tricks or habits to get it back. They can also start to get inappropriate ideas about their own level of importance. Maybe your dog got very little undivided and pleasurable attention, or praise, in its former home, which is why a sudden bombardment of such things from you will be more likely to 'go to its head'.

Your dog has got to be aware, from the start, that every single member of your household, while essentially benign in character and intent, is nevertheless superior to itself. To get this message across, it is best for everyone to avoid displaying any signs that could be interpreted as possible 'inferiority' by the dog.

The Rules of 'Superiority'

In early days, it is very easy to give a dog 'signals' that you do not have sufficient 'authority' to command its respect. Owners or other household members can often convey this impression to a dog without even realising it, and therefore it can help to have some 'rules' (see below) to avoid it. Here are the main ways we can make dogs view us as 'inferior', and how to reverse this state of affairs:

• By being **inconsistent**. Dogs view authority purely in black and white terms. They are either allowed to do something or they are not allowed to do something. We make our authority look rather more questionable when we will **not** allow a dog to do something one day, but **will** the next

Avoid this by: setting out some strict basic rules for your dog when it arrives - e.g. where it can and cannot go, what it should, or should not be allowed to do, and then get everybody to stick to them

• By routinely letting dogs 'set the agenda' within a household - e.g. allowing them to barge past us through doorways or up the stairs, or dictate when they should be fed / walked / played with. Once they see a 'chink' in your resolve, many dogs will conjure up all manner of attention-seeking tricks - e.g. whining, barking, nudging, general 'nagging' - to put pressure on you to give them their own way.

Avoid this by: never letting your dog 'dictate the agenda' for anything that happens with you in your house. From when mealtimes arise to when walks or games begin and end or when the dog should get attention - only you, and other household members, should decide

Should your dog ever try to 'force the issue' to give you what it wants - by barking / whining etc. as outlined above - then *you must total ignore it* until it has quietened or settled down again, even if this means immediately leaving the room the dog is in if you can't stand its behaviour at very close quarters.

This may be very hard for you at first but you must persist relentlessly and ruthlessly with this strategy. Appreciate that with a new dog these are early tests of will or status that you simply *cannot afford to lose.*

Dogs should never be so 'over-oppressed' or restricted that they seldom get the chance to use their own initiative, or have the freedom to generally 'be themselves' a lot of the time. But this is quite different from a dog who is routinely allowed its own way in all household interactions, or is basically allowed to run the whole human agenda and 'pack dynamics' through 'wheedling', 'bullying' or manipulation of any kind.

• By letting obedience or co-operation become more of an '**optional**', rather than 'obligatory', response - in other words, disobedience never has any suitably deterring consequences.

Avoid this by: making 'defying' *any* family member a far less rewarding option. Do this by only ever giving 'preferable' behaviour or responses from your dog a reward - be this simply your attention or a treat or game. By contrast ignore *completely* any other sort of behaviour or disobedient response - unless this behaviour is particularly destructive or worrying, in which case simply banish your dog instantly to another room or the garden *without a word* for as long as it takes for the dog to quieten down. Keep employing these measures automatically and relentlessly until your dog eventually becomes more responsive or 'amenable' to commands. *For more advice, see 'Attention-seeking Behaviour' and 'Disobedience' in the next chapter. Also never let your dog get anything 'for free'* (see below)

• By letting dogs have a fantastic array of privileges - e.g. treats, toys, food, attention - completely 'for free', and without ever having to do anything for us in return.

Avoid this by: making them *always* do something for any family / household member in return for a 'privilege' even just a 'sit' or 'stay' for five or ten seconds, or a bit longer in the case of 'pushier' dogs.

• By letting dogs have open access to all areas of the house - including bedrooms and furniture - and allowing them to sleep on your bed. Factors which can quickly give it a notion of fairly high status.

Avoid this by: Making dogs stay downstairs - with the exception of their first few nights with you, if need be, as previously mentioned - and restricting access to bedrooms, at least until you can gauge how 'ambitious' or 'dominant' their true personalities are. Dominant dogs allowed free access to beds, bedrooms and household chairs or sofas could later see these as 'privileged resources' worth 'guarding' from other family members.

It can be very hard for many people to avoid falling into any of the above 'traps', or to stick to all these 'rules' consistently. This is because, quite understandably, they do not find being so relentlessly 'firm' or 'strong-willed' with a dog easy, and are perhaps far more gentle or generous characters by nature.

It is also inevitable that our relationships with dogs, at some point, will develop an emotional 'overlay'. In other words, once we get more fond of them we will worry more about being 'too tough' with them or could imagine that we might 'hurt their feelings' through being 'over-strict'. It also has to be said that being 'indulgent' with dogs, and generally 'cosseting' them, for some people, can also fulfil emotional needs in themselves.

Dogs, however, do not stop 'loving' you simply because you are strict with them and, if anything, feel inherently more insecure with owners who cannot convey proper leadership or authority. At the end of the day, either as an individual or as a household, you have also got to decide the following:

1. **Do you want to construct a relationship with your dog affording you the best possible chance of being in charge and control of its behaviour? Or:**

2. **Do you want to be far less 'strict' or assertive and run the risk of your dog becoming rather more of a challenge, or far less obedient later on, as a result?**

The choice is yours.

A united front

Problems can also arise if couples, or households, do not keep a 'united front' - and generally back each other up - on the application of our previous 'rules'. If one member of a household, for instance, or half of a couple, is the only one consistently conveying real authority, the dog can often become a divisive force as it begins to 'pick and choose' who to obey. Parents can experience much the same syndrome, once a child learns to play one of them off against the other, or soon knows who it its most likely to 'get round'.

Similar problems can occur if the dog is allowed to become excessively attached to one person. Frequently in households one half of a couple will say, 'oh, the dog will do anything for him/her, but not me', as if this was either an inevitable or healthy state of affairs. It is not.

Many dogs will develop tremendous affection for 'softer' household members who will dote on them and indulge their every whim, but this doesn't necessarily mean they'll also respect them enough to always do what they ask, when they ask it.

Routinely, owners can accept it as 'inevitable' that their dog will not obey them or respect them when, in truth, the key to this problem often lies in their own day-to-day behaviour towards the dog (again, see **Disobedience**, next chapter). There are dogs who really could try the 'authority' of all but the most strong-willed of characters. Many others, however, will simply do what they like because this is the option we have always - however unintentionally - given them.

'Dominant rituals'

Few owners today have not grasped the notion that people are supposed to be their dogs' 'pack leaders', but the way they are supposed to 'interpret' this role and convey it to their dog can often seem quite complex or confusing.

Countless people today, for instance, are now imagining that the minute they get any dog home they must start a series of 'dominant' rituals - which will range from making the dog always eat last to even sitting in its bed occasionally. However fashionable such behavioural 'postures' have now become, they can never be a substitute, in themselves, for a lack of consistent control or authority in all other areas of the dog's life. In other words, there's no point in making your dog eat last, or in sitting in its bed, if the rest of the time it's allowed to do much as it likes.

Dogs, over time, and through general day-to-day experience, are as capable as any other intelligent animal of knowing the difference between a person merely acting out token postures of authority and one with real intent to be **in charge**.

Not all dogs, however, **are** dominant personalities by nature. Some will be far more easy-going characters, and some might actually be quite submissive or nervous. And if you persist, over time, in handing out to them the same more 'oppressive' type of regime that you would use on a naturally more 'challenging' character, it could damage their confidence or just make them fairly miserable.

In the wild, many inherently submissive dogs might get ruthlessly 'picked on' or 'persecuted' by their peers. But this doesn't mean that everything dogs might naturally do to each other 'in the wild' is necessarily the right thing for us to do, too. Wild dogs have little interest in the 'psychological health' of natural 'underlings', but **we do**, because we need our dogs to live happily with us in a sociable environment, which will offer many challenges to their natural confidence. The more we build up their confidence, therefore, the better they will be able to cope with this environment.

Shyer or more submissive dogs

From the above, you may begin to appreciate that effective 'pack leadership' does not really rely on one single formula or approach, but has to be tailored to the personalities of different dogs. Different dogs will often require different tactics, or 'leadership styles' to get the best out of them, whether this is in training sessions or in terms of general behaviour.

Shyer, or more submissive dogs, for instance, will react far more adversely to being shouted at than bolder and more confident ones. But as they can tend to be far 'hungrier' for your praise and general approval, this can also make them more eager to please you and thus easier, in many ways, to train. The best way to handle such dogs is to always go overboard with praise the moment they do something right, and really try to boost their self-esteem in all areas of life. If they do something 'wrong' around the house, correct them instantly in a firm but calm way, then return to a more relaxed mood and don't belabour the point.

Dogs like these often find your obvious disapproval quite **upsetting**, so through prolonging your displeasure you can soon start to undermine their confidence. Also try to appreciate that dogs cannot understand the concept or point of lingering resentment in an owner's mood or body language. It is a purely human form of behaviour, and because it lacks explanation to dogs, it can only make them feel more uneasy and insecure.

When dogs with more submissive natures do something 'wrong' in training, **don't say or do anything harsh, as this could instantly reverse any progress you have made.** Merely give them a brief word of praise for whatever effort they have made for you, and by contrast go absolutely overboard with praise and treats the instant they get something right. The obvious difference between these two reactions from you will soon make it clear to the dog what is the 'right' thing to do without undermining its confidence in any way.

Just because you have a naturally shyer or more submissive dog, however, this doesn't mean that you shouldn't still convey appropriate '**authority**' to it, via consistency of action, and firmness of resolve to instantly check or correct less acceptable behaviour, even if your treatment of it in the main is fairly calm, gentle and reassuring.

Indeed, in many ways, more timid or submissive dogs can frequently have an even **stronger** need to be 'lead' by someone conveying sufficient authority, because this makes them feel more protected. If you cannot give them this sense of protection, then it stands to reason that they will feel more insecure. If your dog is both naturally nervous **and** unsure of your competence as a 'leader' then it can also have an increased risk of becoming more 'defensive', aggression-wise, to others - if only through a fear that it cannot rely on you to safeguard its welfare. There will be much more on nervous / defensive or fearful **Aggression** in the next chapter.

More 'dominant' characters - and do you really have one?

Dogs who are by nature more 'forceful' or 'dominant' characters, as we have already outlined, will obviously need to be handled somewhat differently from more 'submissive' types.

Do be aware, however, that it has become depressingly routine or fashionable nowadays for dogs, or their behaviour, to be wrongly classified as 'dominant', in the sense that such dogs would be 'natural leaders' in the wild. In turn this would appear to instantly explain or 'excuse' many forms of conduct in a dog of which we'd otherwise take a far more critical or intolerant view.

In truth, logic alone should tell you that natural-born leaders in any social species tend to be the **exception**, rather than the norm. Just like there will always be thousands more foot soldiers than generals, and numerous contenders for a sports title or top job that only one person truly has the wherewithal to win. So although you might like to **think** that your dog's behaviour means it would have been a 'natural leader' in the canine world, this is much like every parent thinking that their child is a born prime minister or intellectual genius.

Understandably, many owners will find it more preferable to be told that their dog's behaviour is due to the fact that it was born to be 'naturally dominant', because this can clearly reduce the possibility that they might have contributed to its 'problems' in some way, and can even seem to give their dog some superior sort of 'cachet'. What it will not do, however, is solve your dog's **real problems** if it isn't actually 'naturally dominant' at all - but just insecure, maybe, or frustrated.

This apart, it could just be a common, opportunistic 'rank challenger' of the dog world. In other words, an everyday middle-ranking sort of dog, continually trying to give others the impression that it is a whole lot tougher, or more important, than it really happens to be. And this it will continue to do until owners, or other dogs, finally 'call its bluff'.

As a crucial requirement for solving problems is to have them accurately diagnosed in the first place, if you cannot judge for yourself whether your dog is really a 'naturally dominant' character, or whether this is actually a key factor in its behaviour, seek the most **experienced** or

qualified advice you can get to gain an accurate assessment - even if it means getting more than one opinion. The correct opinion will be the one that offers the most sensible, or logical, explanations and solutions for your dog's behaviour.

Dealing with 'stronger - willed' dogs

Dogs who are truly 'natural leaders' in character can often command an obvious respect from their peers without much conflict. You can tell a lot about your own dog from the way it interacts with others - providing, of course, you know what you are looking for. Classic fearful/ defensive aggression, for instance, can be routinely misread as a sign of 'dominance' by owners, when it is anything but.

As we have already outlined in this book, a dog with a forceful nature can be pretty hard work if your own personality is not a fair match. Dogs like these will not only be far more conscious of any subtle 'lapse' in your authority or will, but will also be far more likely to try and exploit it to their advantage. The naturally 'ambitious' dog however, unlike us, would not view this approach as in any way 'exploitative' or 'ungrateful'. It will just see it as a logical, opportunistic reaction to any apparent 'weakness' in the chain of command.

Dogs like this can also be very independent-minded. In other words, it will matter far less to them, instinctively, to please you than it would to other dogs. Which is why they have to be 'reminded' of why it matters to please you, far more often and consistently, through 'earning' all resources you put their way (see below, and also **The Rules of Superiority**, a bit earlier).

Often **castration** can be recommended for male dogs with aggressive dominant tendencies, or forms of behaviour. It can help in some cases, but be aware that to get any real 'improvements' in the dog's behaviour, castration also has to be backed up with re-training. Preferably with the aid of good professional guidance, you'll need to teach the dog to behave or respond generally in a more acceptable / non-confrontational way.

Sometimes taking a really 'dominant' dog - or one who imagines it is - into a new household can be a bit like initiating a bolshie new recruit into the army. A lot of 'mind-bending' has to go on to persuade the dog that it isn't really as superior as it might think it is and that, in order to have what it needs from life, it will have to reduce personal ambition in favour of conforming to a more preferable code of conduct.

Owners of dogs like this can routinely forget how much of the 'upper hand' they will always hold in their relationship with them. We, after all, as humans, control all of the 'resources' dogs need to thrive and survive - from food, water, shelter and companionship to treats, toys and even access into the outside world. If we give all these things away 'free' to dogs, without asking or demanding anything in return, no wonder some of them can think us dumb, and themselves pretty superior.

Also never forget this. Few dogs - or humans - can sustain an image of themselves as a 'leader' very long if every attempt they make to gain attention, or 'privileges befitting rank', from others is consistently thwarted or ignored.

'Superiority' or high 'self-esteem' in dogs, as in humans, is a state of mind that usually hinges on external reaction. In other words, the more favourable a response an 'ambitious' dog gets from its 'pushiness', and the more frequently 'pushiness' works, the more 'pushy' it will want to be in future, to test the boundaries of its own ambitions.

As previously stated, dogs who have been classified as 'dominant' will not always be typical, natural-born 'leaders'. They can equally be nature's more mundane, opportunistic bullyboys or thugs, who will thrive on aggressive or 'pushy' strategies and approaches as long as they are allowed to, and as long as such strategies and approaches keep on paying off

If, however, you never let the 'pushiness' or aggressiveness of such dogs **work** - in other words, the dog only ever gets rewarded, or access to vital resources, for behaviour **you** would prefer instead - then this can tend to put a rather different slant on things.

Earlier in this chapter, we looked at the strict **'Rules of Superiority'** which will need to be applied to keep more ambitious or 'pushy' dogs in check, hopefully before they can ever reach an aggressive stage (though if this stage does arrive then please, as ever, the instant it does, call in some **professional help**).

As the owner of a dominant dog - or one who imagines it is - you will probably have to apply these 'rules' **religiously** and **always**. It is also **inadvisable, as consistently outlined in this book, to ever let a truly dominant-minded dog sleep on your bed,** or even in the bedroom. Later on it could become possessive not just about the bed, but perhaps about one half of a couple, too - which certainly makes life difficult, if not potentially dangerous.

Fighting or 'harassing' other dogs

If dominant-minded dogs have a tendency to attack or generally 'harass' others when out, then you owe it to other dogs and their owners to keep your own under suitable control. And if your dog is pushing other dogs to the ground violently and holding them down by their necks, then please do not think it is **only trying to play**. An awful lot of dogs do not appreciate 'play' like this - and neither do their owners. Further, if you shout or hit your dog when it lays into others, there's a chance it will be egged on even further by the atmosphere of hostility this creates - or may even think you are backing its actions up.

A dog acting in this way is also 'taking the initiative' over confrontations which it shouldn't be allowed to do, if you are its 'boss'. So if you cannot trust your dog, when out, not to try to give other dogs a hard time, keep it on the lead when other dogs are around and, when they pass by, avert the dog's focus and eye contact away from them and back on to you **immediately**. Do not be harsh or aggressive about this in any way - simply be calm and encouraging but also **firm**. Every time your dog turns its focus away from another dog and back to you it should instantly be rewarded with praise, and perhaps also a really tasty treat or favourite toy.

Your dog must be taught in general - even if this takes some time, and you will probably need the help of a good trainer for best results - to instantly put its focus on you, on command, and away from anything else that might be going on around it. When other dogs pass, you can then get its attention in this way and ask it to sit or lie down - still not letting it look at these other dogs - until they pass by. Additionally, remember to keep praising the dog well every time it does not react adversely to other dogs passing by it.

Eventually your dog should learn that when dogs pass or come near, it must then focus on you for its 'cue' as to what it should do next. This way, **you** are dictating to your dog what it should do in the presence of other dogs, rather than **merely reacting to its own actions towards them**.

An additional precaution would be a basket-type muzzle to prevent your dog using its teeth too forcefully on others. For proper advice on **muzzles** and how to use them, see next chapter (at the end of the **Aggression** section).

Other owners will appreciate this consideration on your behalf. You might find it hard to accept that your dog, due to its nature, cannot run around 'playing normally' like other dogs, but sadly what dogs essentially are - rather that what we'd prefer them to be - is something every owner of every dog has to accept at some time, if only to minimise upset and conflict for ourselves and others.

In essence, the key message a truly 'pushy' dog needs to get is that you are in charge, and that it will always be in its best interests to accept your authority or comply with your commands. Any other options bring zero rewards. It might sound rather drastic or hard. But believe me, living with a forceful and powerful dog who ostensibly 'rules the house' can be a whole lot harder and potentially also nastier. Especially if your dog's ambitions later lead on to **Aggression**, which is covered in the next chapter.

How not to be a pack leader

Some people seem to have got it stubbornly into their heads that being a 'pack leader' means they have to do a lot of 'rough handling'. They have to shout at their dog or shake and shove and prod it around and generally be hostile and aggressive towards it because - that dear old chestnut again   - 'this is what 'top dogs' would do in the wild'. Or so they think, and amazingly this is always with the full benefit of **never** actually having been a top dog 'in the wild', to see how truly effective their actions would be on the wrong dog, or on a dog they could not easily intimidate.

Actually, 'in the wild', if you behaved this way to the wrong dog, there's a chance it would take your throat out. Are you ready for this possibility? A pack leader's job 'in the wild' is just that - to **lead**. This means providing **security** and making decisions that will best safeguard the welfare of the pack as a whole. It means earning trust and respect from others who have put their faith in your 'superiority'. It is not about going around senselessly persecuting or terrorising other ranks for the sake of it, because this is simply exploiting power without fulfilling any of the other obligations attached to it. By behaving in this pointlessly hostile and aggressive way, you might **think** you're a 'pack leader', when what you really are is just a more mundane, old-fashioned bully.

Dogs who are perpetually bullied can feel stressed, frightened, continually apprehensive or increasingly resentful. None of these feelings put a dog in the right frame of mind to think clearly or to perform well to our commands, and some dogs can be potentially very dangerous if pushed to 'breaking point'. So bullying is unkind and bullying also **does not work**.

The ideal leader

Before we go on to our next section, about teaching dogs basic commands, let's hope that this is the sort of 'pack leader' you are aiming to be:

- One who essentially **understands** his or her dog and tries hard to read its feelings

- One who has earned his or her dog's trust, respect and affection through everyday consideration and consistency of action and character

- One who, although not always perfect, is never unnecessarily harsh or unkind and will always do their best to make their dog feel protected and secure

- One who, although demanding unwavering co-operation or 'obedience' from his or her dog when necessary, does not take this 'privilege' for granted, and will always let the dog know when its efforts are appreciated

- One who, above all, understands that with the power of holding a dog's loyalty and dependency in your hands also comes the responsibility never to betray its faith in you, or to ever willingly expose it to fear or harm

If you get all that right, and conveyed to your canine partner, you have the basics for an excellent 'working relationship' - and that's a really wonderful gift to have earned. And even if you're not there yet, there's nothing to stop you continuing to try.

People who try harder and longer to give dogs the sort of lives and 'leadership' they need might find the difference this makes quite remarkable. But ultimately, should it really be so surprising that the more we put into relationships with dogs, the more we will always get out of them?

Teaching your dog some basic commands

Although this ambition won't always be out of the question - see Chapter ten - most owners do not want to train their dogs to 'Obedience competition' standard. All they want is a dog they can feel in reasonable 'control' of, and with whom they can perhaps master the following:

• **Recall, or to come when called**

• **Sit**

• **Down**

• **Stay**

• **Walking properly on the lead**

The above really represent basic 'good manners' in a dog, together with respect for an owner's authority. In a moment we are going to look at how to achieve these things, and why these exercises sometimes fail. First, however, remember that dog training is something which every member of a household, or family, needs to get involved in, in order for it to work consistently.

Commands always have to be given in **the same words and tone, and hand signals** (where appropriate), otherwise the dog will get confused, and also with the same level of **authority**, otherwise - as previously outlined - the dog might start to 'pick and choose' who to obey.

Not all dogs can learn things at the same speed, or will find it as easy as others to reverse previously acquired 'bad habits'. If you find yourself getting frustrated or aggravated by this, remember that patience is the hallmark of all good teachers, as well as the key to most successful final results.

Now let's look at all these training exercises in detail.

Coming when called, or 'recall'

Owners can often find reliable 'recall' of a dog - particularly when out - one of the hardest things to achieve. Usually, however, this is because they are simply not seeing the whole exercise from the dog's point of view.

For most dogs, going out on a walk, and being let off the lead, represents one of the greatest highlights of the day. It is exciting, because they are able to temporarily escape the confines, and perhaps more mundane surroundings, of home, as well as - it must be said - the close proximity of an owner forever attempting to control what they do.

It is also highly distracting, because suddenly there is a whole range of different smells to explore, sights to see, or new dogs to meet.

Faced with all these excitements and distractions, what do you imagine makes boring old you, whom the dog spends hours with every day, so irresistible by comparison that it will want to rush back to you the moment it is called? A dog needs to have **better reasons** than this to want to come back fast, as we shall outline in a moment.

First, however, let us look at some of the classic ways **not** to get a good recall.

1. **By trying to use fear as an incentive.** If a dog takes its time to come back, some owners will get progressively heated or angry. They will shout at the dog in an increasingly hostile manner to get it to return, or will yell at it harshly and even hit it when it eventually does come back, as 'punishment' for returning too slowly, or for 'taking its time'.

The dog, however, will not associate your hostility and punishment with coming back to you too slowly. It will just associate it with **coming back to you**, full stop. So next time, it will be even more slow, or reluctant to come back to you, to put off the dreaded moment when it must face your anger and disapproval. **For this reason, never, ever scold or punish your dog when it comes back to you at any time, no matter how long it has taken to do so.** You are just making future good recalls less and less likely.

2. **By giving recall unfavourable associations.** A lot of owners can get into the habit of only calling their dog back to them when they want to put it on the lead and / or take it home, or stop it playing with other dogs. Dogs soon get wise to this sequence of events, and will subsequently want to delay coming back to you in order to prolong their freedom and fun.

3. **By generally being too 'available' to the dog.** How many owners will you see falling into the trap of calling their dog to them, then waiting or hovering around it until it finishes what it is doing? This way, your dog soon gets the message that you will always be hanging around waiting

for it, so what's the incentive to return to you in a hurry? In truth, as a proper 'pack leader', you shouldn't be waiting around at your dog's pleasure. Your dog should be the one constantly worrying about where **you** are and what **you** are doing, and not the other way around.

How to improve 'recall'

One of the best ways to get a good recall trained into a dog is to start early. If a dog isn't taught to come back quickly to its owner as a young puppy at home - i.e. when it feels most dependent on you, and is in the least distracting environment - then it will obviously be harder to get the same level of response when the dog is older, more confident, and has access to numerous other diversions for its attention.

Clearly this option won't be available to owners of most rescue dogs, but there are still ways that recall can be greatly improved in them. The first thing you need to do is choose a distinct word or **sound** - e.g. a whistle - that is going to represent your 'recall command'.

If you'd prefer a word, pick something short and clear - e.g. 'come!' - and always pitch it in a high, loud and inviting tone. I wouldn't pick the dog's name for this exercise, as the dog will hear this word umpteen times a day in a wide variety of different tones and circumstances. This means it won't be so easily distinguished as a command. If you have several dogs, then it might be worth training them all to respond to the same special 'recall' command or sound.

Once you have picked your word or sound, the next thing to do is to build up highly pleasurable associations with it. You do this by using your sound or word, firstly in the home, every single time the dog is about to experience something good - e.g. a meal, a game, a treat, a walk. **Do not use this sound or word any other time in the home and, initially, also ensure that your dog never gets a meal, treat, game etc. without responding first to this sound and coming to you.** Also praise the dog well when it comes to you.

Once your dog is reliably coming to you each time it hears the 'recall' sound, then start to make things a little more testing. Progress on to only giving a reward to the dog for the **fastest** responses to recall. If the dog can expect a reward for any response - fast or slow - to the recall indefinitely, then its incentive to hurry will be greatly reduced. Similarly, should responses to one special recall 'cue' begin to get poor, you can always change your recall sound / word again for better results, rebuilding pleasant associations with it as before.

Added incentives

Having, in this way, established a 'recall' command in your dog's mind, here are other things you can do. First, get one or two toys for your dog that you know it will find irresistible - some dogs might prefer ball or 'tug' devices, others something fluffy or squeaky to shake and charge around with.

Your dog is only **ever** going to get to see, and use, these toys on one occasion only. And that's when it comes **rapidly back to you**, on command, when you're out somewhere. The rest of the time, keep them hidden somewhere at home out of sight. The preserved 'desirability' and 'novelty' value of these toys will be an added incentive for your dog to come back to you to get them. If you have a dog who is particularly food - orientated - or, some might say, downright greedy! - you can use some special treats as an alternative, or additional, incentive for coming back fast.

It's important, however, to eventually get the message across to the dog that it will only get the abovementioned rewards for coming rapidly, **not** just for ambling back in its own good time. To help get the urgency of this command across initially, it might help to attach a long line to your dog's collar. Should it not come quickly back to you on command, you then have the option of reeling it back to you to make it clearer what is required.

Do remember, however, to always praise / reward the dog well for coming back to you even in this more 'forced' fashion, and don't be too harsh in your 'reeling'. Keep things light and enthusiastic and encouraging - otherwise your dog might get frightened or worried and decide to dig its heels in or have a 'sit down protest' each time you try to pull it back to you. When you are out, the moment you pick to call your dog back to you is also **crucial**. If its attention is intently focused on a fascinating smell or another dog, wait for this attention to momentarily shift away before calling the dog. You want your dog to get into the habit of coming quickly on command. It is far more likely to do this when its attention is not intensely fixed on other distractions.

So now you have got a 'recall' command properly 'programmed' into the dog's mind, and you are making the option of coming back fast to you far more appealing. When your dog comes back to you fast, however, for its toy or treat and praise, **do not then follow this response with putting it on the lead and / or going home.** Instead, send the dog off again to enjoy itself - perhaps with its special toy - and have fun. Recall your dog, reward it, then send it off again several times during the course of a walk, so that it will never associate coming back to you with the end of its fun. When you do need to put the dog on the lead and go home, don't call it. Just wait until it is near you, then gently move over, put the lead on, praise the dog and give it a treat.

When you call your dog back to you, it's also very important **not to wait for it.** Keep moving - or better still, rush off, as if in response to some urgent mission, or as if you are about to go off and do something exciting. If you get the 'theatricals' of this right, your dog will find it hard to resist following you. It's often a good idea, too, when out, to regularly make your dog think that you are deliberately trying to 'lose' it. Hide behind bushes suddenly, when your dog is not looking, or keep switching direction on a normally predictable route.

It might seem like a cheap psychological trick, and other dog walkers and passers - by might think you half deranged. But, in terms of perfecting an even better recall, it also happens to work. Unless of course, you become so skilled at 'trying to lose' your dog that you actually do! Needless to say, you shouldn't ever let this happen, neither should you 'lose' your dog or get it to rapidly catch up with you in areas where it could come to harm - e.g. near busy roads.

'Sit'

Owners usually find **'sit'** one of the easier exercises to teach. This is because, when they call their dog to them, holding a treat or toy above its nose, sitting down in anticipation tends to be the most logical or natural thing for it to do.

It's still important, however, to get the **timing** of the command right. When initially teaching this exercise there is no point in saying 'sit', for instance, if the dog has already sat down. You say it **as** the dog is sitting down to get the association right. As with many other training commands, it's also a good idea to accompany your verbal command with a **hand signal**, to make it as clear as possible, because as a species, dogs communicate more via body 'signals' than voice sounds or tones. Signals will also work better at distance, or for dogs with less acute hearing. The common hand signal for 'sit' is an arm raised with palm facing upwards.

Sometimes more nervous or less confident rescue dogs, or dogs who have been dealt with aggressively in the past, can find it hard to sit directly in front of an owner, making eye contact. Not because they are 'daft' or 'awkward', but because this posture requires them to adopt canine body language they feel could easily be read as confrontational. Thus, in an effort to 'appease' or minimise any chance of conflict, they may prefer to sit at an oblique angle to you with head or eyes averted, or at your side, instead.

If this is good enough for you, leave it at that. If not, a lot more work will have to go into building up the dog's overall confidence, both in itself, and in you, before it feels it can perform this exercise with absolutely no chance of an unpleasant side effect. Whatever you do, however, do **not** keep trying to shove, force or generally 'bully' a dog into the 'sit' position yourself, as you will just make it anxious and also possibly give it very negative associations with the word 'sit' in future. Be **patient**. Remember, anything a dog learns in an atmosphere of patience and **kindness** tends to be absorbed better and repeated far more readily later on.

'Down'

'Down' can be best taught, initially, as a progression on from 'sit'. While your dog is sitting down, hold a treat in your hand under its nose. Once your dog has registered this, gradually lower your hand with the treat in to the floor, encouraging the dog to go down after it. As it is actually in the process of lying down to get it, say the word 'down'. Then reward the dog with the treat.

Once you have got this procedure perfected, start moving further and further away from the dog when you give the command 'down'. Increase the distance only a little at a time, and signal 'down' by lowering your arm down to the ground, palm downwards. As with the word 'sit', however, do say 'down' in a firm but **civilised** tone. Dogs generally have good hearing, but this doesn't seem to stop many owners yelling commands at them more as a form of verbal abuse than as an instruction they'd simply like them to comply with.

This in turn can make a dog feel tense or begin to see training as a form of **bullying** or **persecution**. It is also completely unnecessary. If every teacher at your school had begun your lessons with a mega-decibel scream, it's unlikely that you would have found the learning process either easy or enjoyable.

Remember too that later on you might be required to use the 'down' command at distance, to save your dog from potential danger. On these occasions you really will have to use far more volume, but if your dog is already 'deadened' to the sound of you shouting, a loud command will inevitably have less impact in terms of stopping a dog in its tracks.

Getting a dog to go down quickly on command when out - the **'emergency' down** - can take a fair bit of initial practice, especially if your dog seems intent on chasing something. If a dog won't readily go down on command when out, you could try attaching a long trailing line to it. Each time the dog takes off and ignores your 'down' command, give this line a good tug. Do not do this by throwing out your arms to pull with your body. Instead, do it by placing your foot on the line. This way, because you have not moved at all, your dog will more readily get the impression that it was its own failure to comply with the 'down' command, rather than its owner's actions, that caused the enforced halt - a subtle but vital difference of perception when attempting to perfect this exercise.

When out, do not carry on a walk until your dog has obeyed a command to go down. If you repeat this exercise often enough, and consistently enough, starting with short distances away from you and then progressing to greater ones, your dog should eventually get 'programmed' into believing that going down, on command, is really the most practical thing to do, especially if it wants to carry on its walk.

If it will not go down quickly when off the trailing line, then put it back on the trailing line and continue to repeat the exercise until its responses are more reliable, especially at greater and greater distance away from you. If it eventually goes down quickly on command, you can then remove it from the line as an additional 'reward', and congratulate yourself for a fine achievement - only putting the dog back on the line should its response subsequently deteriorate.

Do not ask a dog to do more than two or three 'emergency downs' during a walk, however. Not only can this be tiring for it, it will lessen the 'urgency' of the command in its mind. Once your dog has learned to respond to this command really reliably you can make it a far more intermittent, rather than daily, exercise.

'Stay'

'**Stay**', like 'down', will always be an important command to teach your dog. Not just to keep it out of possible danger or trouble, but also to prevent it following you into places or areas where you do not want it to go.

If a dog is being particularly troublesome or annoying in its behaviour - e.g. it is constantly 'nagging', barking or whining to get attention - then meeting this with a command to immediately go down somewhere and stay until you say otherwise can be quite a deterrent. It is also a way you can calmly assert your authority over your dog without unnecessary unpleasantness or conflict.

Many dogs, and particularly those who have been allowed to become excessively attached to their owners, might initially find the 'stay' command hard, and harder still if they are asked to stay somewhere while you go out of sight. One also has to bear in mind that many rescue dogs might have frightening past memories of abandonment, or of having been left lengthily on their own when owners departed. This could naturally make them more anxious about the prospect of not following you somewhere, when their instincts demand that they should.

For such reasons, 'stay' should be taught in gradual stages. Start off with your dog on a lead and by your side and, preferably, lying down - as this will make it less likely that it will immediately follow you when you move. Take a few steps away from the dog. If it stays where it is for just a second or two, say 'stay' **while it is still staying.** At the same time give your dog a 'signal' to stay, such as a hand outstretched in a 'pushing' position, about two feet in front of its head - unless it is particularly hand-shy. In which case, make this gesture more to the side of it. Then reward your dog with a treat and praise. Keep working on this until you are able to let go of the lead, while the dog stays where it is on command.

One of the golden rules of the 'stay' exercise is that, once finished, **you should never call your dog to you.** Instead, **you** go to **the dog**. Do not immediately touch it or praise it as it might immediately leap to its feet and, in so doing, end the exercise for itself, rather than wait for you to tell it when it can move. By always going to the dog, rather than getting the dog to come to you, you are also lessening the chances that the dog will follow after you, if only in the mistaken belief that this is what it should do.

While your dog is still staying where it is, come over to it and stand by its side. Wait a couple of seconds, then bend down and praise the dog **while it is still on the ground.** Then let it get up. This way it knows it is being praised for staying down, **not** for getting up to greet you.

From 'down-stay' you can then move on to a 'sit-stay', once the dog has more idea of what it should be doing. If you are going to attempt stays 'out of sight' again, only build these up **very gradually**. Start by going out of sight - very slowly, not in a rush - only for a second or two before coming back, and then slowly increase the time A golden rule for this exercise is to **always return to the dog in the exact direction from which you left it,** so it won't be looking elsewhere, or worrying that this is where you might be. Remember, your dog has got to completely trust, without any doubt, that when you go out of its sight you will **always** be returning. Do not underestimate the sort of 'leap of faith' this might require some dogs to make, until enough repetition and practice of this exercise has been undertaken to put them more at ease.

Walking properly on the lead

As previously mentioned in Chapter Four, dogs who relentlessly pull on the lead can infuriate or frustrate their owners - if not incur them aching backs, shoulders and arms! Every walk can turn into a battle of wills and muscles, and ruin the general experience of taking a dog out.

Most rescue dogs will pull on the lead for any or all of the following reasons:

- **Because no one taught them how to walk properly on the lead when they were puppies**

- **Because they are intensely excited about going out**

- **Because they have learned that this can get them somewhere quicker - particularly if they are quite big and strong**

- **Because they are actually trying to 'escape' the pressure you are putting on their throats and necks**

Owners who commonly think that the answer to this problem lies in yanking a dog around by its neck in a **check (or 'choke') chain** should ask themselves how much they would relish such an experience. Check chains, when aggressively used over time, can cause considerable injuries to dogs' throats, necks and spines and to my mind, certainly, there is no more sickening and distressing a sight than these devices being routinely misused by heavy-handed owners to the point where dogs gasp, gag and retch.

This apart, if owners have to yank at these things every few seconds while out on a walk, in order to keep their dogs relatively near their sides, then clearly, as a device to stop dogs pulling, they are also **not working**. If anything, check chains can make a dog pull even harder, in a desperate attempt to counteract or escape the torturous pressure or pain around its neck and throat.

So forget about check chains. Instead, you could try a far more kinder and effective device like a Halti or Gentle Leader (available from most pet stores or through some training clubs). Basically these are like headcollars for dogs. The lead fits on to them and they work, much like a halter on a horse, through reducing the 'leverage' potential a dog would otherwise have with its neck and shoulders in a traditional collar.

The drawback with the above, however, is that many dogs do not like the feel of the straps round their heads and noses, and may rub continuously at them, or try to remove them with their paws when out. If fixed too tightly and repeatedly pulled too hard, they can also leave marks or bald patches on the head and nose, and I've known many dogs who can still contort themselves into postures which allow them to pull hard on the lead, Halti on or not.

Further, such devices are only really hampering a dog from being **able** to pull, rather than preventing it from **wanting** to pull, which is quite a different thing.

To stop a dog from wanting to pull, you need to make the act of pulling completely unrewarding. To do this, walk out as usual with your dog on a slack lead. Your dog should be kept on your left at first, before moving on to walking it on both sides of you. If you get the dog initially used to walking just on one side of you, it is less likely to keep cutting across in front of you, switching from one side to the other.

Give your dog a good length of lead but as soon as you feel it tighten, **stop dead**. Then immediately call your dog back to your side. **Do not** go to join the dog instead. It is not only more of a hassle for the dog to have to keep coming back to you, it is also ensuring that the dog's pulling only has the effect of making it have to go backwards and **never forwards**.

Once the dog has come back to your side, wait a moment, and then carry on. Next time the lead goes tight again, repeat the whole exercise and keep repeating it until eventually the dog learns that the key to any continual forward progress is to stay near your side, and on a slackish lead.

This can, I'll admit, be really tedious work for you and the dog to begin with - speaking as someone who has gone through this 'conditioning process' many times. If you do not check the dog in this way, however, **every single time** it pulls ahead, the eventual success of the exercise will be greatly undermined. Keep at it consistently and you really will start to see marked improvement in a matter of weeks or less. And what a relief it will be.

Last points on training

Before we move on to deal with the subjects of rescue dogs and children, and rescue dogs and other pets, let us first recap on some of the most important points about training. And they are:

- First, build up a good 'bond' with your dog, establishing its respect for you and trust in you, as well as its general belief in your authority. Additionally your dog has got to understand that 'no' **always** means no and never maybe - and that disobedience will never be rewarded.

- Find a good trainer, or training class, neither of which should advocate methods using any form of harsh treatment or punishment-based techniques. Further, training classes should always be places where you and your dog have fun together and you get the feeling also that, together, you and you dog are really achieving things that are worthwhile and of benefit to your entire relationship, either at home or elsewhere.

- Train **with** your dog. You and your dog need to work together as a **team**. 'Training' is also not something that just happens at training classes. Whatever you learn there of benefit must be applied and practiced everywhere else with your dog on a daily, consistent basis for best results.

- Make your commands **clear** and as easy as possible for the dog to understand. Also appreciate the value of constantly 'reinforcing' right actions by rewarding them instantly, and repeating them frequently enough for the dog to 'programme' them into its mind - but not so often that the dog becomes over-tired, bored or stressed.

- Similarly appreciate that shouting aimlessly, or in an irritated fashion, at your dog - e.g. 'stop that!', 'behave yourself!', 'get out the way!' is no substitute for a proper **command**. Abstract phrases like the above make no sense to a dog. All that makes sense to a dog is a command it has been taught to understand and respond to. When you want your dog to do something, or not do something, use a **command** it can understand and respond to, not meaningless words.

- Be **patient**, and learn to read when your dog is stressed or distracted, or for some other reason finds it hard to do what you ask. In such cases, lay off the pressure.

- Make training **always** have rewarding and enjoyable associations. Keep training sessions regular but short and always end on a good note, and with a game.

- Never try to **bully** your dog into doing something for you. It's unkind and, ultimately, it also **will not work**. Also remember that, in terms of good performance, there is no substitute for a dog who willingly wants to co-operate with you and please you.

- Use food treats in training to get a dog to quickly realise that it has done the 'right' thing. Thereafter, use them only to reward the quickest or best responses to a command. By contrast, use praise **lavishly** and **often**. To many rescue dogs, who may rarely have experienced much of it in a past life, praise really can be a quite thrilling - and highly motivating - pleasure.

- When it comes to learning and progress, work at your **dog's** ideal pace, and not your own. Let it makes mistakes without fear of intimidating disapproval or punishment - and don't forget to have **fun**.

Rescue dogs and children

Rescue dogs, or puppies, can be a great addition to 'the family' for most children, but problems can arise if interactions, or growing relationships between them, aren't adequately supervised or handled.

To minimise potential conflicts or 'rank' challenges, as previously outlined in this chapter, all dogs need to be taught that within the hierarchy of the family 'pack', children will always be superior to them, or carry more authority than them. But in return children must **not** abuse this position through being allowed to tease or torment dogs in any way. Such a state of affairs could rapidly lead to a dog feeling resentful or threatened by the children's presence. This in turn can be a starting point for retaliatory or 'defensive' aggression as self-protective instincts kick in.

Very often puppies or dogs are condemned or 'demonised' for snapping at children, when all they have really done is get over-excited during a heated game of 'tug' or 'chase', or crack under the weight of **intolerable** harassment or torment at youngsters' hands.

In other words, they have either had natural hunting instincts suddenly triggered, or are merely reacting as a dog would to another who had pressurised or persecuted them unduly, in an attempt to make them 'back off'. In other cases, the 'correct' relationship between a dog and a child or children might never have been satisfactorily established in the animal's mind, thus leaving its actual 'inferiority' to them in doubt.

Dos and don'ts

Because young children cannot always know when their actions are making a dog anxious or uneasy, or read the appropriate signs of stress in its body language - e.g. panting, yawning, pacing around in an agitated or 'cowed' manner, trying to escape the room or the children's attentions - they should **never** be left alone unsupervised with puppies or dogs, until they are old enough to deal with them in a calmer and more responsible way.

So much grief, over the years, between children and dogs might have been spared if these basic rules had been stuck to:

- **Never leave a baby or young child unsupervised with a dog or puppy anywhere**

- **Never allow a child to smack, tease, or torment a dog or puppy in any way,** and this can mean anything from pulling its fur or ears and yanking it about forcefully on a lead to shouting at it or bullying it with endless repetitive commands - all of which can be highly stressful for a dog of any age. Never forget to remind them that dogs are **not toys**.

- **Never allow children to engage in boisterous 'rough and tumble' games with dogs** on the floor, which could end in nipping or biting should the dog suddenly feel defensive or get over-excited. This is particularly crucial with bigger puppies (or dogs), who can soon learn their own physical superiority to a child through such 'tussles', and may later seek to exploit such an advantage.

- **Never put a young child in sole charge of a dog when out.** In the case of bigger and more powerful dogs in particular, this can lead to many problems. It is also a responsibility a young child simply isn't equipped to deal with, and shouldn't be expected to.

- **Never allow children to pester or harass a dog or puppy when it is eating, trying to rest in its bed or 'den' or on any occasion when it is clearly in need of peace.** A dog's need for rest and solitude, when it needs it, is essential to its psychological well-being and has to be respected.

- **Never allow children to play any 'mouth' games with puppies or dogs** - e.g. encouraging 'play-biting' in puppies or tussling with puppies or dogs over 'tug' toys or other items where things could soon get over-heated.

In return for such considerations, however, puppies and dogs will also need to learn to respect the children they will be living with, so from the start they must:

- **Always be encouraged to obey a child's command** - though such commands should **only** be given when absolutely necessary - not simply as some form of 'entertainment' for the child. They should also be given in a calm, firm but non-aggressive or 'bullying' tone for proper impact.

- **Never be allowed to beg or snatch food off children, or forcibly grab toys off them.**

- **Always be discouraged from chasing children, jumping up on them and / or knocking them over.**

It can also help to get children to regularly groom and feed the dog, as well as participate in its training. The more 'involved', generally, children become in a dog's everyday life and welfare, the greater the 'bond' they can build with it.

Child / dog conflict

If a puppy or dog shows any sign of what appears to be totally unprovoked aggression towards a young child, then **this has to be taken very seriously.** One of the best things you can do should this arise is to immediately banish the dog out of the room and perhaps into the garden, without saying a word, allowing all parties to 'cool off' a little.

If you shout at the dog, it is getting the reward of your **attention** for its actions, and if you physically punish it, it could start harbouring resentment towards the child, or could make a dangerous association between the child's presence and pain or fear.

While your dog is 'cooling off' in the garden, or another room, for five or ten minutes - don't leave it too much longer - you should ask yourself the following things:

- **If the dog or puppy has already had a previous home, is it possible it was teased or ill treated by children** or a child there, leaving it with 'fearful' reactions towards them? If so, you may need to re-establish the dog's trust in children (see Chapter seven on dealing with 'Fearfulness')

- **Is it possible that your child might have frightened the dog,** prior to it reacting aggressively - only you didn't see it, or could not correctly interpret the situation from the dog's point of view? If so, you will need to be more vigilant in future, and your child will need to be taught how to better respect the dog, as previously outlined. If the child is too young to know how to do this, then the dog and child must be kept apart until you have decided how to best resolve this situation

- Having weighed-up the above, **do you feel capable of resolving this situation yourself,** with the benefit of some independent and skilled professional help or guidance? Or do you feel that you could never trust the dog again?

If you do not feel that you could ever trust the dog again, or feel unable to assess whether it really is capable of doing your child harm - rather than just sending 'warning signals', or getting over-excited in play, then it may well be better off in a new home without children. However reluctant you might feel about this option, your first priority is your child's welfare, and the dog would also not be happy in a home full of constant unease and tension about its behaviour - not to mention the numerous banishments into the garden!

What complicates this issue, however, is how differently it can be handled by different households or families. Some parents might become near-hysterical when a dog or puppy snaps at their child, others - and particularly those with far more experience of dogs - will be far more pragmatic, or judge that the child must have provoked the incident in some way. In a lot of cases, with older children in particular (i.e. over four or five years of age) an earlier state of conflict with a new dog or puppy can resolve itself, purely over time, as they learn to trust each other, treat each other with more respect, and also share a lot of 'fun' or positive experiences together.

Some breeds of dog - e.g. some terrier varieties, and Border collies - can have hunting / chasing instincts which make them incompatible with younger children. At the end of the day, however, with or without professional advice, only you can decide whether your own situation is worth persevering with, and has much potential for improvement, or whether your puppy or dog really is too dangerous, or unreliable, to live closely within young children's company.

The best of friends

So far we have only looked at possible conflict that could arise between dogs and children, and why, and how this should best be approached. What also has to be said, however, is what tremendous pals children and dogs can be once their relationship is put on the right footing, and also what incredible comfort and pleasure they can offer each other once they have built up mutual trust and affection over time.

In many households, dogs can fulfil so many roles in children's lives, from nanny or minder, to unique confidant and best friend. Children and animals, in general, often have a capacity to 'connect' on a wavelength of understanding that can be quite unique, as many studies over the years have shown.

Through dogs, children can also learn so many valuable lessons about responsibility and commitment and the duties of being a friend. And such an impact can a dog's devotion, in return, have on a child, that it is something it will never forget for the rest of its life.

Rescue dogs and other pets

Previously in this book (Chapter two), we have looked at issues concerning 'predatory instinct' in dogs, why this might make them a risk to other smaller pets, and also how important it is, when choosing a rescue dog, to pick one less likely to upset the 'hierarchical status quo' among other dogs - or another dog - at home.

We also know, however, through earlier coverage of these subjects, that how dogs behave in a kennel environment, or when they first come home, will not always be a true indication of how they might behave later, once they feel more settled and secure, just like we know that 'equality' in relationships is not a concept dogs tend to grasp.

Having quickly recapped on all this, now let us look at how all the above might relate to the new dog you bring home, and how well or not it might settle in with existing pets. First:

Other dogs

Maybe you thought you did everything possible to ensure that your new rescue dog was going to be compatible with a dog, or dogs, you already had at home. You introduced it to your own dog or dogs on neutral territory, or at the rescue centre, and all seemed to go well. Maybe all seemed to go well during early weeks, too, as your new dog kept a respectful distance from your own dog or dogs, or behaved in - at least in line with your expectations of how a 'newcomer' should act - in a suitably apprehensive or 'humble' manner.

And maybe you never have many further problems on this front. If you do, however, and find that suddenly one day there is uproar and conflict developing between the new dog and another, here are some possible reasons why:

- **Your new dog, having become much more confident in itself and its new surroundings, begins to imagine it is naturally more 'superior' to another dog in your household and is therefore starting to challenge its existing status**

- **You have inadvertently 'upped' the status of your new dog, by giving it so much more attention, generally, than another dog, or other dogs, leading to resentment from another, or others, and possibly also fuelling the new dog's own notion of growing status**

In the wild, dogs would normally settle these common 'rank disputes' by themselves. After much posturing, and sometimes varying degrees of aggressive display, one dog will arise as naturally more 'inferior' or 'superior' to another. Thereafter, providing the status level at issue wasn't so keenly or violently contested that it resulted in a literal 'fight to the death', this leaves the 'inferior' dog with the option of leaving, or being banished from, the pack if it can no longer live in harmony with its superior rival.

Dog generally understand the true risks of entering into an all-out confrontation which they might not win, or which could seriously injure them. Which is why so much of their 'status-seeking' behaviour can revolve around 'needling' or 'intimidating' the opposition to see how 'tough' it really is. It is a 'risk-assessment' strategy. So much can be at stake for any dog who loses out in a more serious confrontation that it is crucial for it to first weigh up its odds for success.

Some dogs are better at intimidating potential 'rivals' than others, and some are more easily intimidated. Or in other words, some dogs are better at conveying the 'impression' that they would win any confrontation, and others are more reluctant to have to face one. Which gives us the key to why so many rank disputes can be settled through 'posturing' alone, and also why 'superiority' can sometimes have less to do with the size or age of a dog and more to do with its individual capacity to 'psyche-out' the opposition.

Dealing with conflict

Now we have a better idea of why dogs can 'fall out', we also have to realise that the way in which most dogs live today - with human owners in a domestic home - can greatly interfere with how they manage their own 'rank disputes' by themselves.

For a start, a dog who has come off the 'worst' in any 'rank tussle' does **not** have the option of leaving 'the pack', unless we arrange this option ourselves. Instead it has to stay in the same home, and on the same territory, as its more superior persecutor, which can lead to considerable stress for the 'underdog' and seething resentment in its rival.

In our own well-meaning way, we can also make matters worse by 'sympathising' with the underdog - and showering it with far more attention, fuss and treats or whatever to 'make up' for it having such a rough time. Maybe we will also think, or hope, that such treatment of the underdog will 'send a message' to its rival that it ought to be 'nicer' to it, or make more effort to 'get along'.

But sadly these are purely 'human values', of little relevance to dogs. So although your 'underdog' might relish the attention showered on it, its rival will simply get even more resentful. It might also get more determined, as a result, to put the 'underdog' in its 'rightful place', which means even more, rather than less, displays of open hostility or aggression directed towards the underdog by the rival.

Although it might go against the grain, or prove - understandably - incredibly difficult for owners to see through, the way to improve a situation like this, between two dogs, is to **always favour the superior dog**. In other words, the superior dog will always be the one who is greeted first when you come home, gets in or out of the car first when you go out, eats first, has the first approach for treats or toys etc. If you have two dogs of the same sex, it can also help to get the inferior one neutered to further increase its obvious 'lower status'.

Through all these measures you are simply restoring a more 'logical' pack system, wherein dogs are treated in a way befitting their 'rightful' status. You will also be more likely to reduce the potential for conflict. So if you want to keep two dogs with such a 'status problem' under the same roof in relative harmony this, I'm afraid, is what you must do.

Another option for owners with dogs continually - if not sometimes literally - at each other's throats is **to house them and handle them completely separately,** so that they never have a chance to get into a conflict. This is often the only viable option if two dogs are so evenly matched in their status ambitions that one will never accept itself as inferior to the other. Or if there is a continuing fear that one dog might really do the other serious harm. I know owners who manage such segregation with considerable success, but the dedication, discipline and sheer everyday logistics the feat demands is not practical for everyone.

At the end of the day, if you care enough about both dogs involved in a 'status dispute' you will find the resolve to tackle their problems in the only 'workable' ways. Otherwise, very sadly, you may be faced with the option of having to rehome one of them elsewhere.

Dogs and cats

When it comes to rehoming rescue dogs with existing cats, you have to put your cats first. Not just because they were there first, and you love them, but because cats can easily take 'umbrage' when they feel their territory or physical security has been put 'under threat' and may subsequently leave home for somewhere 'safer' as a result.

Most cats will find it easier to get used to a new or strange presence in the house **gradually**. For this reason, it is a good idea to bring back an item, or items with your new rescue dog's scent on before it actually comes home. Most rescue centres or agencies should help you in this mission by leaving a largish old cloth in the dog's bed for you, or you could rub the dog down well with this cloth yourself, and then bring it home. Cut it into about three or four pieces, then leave these around your house for your cat, or cats, to get used to. They will probably be highly curious about the new scent and, knowing most cats, also look suitably appalled.

Next, again before your bring your rescue dog home, set up some self-contained quarters - e.g. with beds, litter tray, food and water - for your cat or cats to retreat to when the 'newcomer' arrives, should they wish to. These quarters could just be a bedroom, but even more ideal would be a room or place they could come in and out of, if desired, without encountering the dog.

When you eventually bring the dog home, **do not just stick the dog and cat, or cats, in one room** and 'leave them to get on with it'. You do not know your new dog well enough to know how it might react, and your cat(s) could well be terrified. Instead, while the dog is restrained somewhere, but can see what you are doing, make a big fussy greeting of your cat(s). Your dog needs to get the message, early on, that the cat, or cats, are members of your 'pack' and not prey or any other form of undesirable intruder.

It could well be that your cat - or cats - scarper in horror the moment they see the dog. If so, wait for them to return. It might be a long wait, but when curiosity or hunger eventually gets the better of them, they should hover somewhere at a safe distance, where you can go over and reassure them. Give them more fuss than normal to make them feel less threatened.

Over the next few days, continue to keep the cat(s) and new dog apart - i.e. the dog kept on a lead or line when the cat(s) are around - while still allowing them to see each other. Watch your dog carefully. Is it taking the presence of the cat(s) in its stride, and looking only vaguely interested, or does it look highly excited, barking or growling and lunging forward in its eagerness to get at it or them?

If the former, you may soon be able to 'stage' a closer meeting between the two parties (more details in a moment). If the latter, your dog might still be excited by the 'novelty' of the presence of cats at such close quarters, and may want to investigate them more fully, without necessarily wishing them harm. There is, however, still a possibility that your new dog **might wish them harm**, or might chase them in a frightening way if given the chance.

You must not allow this to happen, because you will have ruined any progress made in trying to win the trust of the cat or cats. To increase their sense of security, your cat or cats need to know not only that they have a 'bolthole' to go to away from the dog, if need be, but also that you appear to have some control over the dog's actions. In other words, when they see you with the dog, they can feel less frightened. By allowing the dog to escape your control and chase or harass the cat or cats at close quarters, you have shattered this precious illusion of 'safety'.

If your dog has not calmed down its generally 'excited' or even 'aggressive' reactions towards your cat or cats over two weeks, say, then it might well be time to reconsider whether you can viably home it with them long-term. This apart, owners - or cats, for that matter! - do not necessarily have to be dog experts to know, instinctively, when a dog's intentions towards another animal don't appear to be anything other than harmful. If these are your instincts, go with them. You then have the option of having to return the rescue dog, however reluctantly, or of spending the years ahead consistently keeping your cat(s) and dog physically separated at all times.

This might sound straightforward in theory, but in reality living in constant fear that your cat(s) and dog might one day cross paths can involve tortuous logistics and can also be highly stressful for you, as well as the cats. Providing, of course, that the cats are actually prepared to stay around long enough to get this stressed.

Closer encounters

Let us suppose, instead, that your early meetings between dog and cat(s) have actually gone quite well. Your dog and cat(s) may remain curious about each other, but there is no hint of any really potentially harmful 'predatory instinct' in the dog. At this stage, gradually introduce closer and closer meetings between them.

Still keeping your dog on the lead, wait for your cat or cats to go into the garden, or living room, and follow them there with the dog until eventually you can get quite close to the cat(s) without them running off. Encourage your dog to look at you and not the cat or cats, and when it does so, praise it and give it a treat. Also praise it and reward it for not reacting at all to the presence of the cat or cats.

By this stage, in the true spirit of familiarity breeding contempt, there's a chance that your new dog and cat or cats will now be bored to tears with the sight of each other. Which is actually quite a good thing. Bolder cats might even want to approach the dog for further investigation, which they should be allowed to do. And again, if your dog doesn't react in any adverse way, reward it. At this point, you should be able to let a dog have the full length of a long trailing line to see if it will approach the cat in a friendly or merely disinterested way. If it does, give it this exercise praise again. If it lunges forward in any kind of threatening or frightening way, reel it back very quickly, and do not try again until all parties have calmed down a bit.

Providing all eventually goes well on this front, it should not be long now before your dog and cat or cats finally settle in together or, at best, learn to tolerate each other's presence, although still never, **ever** leave a dog alone with a cat until you are absolutely sure it can be trusted - and with some breeds or individuals with keen innate hunting instincts (especially sight hounds, e.g. greyhounds or lurchers, and many terrier breeds, as previously mentioned) I'm not sure I'd ever take this risk. All the above might seem like a pretty drawn-out exercise. But if it will help ensure the trouble-free companionship of your new dog and existing beloved cats over years ahead, surely it is worth it.

Most cats, in any household containing dogs, tend to end up ruling the roost anyway. But do not tell this to your rescue dog. At least not at first.

Other pets

Some dogs seem able to live in harmony with all kinds of small animals - e.g. rabbits, hamsters, guinea pigs - they might otherwise consider 'natural prey'. Often this is because they have fairly low levels of predatory instinct, or because they have been raised with such animals since they were puppies, or because owners have made it sufficiently clear to them that they must not be chased or harmed, and they have never seen it fit to challenge this state of affairs.

With rescue dogs, you cannot be sure how many - if any - of these 'inhibiting' factors will apply. For this reason, my advice about rescue dogs and other small pets - particularly those who are easily shocked or frightened - is fairly simple. **Keep them apart. Always.** This way you will never have to deal with the consequences of being 'wrong' about your dog's capabilities.

Having now covered all the issues that can be involved in training your dog, building up a 'healthy' relationship with it, and generally settling it into its place within the household, we are going to move on to the great subject of **'Behavioural Problems'** in dogs. How to recognise them, what might cause them, and how to deal with them.

Chapter Seven

Help Again! Your Troubleshooting A-Z Guide To Possible 'Behavioural Problems' in Rescue Dogs. How To Recognise Them, What To Do About Them, When To Call In More Expert Advice

It's incredibly easy to get worried, panicky, angry or just downright neurotic about the way dogs behave, or to imagine that we are the only person in the world whose dog has got a certain 'problem', when we clearly are not - and it can be both isolating, and unhelpful, to think so.

Moreover, the longer we live with dogs on such intimate terms, the higher our expectations become of their behaviour, and the more likely we are to react adversely to canine conduct that we do not like, find baffling, inappropriate, or simply inconvenient. In doing so, however, we can forget not only how different dogs essentially are from us, as a species, but also how much we can put dogs under pressure when we do not sufficiently understand their own needs or 'point of view'.

If we want, to make it sound so much more mysterious, scientific or complex than it often is, we can call any canine conduct that we do not like a 'behavioural problem'. Or we can try to view it in a slightly more straightforward light. Dogs are doing something we'd rather they didn't do. So first we have to find out why, and then we have to try to change or modify it.

Not all rescue dogs will have 'behavioural problems', but to be forewarned of what these 'problems' might be can be of use to any dog owner some time. Remember, too, that the more 'stressed out' you get about your dog's behaviour, the more this will feed down to the dog. Dogs don't need to know the reasons for our stress to become adversely contaminated by it. All in all, before we move on to our 'troubleshooting A-Z guide', these are the most important points to keep in mind about any behaviour in your dog which you view as a 'problem', or something it is necessary to change:

• **Get the best advice you can (see end of book) about it as soon as it starts or becomes apparent.** Too often owners will wait until a problem has reached 'crisis point' before seeking help, making it that much harder to reverse or solve

• **Dogs do not change or 'grow out of' bad habits that they have found rewarding** in some way. They only change them when they are made less rewarding, or appropriate, or when the 'fear trigger' activating them is lessened or removed.

• **Do not feel a failure.** This doesn't help you or your dog. Remember you are responsible for controlling how your dog **behaves**, and not for what it essentially **is**, genetically, as a character. Only its parents, or its breeder, can take the credit for that. Similarly you cannot take the blame for any psychological 'damage' or problems caused by former owners - you can only try to remedy such problems as best you can.

• **If you have been given advice to 'solve' your dog's 'problem', these are the criteria any 'solution' should meet. First,** it should not involve any form of harsh or unkind treatment. **Second**, it should make sense to both you and your dog. **Third**, it shouldn't result in any harmful or unfavourable consequences. In other words, a 'solution' shouldn't have the potential to give you **another** consequent problem, on top of the one you were trying to resolve.

• **Always try to see a problem from your dog's point of view.** It might not make it any easier to live with but it could make it look far less 'frightening' or 'weird'.

• **Don't panic.** Hard as this might be. Panic has no function in solving dog problems. Remember to give yourself plenty of 'cooling off' periods, away from your dog, in moments when it really tries your patience or nerves.

Also note these crucial points:

• **Behavioural advice contained in this section can only be viewed as general guidelines to dealing with common problems an owner - or owners - may experience with a dog. What must always be remembered, however, is that every dog is different, in terms of the precise factors - genetic and / or environmental - that may have contributed to its own individual problem or problems. The key to successfully tackling most dogs' individual problems, therefore, usually lies in how accurately these have been diagnosed in the first place, and how skilfully 'solutions' have subsequently been tailored to them.**

• **Because of the above, owners should seek additional professional advice whenever possible to tackle any 'behavioural problem' in their dog, and *always* in cases where any form of aggression is involved. This is because, by trying to 'fix' things yourself without professional help, you could well make an existing problem worse, or put yourself or others in danger.**

A

Aggression

Aggression is a form of canine behaviour most likely to get owners in a panic. In the main this is because it looks scary and **is** scary - and also because we frequently cannot understand it. When you cannot understand the motivation or likely 'trigger' for aggression in a dog, then you also cannot easily prevent it, control it, or always predict when it might occur - all of which makes it scarier still for most owners to deal with.

So let us start this section by first making dog aggression a little less of a 'mystery'. Let us appreciate that within canine society, aggression of some kind, or at some level, will be a pretty standard **and natural form of communication.** It is also a **basic tool for survival.** Dogs without the ability to use aggression when required cannot hunt, protect themselves, their young, their pack or their territory and cannot compete with others for valuable resources.

Very few dogs, therefore, will not have the capacity to use aggression at some time, and in some form, given the right stimulus or trigger. So what remains at issue is **why some dogs will be readier than others to use aggression,** particularly in more extreme forms, and **what circumstances are most likely to trigger aggression in individual dogs.**

In the main, dogs are more likely to use aggression if:

- •They feel frightened or threatened or not adequately 'protected' by their 'pack leader'
- •They are unwell, injured, stressed, in pain, are restrained or confined - i.e. if they generally feel more vulnerable in the face of a possible threat
- •They want to protect a valuable 'resource' - e.g. food, territory, 'rank', a potential breeding / sexual partner
- •They have high predatory / hunting / guarding / defensive or 'rank competitive' instincts
- •They were not adequately socialised as puppies, or taught to 'inhibit' their bite
- •They have found aggression an extremely rewarding strategy in the past

Now let us look at all these factors in greater detail, should one, or a combination of them, explain what could be happening with your individual dog. Then we will consider how they might best be tackled.

Fright or threat

As previously touched on in this book, a dog's perception of what is 'frightening' or 'threatening' will always conform to its own sense of 'logic', because it cannot 'rationalise' the world it lives in as we can. In other words, it cannot **know** that something its instincts tell it is potentially threatening is really safe or harmless. It can only decide to take the view that something is threatening, or decide to take the view that it is safe, until it is led to believe otherwise. And then it will react accordingly.

Nervous / Defensive or Fearful Aggression are basic terms used to describe dogs whose aggression is primarily triggered through fear, or a perceived sense of threat. Although any dog could have this tendency, it appears to be most common in breeds, or crosses of breeds, with particularly sensitive or 'reactive' temperaments - Collies and German shepherds being two typical examples. It can also be greatly exacerbated by owners wrongly handling it, or through the dog not feeling confident enough in its owner's authority / ability to protect it (see **'Role confusion'** a bit later).

To the untrained eye, dogs like these can simply seem incredibly 'hostile' towards any strange person or dog. And as they possibly bark, snarl or lunge at them, in a rather unnerving way, you'd imagine that this was purely very intimidating behaviour on the dog's behalf, rather than anything to do with its own sense of fear. **Which is entirely what the dog wants others to think,** in order for this strategy to work.

To the dog, what it is doing makes perfect 'sense'. In its mind it is likely to harbour a notion that any strange person or dog it sees could wish it harm. Therefore, the nastier or more frightening it makes itself look, the more the chance - or so it reasons - that this 'threat' will go away.

Unfortunately - but quite understandably - what will most strange people, or dog owners do, when faced with such a grisly and disturbing spectacle? **They will go away** - and fast. Or the owner will take their 'hostile' dog away, fast. So the dog thus finds that this 'defensive strategy' has worked brilliantly, and it will be even more motivated to use it again. Sometimes 'triggers' for such behaviour - as we outlined in Chapter five under **'Early aggression'** - will not exclusively be strange people or dogs. They can also be any object or situation that suddenly makes the dog feel uneasy or afraid.

Potential reasons for this problem in your rescue dog include:

- **Individual genetics.** In other words, its genes make it more naturally inclined than other dogs to react in a fearful or defensive way.

- **Poor early socialisation.** In other words, the dog was not exposed to a wide enough variety of strange new people, dogs, sights, sounds etc. during its early puppyhood and thus could not learn, or was not encouraged, to react to them without fear, during this critical phase of development.

• **'Proven' fears.** In other words, the dog has learned, usually in its past life, that certain-looking objects / people / dogs etc. really **are** threatening and have already caused it previous terror and / or pain.

• **The tendency for its 'defensive' behaviour / aggression to always be rewarded.** Either because the owner has always taken the dog away from the 'threat', or the 'threat' has always gone away from the dog, when it behaves aggressively. Or because the owner has tried to 'soothe' or calm down the dog, which could make it think its response is 'right' or 'appropriate'.

• **Former owners 'reinforcing' the dog's sense of fear or threat** when encountering stranger people / dogs etc. by shouting at it or yanking hard on its lead.

• **The dog's confusion about its own place in the 'pack hierarchy'** - or lack of faith in its owner's ability to 'protect' it whenever a possible 'threat' comes in to view.

What to do

The most urgent priority with any dog displaying nervous / defensive or 'fearful' aggressive tendencies is to **spot the problem as early as possible**, and also to **get it correctly diagnosed**. A good dog trainer or behaviourist should be able to spot classic giveaways of this sort of aggression in a dog - e.g. ears back, crouched body posture, avoidance of direct eye contact - even if you cannot.

Next, understand that a distinct **'genetic factor'** in this sort of behaviour can make it rather more complicated, or harder work, to deal with. In other words, dogs - much like us - will generally find it easier to change habits they have **learned** than they will to **alter fundamental aspects of their character**. There is always room for hope, and improvement, in all cases - but do bear this in mind. It might also help to try and get established - through good behavioural assessment - whether your dog's responses are likely to be more 'genetic', rather than 'learned', in origin.

Once fear has been established as the chief cause of your dog's aggressive behaviour, you will then have to follow a regime to 'de-demonise' the 'triggers' causing your dog to react so defensively. In short, the dog has to learn that its hostile reactions to other dogs, strangers, etc. are ultimately both **unrewarding** and **unnecessary**.

If, for example, your dog reacts most violently to strangers when you are out, or when they come to your house, then you must find a way of illustrating to the dog that they are not so frightening as it might imagine. And equally, it needs to learn that aggressive responses won't always work, or get it what it desires - i.e. the 'threat' invariably going away. Most effective strategies for combating 'fearfulness' or fear reactions in dogs can follow similar lines, and will be covered in full under **Fearfulness** later in this chapter, should you want further advice.

'Role' confusion

Previously mentioned factors apart, it is important to understand that, in or out of the home, many dogs will 'fly off the handle' when encountering strange people / dogs - e.g. rush forward and bark or appear threatening - **because they genuinely believe that this sort of defensive behaviour is part of their 'job' or 'responsibility' within their 'pack'.** In other words, their owners have not conveyed themselves convincingly enough as pack leaders.

How many owners do you see when out, for instance, who allow their dogs to run or walk miles ahead in front of them, and also be the first in the 'pack' to encounter any new person / dog who approaches? Both these 'jobs' or prerogatives belong to the **pack leader.** By constantly allowing your dog to tear ahead up to others like this, you are inadvertently 'promoting' it to a role - e.g. pack defender or pack 'threat assessor' that should be **yours alone.** Moreover, many less naturally confident dogs might find the responsibility of being 'elected' pack protector in this way so worrying or daunting that their behaviour will become progressively more defensive towards others as a result.

Do also note that by shouting at your dog when it rushes ahead barking or looking aggressive towards others - whether inside or out of your home - you are merely giving your dog the impression that you are 'backing it up' in its hostile stance. **So do not shout or be aggressive in any way with your dog when it rushes ahead, or you will just make the problem a whole lot worse.**

To overcome excessively defensive behaviour like this in a dog, a priority is to make it clearer to the dog who really is in charge of the pack. To do this you must ensure that both at home and anywhere else, you are applying **The Rules of Superiority** mentioned in the last chapter.

Apart from this, should visitors call at home, do not let your dog just charge up to them at the front door, barking or growling. Make the dog wait behind you in a 'sit' while **you** answer the door and encounter the visitors **first.** Remember this is **your** job as the pack boss, and **not** your dog's. If your dog will not wait and always tries to have a 'race' with you to get to the front door / visitors first, keep a lead permanently attached to a fixed point - e.g. bottom banister rail - in the hall behind you. Then make a habit of **always** clipping your dog's collar to this each time the doorbell rings, or until it can be trusted to stay back on command without being restrained in this way.

Once you have greeted your visitors and brought them into the house, should your dog continue to be hostile or excitable, tell your visitors to totally ignore it. Once your visitors have settled in, and your dog has quietened down, only then let it come and greet them in a civilised way. If your dog does not quieten down, or you do not feel that you can trust it with visitors off the lead, see the **Fearfulness** section, should fear be the root cause of its problems.

When out with your dog, it may be impractical to never have it walking / running ahead of you at some time, but what really matters is that it comes back **instantly** to you, on command, as soon as other people / dogs are seen approaching (for tips on better **Recall** see last chapter). If your dog won't do this, keep it on a long trailing line (as outlined again in the last chapter) until it finally learns that the '**come**' command from you is not a take-it-or-leave-it option. Do always reward your dog well with praise or a treat, however, each time it does come back to you - even if on the line - to improve its motivation to do so.

It is **very important** that you, and **not your dog,** makes the first social contact - even if this is just verbal - with any approaching people or dogs, while your dog stays close by your side, or even behind you. And by now, should you be doing everything right at home as well as when out, your dog will be getting the message that **you** are one, as 'boss', who sorts out how approaching dogs / people should be dealt with or greeted, and not itself.

This simple 'clarification of roles' can take enormous pressure off many dogs. They now no longer have to worry about the responsibility of accurately assessing threat or defending everyone else. All they have to do is take their cue from the 'boss'. If the boss isn't worried by most stranger people or dogs, then neither should they be. By the same token, however, as 'boss' you should also ensure that you **never knowingly lead your dog up close to any other dog which could do it harm or badly frighten it,** because this is a damaging betrayal of the 'trust' it has placed in your judgement as 'leader'.

Bad handling

As previously touched on, one of the most **disastrous** - and **potentially very dangerous** - things you could ever do to dogs with fearful-aggressive or over-defensive tendencies is to retaliate with aggression yourself. You will simply strengthen their notion that the world is a pretty unsafe or unreliable place and also undermine their trust in your will or ability to always 'protect' them. All these factors can only increase - rather than reduce - their desire to defend themselves even more readily, or aggressively, in future.

It really is quite tragic to consider how many dogs with 'fear aggressive' problems are put down every year, purely because the real cause of these problems was not recognised early enough. Either that or their problems were handled in the most harmful or inappropriate way. You may not be able to 'cure' all dogs with nervous / fearful or over-defensive aggressive tendencies, but if you care enough about your particular rescue dog, at least you can have a darn good try. If only to make life that little bit more pleasant, and less stressful, for you both.

Vulnerable reactions

Before beginning a 'treatment programme' for aggression in a dog - particularly one you do not yet know well, or one whose aggression seems rather more 'out of character' with its normal self - **it is always a good idea to first get the dog properly examined by a vet.** This is because a source of pain - e.g. toothache, infected ears, bad arthritis - or an underlying medical condition, could lie at the heart of its need to react so 'defensively' towards others.

Other reasons for your rescue dog feeling vulnerable, and thus more 'defensive' in its reactions include:

- **Feeling generally 'under pressure' at home.** We know ourselves that when we feel anxious, stressed, or generally challenged by the restrictions and demands of the environment we are living in, we are likely to react in a far more 'irritable' or 'snappy' way. Unfortunately, however, not all owners can recognise or appreciate the factors that are most likely to put dogs under pressure.

- **Being tied up somewhere or confined within a restricted space - e.g., a car.** Some owners might discover that their dogs become 'abnormally aggressive' towards other people, or dogs, in these kinds of circumstances, but this is not really so baffling. The dog simply recognises that the option to flee any possible threat has been taken away from it, leaving it with the only other 'logical' option - to its mind - of staging a hopefully very deterring display of hostility. The level of the dog's reaction in these circumstances can once again depend on its own individual character, as well as the possibility that it really did experience something highly frightening or threatening in the past, while tied up or in the car.

What to do

In the case of dogs **'under pressure'**, see **Anxiety**, p.158, ,and also the next chapter.

In the case of dogs reacting defensively within the car, see the **Fearfulness** section later on in this chapter, and **Car travel problems.**

This apart, be aware that some dogs will react aggressively when left inside a car not so much because they are 'fearful', but because they are actually **'guarding'** the car as a prized 'resource'. A lot of owners will not discourage this because, logically, they see this as no bad thing and possibly a deterrent against car thieves. However, a dog who takes - as some will - to eventually **guarding the car from its own owners,** or other invited passengers, is clearly a much bigger problem. If it is your problem, see below, and also the **Possessiveness** section in this chapter.

Protecting resources

Items dogs may choose to 'guard aggressively' can be basic resources of survival - i.e. food, a potential sexual / breeding partner, territory (the latter can include a car's interior or a certain room) - to any range of items or 'trophies' they might view as reflective of their 'rank' or general 'standing' within a pack, from toys to owners' possessions they appear to take a delight in 'stealing'.

Reasons for this in your rescue dog include:

• **A past life where it had to fight, or compete heavily, with other dogs for food** or other important resources, such as owner attention.

• **It has naturally higher and stronger 'guarding' or 'defensive' instincts**

• **It has a high notion of its own 'status'**

• **It was never discouraged from 'guarding' or 'stealing' things when younger** - or, worse still, soon learned that aggression made it win every confrontation over an item with an owner, by making him or her back off and leave it with its 'prize'.

• **It was so roughly handled, or punished, by owners for 'guarding' and / or stealing things** that this subsequently made it even more defensive when people approached to remove items in its possession.

• **It discovered that stealing things was a highly effective way of gaining owner attention**

What to do

For advice on tackling all the above, see below and also the **Possessiveness** and **Stealing things** sections later.

Naturally strong aggressive instincts

We can seem to find it surprising that some dogs are much more aggressive than others in their behaviour, yet find it unremarkable that people will vary in much the same way. Some people, for instance, can barely drive a mile down the road in their cars without unleashing a torrent of abusive words and gestures at other motorists or pedestrians, whereas others could travel the same distance, in the same circumstances, with utter - or comparative - serenity (and probably far lower blood pressure). Some people, like some dogs, may be hostile and aggressive because this is the only 'behaviour model' they've ever been presented with in their lives, by parents - or, in the case of dogs, by owners as well. And sometimes people and dogs resort readily to aggression simply because this is **the way they are made.** They have naturally 'shorter fuses', or their individual make-up predisposes them towards more violent or confrontational behaviour and reactions.

When we say that a dog has 'naturally strong aggressive instincts' then - apart from fear/ defensive factors already covered - what we'll often find is that it can have any or all of these following factors in common:

• **It is of a breed or type deliberately developed, originally, to have powerful guarding/ hunting instincts,** making for a more 'assertive' character

• **It is a naturally dominant character,** with a high opinion of its own status, and also highly motivated to both seek and protect a superior 'rank'

• **It is a young male dog,** whose behaviour may be additionally influenced by powerful surges of testosterone

What to do

First, understand that when you choose a certain breed or type of dog, you also stand a chance of selecting the temperamental characteristics and instincts that go with it, as previously outlined in earlier chapters. Think hard about taking on dogs with high predatory / hunting / guarding instincts if you feel these are traits you would find it hard to control or manage.

Many people are attracted by the idea of owning powerful big dogs from hunting or guarding breeds - e.g. German shepherds, Akitas, Rottweilers, Dobermanns, but unfortunately usually the greatest part of this attraction comes from imagining that they will have an imposing or impressive-looking dog which will still be fairly easy for them to control, or whose accompanying temperament and instincts will present few problems with other people or dogs.

What they do not consider is how they are going to handle these dogs should their more aggressive or challenging instincts prove **not** to be so easy to contain or control. Or how unsatisfactory, long-term, it can be to own a dog you can only ever take out on a lead and wearing a muzzle, for fear of the harm it might do others.

In the case of more **dominant-minded** individuals, see last chapter - **'Dealing with stronger-willed dogs'** and **'The Rules of Superiority'** - for how to manage them more effectively.

Young male dogs, like young male humans, can have levels of testosterone - and energy! - which can rapidly be turned into aggression towards others without adequate anticipation, control or management of their instincts. The situation will be worsened if they had a puppyhood lacking in proper discipline, and discouragement of biting, or without the chance to socialise with other dogs in a non-confrontational way.

It is vital that dogs like these are not given ample opportunity - see below - to have more aggressive instincts rewarded in any way. They will also benefit from training wherein owners consistently assert their 'control' and 'authority' without ever forcing a confrontation (see **The Juvenile Period,** Chapter four, for more advice on this).

Dogs who are **kept active, physically and mentally,** and who are **taught to focus intently on their owners, and their owners' commands,** will also have less opportunity to focus on aggression towards others instead. A good dog trainer should be able to give you more detailed advice, and examples, of how to bring this about.

Castration can have varying results in reducing aggression in young male dogs, depending on what age it is done and - as mentioned previously in this book - whether or not the operation is backed up with retraining the dog to behave in a less 'confrontational' way. This is something you may wish to discuss with your vet.

Rewarding aggression

Throughout this section, you have probably begun to realise how easy it can be to 'reward' dogs for their aggression, without necessarily being aware of it.

For instance, we reward a **'fearful'** dog for its aggression towards others by instantly removing it from these 'threats' the moment hostility is shown.

We reward dogs for being **aggressive** towards us by getting into confrontations with them which we will then lose, because their hostility intimidates us into 'backing off'.

Similarly, if we constantly allow **young male dogs** to get into confrontations with other dogs which they win, or let **any dog roar triumphantly off after a fleeing postman** or delivery man, this is such an 'ego boost' for the dog that it will feel compelled to repeat the same actions again.

Every single time a dog enters into a confrontation that it appears to 'win' in any way, then it will want to repeat the experience. **So we have to do everything in our power to avoid dogs getting into confrontations with us, or others, in the first place** - and teach them that different or more 'preferable' ways of behaving, other than aggressively, will be far more rewarding or appropriate in the long run.

We also have to bear mind how much we can reward aggression in dogs simply through **giving it so much of our instant attention.** It is pretty hard to ignore an aggressive dog, and dogs learn this lesson very fast.

If you shout and scream at your dog when it is being aggressive, incredibly easy though this is to do in a moment of panic, be aware that this can not only lead to an even more 'hostile' atmosphere - it can also **give your dog the notion that you are 'backing it up'** or 'urging it on' to greater hostility.

Instead, in any scenario where your dog is being aggressive towards others, it is better to try and stay calm, and then do your best to redirect your dog's focus immediately back on to you in a firm but steady voice and tone. This is something you should be practising a lot with your dog in general - preferably with the help of an experienced trainer - and in a variety of different contexts, using toys or treats if necessary to begin with, to effect the fastest responses.

Once you've managed to get your dog's focus quickly back on to you, in many different situations, and in anticipation of what you are now going to ask it to do - e.g. sit, go down - then praise it effusively for its cooperation each time. It is important that the dog eventually learns that compliance with **your** wishes, rather than any of its **own** aggressive responses or initiatives towards others, will be the only thing that gets it some highly rewarding attention from you.

All in all, solutions to aggressive behaviour in dogs generally revolve around these key things:

- **Sufficient understanding, and accurate and early diagnosis of the cause**

- **Improved anticipation and awareness of possible 'aggression triggers'**

- **Avoidance of any scenario likely to lead to a confrontation between the dog and yourself or others**

- **Better overall 'leadership' as well as improved control of the dog through training**

- **The removal, wherever possible, of any 'reward' for hostile reactions**

This apart, be prepared for progress in 'improving' an aggressive dog to be gradual and to take some time, depending on how long it has had hostile or defensive tendencies, and how frequently these have been rewarded in the past. **And be warned again not to send your dog away to 'an expert' to have its aggression 'cured'.** There is no such thing as a 'quick fix' solution to aggression in dogs. There are only longer-term 'modification' programmes which require effort but will keep your relationship with your dog, and your dog's mental well-being, intact. Or there are the 'shorter, sharp shock' tactics which always look and sound so much easier, or more preferable, until you're later left to deal with the psychological damage they can inflict - and even greater problems, potentially, than you started out with.

For aggression that culminates in **Biting**, see relevant section heading. For advice on how to properly use a muzzle, see below.

Wearing a muzzle

To my mind, the modern plastic basket-type muzzle for dogs is one of the best 'problem prevention' tools ever devised. A dog correctly fitted with such a device is able to breathe or pant freely, or vomit should it have to, but at the same time is restricted from using its potentially very damaging teeth on others (though there can still be risks, see below) or from scavenging unsavoury items which could damage its health (see the **Faeces-eating** section later)

When dogs are continually denied the possibility of readily using their teeth on others, they often have to start rethinking the way they socially interact with other people or dogs, once all - out aggression is no longer an option. Owners can immediately relax a lot more. This in turn can positively affect the overall mood of their dog.

A word of warning, however. It cannot always be assumed that any muzzle on a dog will be totally foolproof or bite-proof. In some cases, dogs have been known to work off even the tightest of muzzles, or actually find a way to bite other dogs through the muzzle they have on. So do be alert to these dangers.

Fitting a muzzle

As outlined before, the best type of muzzle to get a dog is the modern plastic basket type, which many pet stores keep in stock. Make sure you get this muzzle fitted correctly in the shop. The dog should have enough room to open its mouth and pant freely inside the muzzle. The straps shouldn't be so tight that they cause real discomfort, but neither should they be loose enough to enable the dog to pull the muzzle off its head with its paws.

Once you're home, a dog needs to get used to a muzzle **gradually**. If you just thrust one on without any preamble or pre-preparation your dog will rightly start to dread it, or will do its best to avoid having it put on.

Here is how to get a dog used to a muzzle:

•**Before putting the muzzle over the dog's snout, put a food treat inside it.**

•**Gently slide the muzzle over the dog's snout, allow it to take the treat, then slide the muzzle off again.**

•**Repeat this exercise a few times, saying 'muzzle' each time you slide the device on. This way the dog can eventually anticipate the device and know what to expect, so will thus be less wary or frightened.**

•**Move on to fixing the muzzle strap(s) behind (and above - if applicable) the dog's head, leaving these straps on slightly longer each time before removing them.**

•**Repeat this exercise in a variety of different contexts - e.g., at home, or out - and at different times of day, leaving the muzzle on for different lengths of time. This way the** dog will not associate the muzzle with specific situations - e.g. strange people or dogs approaching. If it does this it can then calculate when to avoid coming back to you to have it put on, or will hastily try to 'accomplish' the thing it suspects you do not want it to do before you have a chance to muzzle it.

Whenever your dog attempts to drag the muzzle off, keep distracting it by calling it to you and making a fuss of it. It may take some while before **your** dog fully accepts wearing the muzzle without protest, but the above measures, plus persistence, should eventually make this more likely.

Anxiety

Dogs, as first outlined in Chapter five, are no more immune from the effects - or causes - of anxiety or stress than ourselves. It's just that some of the symptoms might be a bit different. The following can be symptoms of anxiety or stress in dogs:

- •Restlessness

- •Lack of concentration

- •Disinterest in 'play' or toys

- •Diarrhoea and / or itchy skin

- •Inappropriate 'scent-marking' or fouling round the home

- •Lack of appetite

- •Pacing continually around and panting

- •Excessive barking and / or whining

- •'Compulsive' habits - e.g. tail-chasing, licking or gnawing paws or other parts of the body

- •Destructiveness

- •**Excessive drinking** (though note, this could also herald a possible medical problem, so if in doubt check this out)

Possible reasons for this in your rescue dog include:

- •Concerns about being in a strange new environment

- •Existing insecurities about its past life or living environment

- •Fears about being left alone or about being confined

158

•Hostility or general 'pressure' from new owners or other dogs in the house

•General uneasiness about someone or something it imagines is threatening to it within the home - Be this something as simple as the 'unfamiliar' sound of a tumble-drier or workmen inside or outside, or a household member whose appearance reminds it of some past fear.

•Insufficient outlets for physical and mental energies

What to do

Anxiety and stress are incredibly common problems in rescue dogs - usually due to backgrounds of upheaval, insecurity, trauma or uncertainty. A spell in kennels can also be pretty stressful for many dogs. The important thing in most cases is to be **patient** and **understanding**. Once dogs have reached pretty high levels of mental stress or anxiety, it can sometimes take months for them to wind down, and expecting far 'quicker' results can only lead to increased unhappiness or frustration all round.

If dogs are going to 'come down' from high stress or anxiety levels, they have to be given a pretty calm, ordered - and tolerant! - atmosphere in which to do this. This means excessive bouts of over-stimulation or excitement should initially be avoided, and likewise any situation likely to 'harass' a dog or push it into some form of confrontation. This includes the dog being 'picked on' by other dogs in your house, or being excessively 'wound up' or pestered by children. Also see **'Stress-related behaviour'** and **'Dealing with stress during early days'**, Chapter five.

Only in really **desperate** 'anxiety' or stress cases could **drug therapy** (i.e. a sedative) be recommended, as a temporary measure to help the dog adjust better to its new home. Your vet could give you more guidelines about this. Alternatively you may want to investigate **homeopathic remedies** that could help reduce anxiety - in which case, see advice section at the end of this book.

If your dog starts licking and chewing its paws or other parts of its body in a seemingly 'compulsive' way, then this must be stopped to avoid serious mutilation. Your vet could provide you with a special plastic collar to prevent this occurring.

Physical symptoms & diet

Symptoms like **itchy skin** or **diarrhoea** can be stress-related, but could also be to do with a sudden change in diet. Itching could also be due to reactive to fleas or other irritants - e.g. household cleaners, dust mites - in your home which stress will greatly exacerbate, so do be aware of this. When rescue dogs first come to your home, it's thus best to ensure they have been treated for common skin parasites and to stick to the previous diet they were on. If you have done this, then the dog's previous diet may not be suitable for it. Or its symptoms may only truly wane once its stress levels have come down. Blander diets, or diets higher in carbohydrate than protein can often have a calming effect on some dogs. Again, see your vet about this.

Exercise and mental stimulation

Sometimes stressed or anxious dogs - and particularly those from working breeds - simply need a better balance of physical and mental exercise in their lives. Too much physical exercise involving chasing things, or getting intensely excited, can actually make them become more, rather than less, 'frenetic' or over-stimulated once they stop or come home. Mental work, on the other hand - e.g. formal training exercises, exercises where they have to use their noses or brains to find food, or work out a distinct 'problem' - will make them calmer. See Chapter nine for more tips on correct **exercise** and **mental stimulation** for dogs.

Where anxiety or stress relate to **Toileting problems**, lack of **Appetite**, **Barking**, **Destructiveness**, **Separation Anxiety** or any responses involving **Fearfulness**, see relevant section headings in this chapter.

Appetite - extreme, or loss of

Levels of 'natural appetite' can vary from dog to dog. Some dogs can be very fussy eaters - toy breeds are a classic example - whereas others could be positive gluttons.

New owners will often get worried about their dog's eating habits. Either it is eating too fast or too much - basically anything it can get its jaws around. Or it is not eating enough, or it is not eating at all.

Possible reasons for your rescue dog 'bolting' or 'wolfing' food down include:

- **Coming from a former household where it had to compete for food with other dogs, or where it was often hungry.**

- **Coming from a rescue kennel environment where mealtimes were often the biggest 'highlight' of the day.**

- **It is just plain greedy!**

What to do

Providing a dog is not obese, and is eating in line with its energy output, many owners might not view the above as that much of a problem. However, if the dog is 'bolting down' food, the chances are it will also be swallowing large amounts of air with it, which in turn could lead to digestive upset, or even a life-threatening condition called **gastric bloat** (see Chapter nine on **Health**), particularly if it is a dog of a larger breed or type more prone to this ailment than others.

If this is a concern for you, then you can purchase - from most pet goods suppliers - a special raised stand to put your dog's food bowl in. The bowl being that much nearer the dog's head level will prevent it from sucking up so much air with its food. It's also a good idea not to feed your dog too soon before or after exercise (i.e. leave at least an hour's gap), and not to allow it to drink excessive amounts of water immediately prior to, or after, eating a large amount of dried food.

If you have other dogs that you feel could be encouraging your new dog to eat faster, feed the new dog on its own, in a separate place. In time, once your new dog realises that regular feeding opportunities can be relied upon, and its food will always be 'safe', this may no longer be necessary. Unless of course, the new dog's food definitely **isn't** 'safe' from your other dogs! In which case, carry on as before with separate feeding arrangements.

You could also try feeding the dog two smaller meals - morning and evening - rather than one bigger one each day. They might disappear just as rapidly, but at least less food means less air to go down with it, and less of a sudden assault on the digestive system.

The most important consideration for any dog that loves its food is that it should not be allowed to get overweight. To find out more about the perils of **Obesity** in dogs, see Chapter nine.

Possible reasons for lack of *appetite* in your rescue dog include:

•**Anxiety.** Anxious dogs, like anxious people, find it pretty hard to eat. For possible anxiety causes see last section.

•**Inhibition.** Some dogs - particularly less confident types-can find it harder than others to eat in close proximity to people, or other dogs, they do not know well. There is also a possibility that mealtimes, in a former home, developed some unpleasant associations - e.g. it was 'bullied' by other dogs, or even had its food dish regularly snatched away by owners in the bizarre, and too common, belief that this would assert 'authority' over a dog, rather than simply give it lasting hang-ups about eating and food that it wouldn't otherwise have had.

•**To seek attention.** Dogs much like children - can soon catch on to the fact that declining food gains them a level of attention they would not have got through eating it in a normal and uneventful way. If they have more indulgent owners, they can also discover that refusing a 'first' option of food can inevitably lead to a better, or more preferable, one being offered.

Needless to say, this tendency is also likely to be more common if the dog has no others in the household to 'compete' with at mealtimes.

•**Illness.** If your dog consistently refuses all food for more than a few days, and has any other accompanying symptoms, such as lethargy, vomiting, or an absence of any bowel movements, then illness, or some possible intestinal blockage - e.g. it has swallowed objects it cannot digest, or pass out of its system - have to be considered.

What to do

In the case of suspected **illness**, or some intestinal blockage, **you must** consult your vet as soon as possible. In the case of **anxiety** - this can often pass. It can be quite normal for dogs in new surroundings to be off their food for a while until they feel more secure, or generally settle in to the routines of your household. If it does not pass, see the last section on **Anxiety**, and also the next chapter on the subject.

Inhibitions about eating

Dogs with **inhibitions** about eating should always be fed somewhere away from the main hustle and bustle of household life, and should also be left to eat quietly on their own - preferably while you are all still in the house, as anxiety about your absence will not help their problem. Never hover over the dog, or try to hand feed it. This may further put pressure on it and increase its apprehension, especially if food had been snatched away from it in the past by other dogs, or former owners.

It could also lead to a dog - see below - whose genuine early inhibitions then develop into a deliberate ploy for attention. If your 'inhibited' dog doesn't eat the meal you leave for it within fifteen minutes, remove it - **without** the dog seeing you do so - and wait until the next mealtime before offering another dish of food. Continually repeat this exercise, with minimum fuss or attention directed towards the dog, and in time it should gain far more positive, or less worrying and threatening, associations with mealtimes.

Attention seeking

Providing your dog is not ill, anxious, or suffering from inhibitions like those mentioned above - i.e. it never looks remotely nervous or apprehensive when a food bowl is presented - the other possible option is that it sees declining food as **a great way of getting your attention.** It is vital to spot this ploy early on and to thwart it by giving zero attention to a dog who will not eat its food. Do not **ever** give it other options and, like above, promptly remove any dish of food that has not been eaten within half an hour with no fuss or comment at all - only **in this case, let the dog see you do it.** Do not offer the dog any more food until the next mealtime, and keep repeating this exercise until the dog eventually realises that its attention-seeking ploy is not working - and probably also that it is getting very hungry.

Natural eating habits

Owners primarily get neurotic about their dogs' eating habits because they expect them to match their own - i.e. one or two set and formal meals a day, every day. In truth, neither dogs' minds nor digestive systems are geared to this sort of regime. A dog's digestive system was originally designed for **gorging and fasting** - which is why so many dogs will routinely turn down meals now and then, for no other reason other than that they have healthy and normal canine appetites.

Dogs are also programmed to be **scavengers** and generally have less natural expectation of gaining food without effort. In the wild what they eat they will either have hunted and killed, or found from opportunistically rummaging around. All of which probably explains why they'll take a perverse delight in turning down your beautifully - balanced, prepared meal, only to guzzle down some horrific bit of old muck in the street.

Ultimately, providing illness is ruled out, your dog maintains a good weight and seems pretty healthy, it's best not to get too neurotic about its eating habits. Few dogs are really daft enough to starve. If there's food around to be eaten, and they really need it, then they'll eat it

Attention-seeking behaviour

The previous section has already given us, as it were, a taste of 'attention-seeking' behaviour in dogs when it comes to mealtimes. If we work on the premise that what a lot of dogs supremely dread - again, like most children - is **to be ignored**, then we'll better understand the efforts they will go to to ensure that this doesn't happen.

Unfortunately, parents and dog owners alike can all too easily **make the classic mistake of giving bad, rather than good, behaviour far more of their attention.** When a child, for instance, is sitting down in a civilised and quiet manner, doing its homework or some household chores for us, how many parents will immediately shower it with lavish attention and praise for being so good? Now compare this with the level of attention you might give to a child when it screaming in a shop, writing on walls or annihilating your cherished herbaceous borders. Hmm - see the problem?

From barking and whining and mounting guests' legs to refusing food or running off with the mail, the amazing range of things dogs will do to get your attention can actually be governed by just one main criterion - a**nd that's that they get your attention.** And even - or especially - if you rant and rail at them like a demented banshee, that's certainly a whole lot better than being ignored.

Reasons for this tendency in your rescue dog include:

• **A past - in a former home, or in kennels - where it received little, or quite limited, personal attention.**

- **It is a naturally 'needy' dog** - i.e. its own confidence or sense of security hinges too heavily on owner attention, or it quickly becomes over-dependent on, or over-attached to, an owner.

- **It has become an 'attention junkie'** through excessive indulgence, early on, from new owners.

What to do

First, start to look a little bit more closely at your day-to-day relationship with the dog. Are you putting sufficient emphasis, in terms of praise and attention, on all the things you'd **like**, or **prefer**, your dog to do - e.g. settle down, come when called, wait patiently for a meal or treat - or are you just taking this 'better behaviour' for granted? And can you generally give your dog **more** attention - in terms of shouting / pleading / cajoling etc. - for disobeying your wishes or commands that you would for **complying** with them?

Can you additionally have a tendency, as an individual, or as a household, to give immediate attention to anything your dogs wants, when it wants it, or to be over-interested in anything it happens to be doing at any given time?

If so, then this all has to change. In future, save praise and excessive attention for your dog **only when it is doing something you'd like it to do, or would prefer it to do.** Whether this is when it is lying down quietly, or just complying with a basic command. Yes, go right over the top, and won't your dog be baffled - before, hopefully, then being rather pleased with itself.

If, on the other hand, your dog is continuing to do things that you **don't** like, then **stop rewarding these things with your attention.** The way to really effectively 'cure' any form of attention-seeking behaviour in your dog is to totally ignore it, **always**, until the dog eventually stops it. Try this if you can, whenever you can, as it will really work well. If, however, this tactic frequently seems too hard to stick to, then it's because dogs are masters at developing, and sustaining, certain forms of 'bad behaviour' that you could only actually 'ignore' if you were in a different town to them - or possibly a different country.

So instead, here are your options. You could instantly make a dog **lie down**, and **stay** still where it is - until told otherwise - each time it does something 'bad', which makes it ultimately pretty unrewarding. Or, if you do not yet have such a level of control over your dog, instead instantly banish it into the garden, **without a word**. If the 'bad' attention-seeking behaviour - e.g. inappropriate digging - has been happening in the garden, then bring it inside instead, and banish it to a room in which it can do little damage.

Leave it 'banished' for a minute or two - unless it starts howling and whining in protest. In which case, leave it until its stops howling and whining for a while, and then call it back in to you. If it repeats the bad - or less desirable - behaviour, keep repeating this exercise. If it settles down, or behaves well, praise it excessively. Eventually the dog should associate the 'bad' behaviour not with your attention but - oh no, another boring spell of 'banishment'. Which isn't very rewarding at all. And certainly not as rewarding as other things you seem to prefer it to do.

A last word of caution on this front, however. **Do be sure that your dog's behaviour genuinely is an attention-seeking ploy, before pursuing the above measures.** If in doubt, get some additional professional advice to be sure. If the behaviour really is **not** motivated by a desire to get your attention, then the chances are you removing all attention from it will not change it significantly in any way.

B

Barking

Dogs will bark for lots of different reasons. Because they are **anxious**, or **stressed**, or bored or frustrated - in which case, the action of barking will alleviate the discomfort of such feelings. Or they will bark to 'see off' any perceived **threat** to themselves or their territory, or bark because they are excited or want attention, or bark because they are lonely and want to 'call' owners or other 'pack members' back to them.

Owners who get pretty frustrated or anxious themselves about a dog's barking - particularly when they are out and the noise drives neighbours mad - need to first consider which, out of the following possibilities, is most likely to be the case with their dog.

Reasons for excessive barking in your rescue dog include:

- It picked up this 'habit' in a past home, or in kennels, to relieve anxiety, frustration or boredom
- It is a dog with a naturally 'excitable' temperament
- It is a dog with heightened sensitivity / reactiveness to all manner of 'strange' or worrying sounds / sights around or outside the home
- It is over-attached to an owner and / or copes badly with being left alone
- It has discovered that barking quickly gets your attention

What to do

First understand that, compared to us, dogs have a **very limited repertoire** of what they can do

165

to 'kill time' or relieve boredom and anxiety when left alone, particularly for long periods (e.g. two hours or more). They cannot read books, watch television, embroider a few cushions, redesign the rockery or generally devise a whole range of more 'constructive' - and quieter - uses for time. So if dogs bark, or get into destructive habits when we're out, then it's usually because they cannot find - or know - any better ways to externalise their energies or anxieties.

Second, appreciate the 'reward' factor that can be attached to many forms of barking. Barking will make a dog feel better because it's a way of displacing anxiety or stress, or it can get a 'high' from just roaring up the garden in full yowling flight, whether or not a 'real' threat is actually there. If you yell and shout at a dog yourself when it is barking - as it is so tempting to do - the dog will then find its actions further 'rewarded' with **your attention**, or might imagine that you are 'joining in' with its enjoyable racket.

Once we have grasped the above, we should see that the keys to tackling excessive barking lie in:

• **Understanding why the dog is doing it, and what it is trying to 'communicate' in doing so**

• **Making barking less necessary or rewarding**

Many dogs with persistent barking problems when owners are out may also be prone to bouts of **Destructiveness**, or can generally suffer from **Separation Anxiety**. In which case, see the relevant section headings in this chapter.

Conflicting needs

This apart, owners seeking quick or 'foolproof' solutions to dogs who bark excessively when they are out should realise that this whole problem usually revolves around, and perpetuates itself, through **constantly conflicting needs**. In other words, owners need to be out of the house at times, without dogs, and dogs in turn need company and stimulation and some can react pretty adversely if regularly denied these things through an owner's absence.

Additionally, dogs left alone will not have their less desirable behaviour - including barking - **checked** or **thwarted** by anyone the instant it occurs. This means they cannot know that what they are doing is 'wrong'. The longer and more often you are allowed to repeat behaviour which makes you feel better, without any immediate negative consequences, the more you will also want to keep on doing it.

Unfortunately the 'simplest' solution to this problem - not to leave your dog alone, or to take it with you when you go out - is also the hardest, or least realistic, for most owners to achieve. If we cannot be with our dogs all the time, however, what we can do is make them better equipped, mentally, to cope with separation without resorting to barking or other less acceptable forms of 'time killing' or anxiety-displacing' behaviour. For more advice on achieving this, again see **Separation Anxiety**.

Some more **sensitive, nervous or generally 'highly reactive'** dogs will bark while you are out because they are disturbed or anxious about people passing outside in the street or by other worrying noises they can hear close to home while you are out. There's a chance they will also do this, from time to time, while you are at home (see '**Alarm barking**' below).

 If you suspect that this could be the reason for your own dog's barking while you are out, you could try some simple measures like moving its bed, or sleeping quarters, away from more 'threatening' places like hallways, windows or front doors to somewhere quieter within the house, and also leave a radio playing in the background to mask other sounds. Tune this into a station with more talk than music. Do not leave this on too loud, however - not only can this worry the dog, but a barking dog swapped for a deafening radio won't be many neighbours' idea of a 'solution' to this problem!

If your dog appears to have got into the 'habit' of leaping onto furniture to bark out of the window while you are out, out of frustration, boredom or worry, move this furniture away from windows, or stop giving the dog access into rooms where it is likely to do this, in order to help break such a habit.

Alarm barking

Lots of dogs - and especially more excitable / reactive breeds or individuals - will bark loudly **while owners are around**, perhaps at the front door or in the garden. Sometimes this will be 'alarm barking', which has a far more urgent and less monotonous pitch to it than other kinds. Basically the dog has perceived some 'threat' outside, near or within the home 'territory' and wants to alert the rest of the 'pack' to it. Frequently owners will be told to ignore this behaviour, like all barking, for fear that it will soon become an 'attention-seeking' ploy.

But what if your dog really **has** identified some threat you should know about - like an intruder, fire or other danger? You would only ignore such things at your peril. My own feelings are that genuine alarm barking should never be ignored. Often dogs will only go on barking frantically at perceived external 'worries' around the home because their 'leaders' or other pack members do not come to check these worries out for them. Or they just shout at them to shut up. Yet until the 'leader', in particular, has checked out the dog's concerns, how can it relax? Worse still, it can feel that the decision as to how an external 'threat' should best be dealt with has been left entirely to itself. This in turn can make it even more anxious, insecure and frantic in its 'barking defence'.

If your dog is barking in alarm at something inside the house or out in the garden, go and check it out. Thank your dog, **in a calm and quiet manner,** for 'telling you' about a possible threat and, should nothing be amiss, simply ask it to settle down again or come back inside if it is outside. If it will not come inside, go and attach a lead to it **without a word** and - again in a very **calm** manner - bring it indoors. Once it has come inside with you, praise it well and ask it to settle down.

So often this simple exercise in reassurance is all that is needed to stop a dog's alarm barking getting out of control. If, however - as previously outlined - you make the mistake of shouting at a dog when it is barking in this way it could think you are joining in with its excitement or panic. Either that or it soon could adapt 'alarm barking' into an **attention-seeking** ploy because of the excessive fuss you make every time it does it.

'Teaching' barking

Perverse as it may sound, another good way to stop a dog barking quickly is to **teach it to bark** in the first place, on command. You do this by getting the dog's barking associated with a word like 'speak!' In other words, every time the dog barks, say **'speak!'** or whatever other 'prompt' you prefer. Once you have taught this, you will then also need to teach the dog a command to stop barking - e.g. **'qui-ET!'** Plus perhaps a hand signal to go with this for extra clarity. Praise the dog effusively and give it a treat when it responds to either command, and you should soon have an anti-barking device more efficient than any other amount of aimless shouting at your dog to shut up.

A final point on this subject. Sometimes **older** dogs can develop more **bizarre or seemingly inexplicable patterns of barking** that are to do with circulatory changes within the brain. The same can be true of any dog experiencing some kind of brain disturbance due to illness or a tumour. If you have any suspicions that this could apply to your dog, do get it checked out by a vet.

Biting

It's important to understand that not all forms of biting in a dog mean that the animal is fundamentally 'bad' or dangerous. Most puppies, for instance, will begin their early lives constantly exploring the people, dogs and general world around them with their mouths and teeth. When puppies are small we tend not to find their constant 'play-biting' threatening, simply because they are small and also young. But we don't find the same behaviour so 'cute' in an adult dog, even if it may still be behaving just as it did in puppyhood, because no one taught it to correctly 'inhibit' its bite when playing, or interacting with others.

In some breeds or types of dog - e.g. Border collies, terriers - 'nipping' can also be just an instinctive hunting reflex, used inappropriately when the dog feels suddenly excited or threatened.

This apart, the most dangerous dogs are always those who will use biting as a **first**, rather than **last**, resort when under pressure or set off by any number of possible triggers. This could simply be due to the way they are inclined, genetically, or because previous owners punished them for giving any sort of 'warning signal' - e.g. growling - in the past. In the main, most dogs will tend instead to give off a series of **'early warning' signals** to show that they threatened, uneasy or are about to launch a 'challenge' (e.g. over rank, territory, or a 'prized' resource) and want others to 'back off' or 'back down'.

In more **nervous or 'defensively aggressive'** dogs, these 'early signals' can include:

•A crouched and sometimes almost half-retreating body posture

•Flattened ears

•Narrowed eyes and averted eye contact

In more dominant, confident or more 'offensively aggressive' dogs, the signals will include:

•A stiff and erect body posture

•Raised hackles and ears

•Direct eye contact

If we do not, or cannot, read these 'signals' correctly, and continue to provoke, pressurise or threaten the dog even further, only then may it feel driven to resort to biting as a last resort, either to defend itself or, if it is a more dominant-minded individual, to secure or protect something important to itself.

Reasons for biting in your rescue dog include:

•It is a deeply troubled dog, psychologically - due to its genetic make-up and / or past

•It was never taught to 'inhibit' its bite during puppyhood

•It is using hunting instincts inappropriately

•It feels under extreme pressure or threat

•It is a dominant-minded individual with a keen desire to protect resources or status

What to do
First of all, be aware that if you have a dog capable of launching a full-scale biting attack on someone visiting the home, or someone encountered while out, it may, under the provisions of

the Dangerous Dog Act, stand a risk of having to be destroyed. **Also, as ever, be aware of the risks of tackling any form of aggressive behaviour in a dog without proper professional help or assessment.**

If you have a dog who has badly bitten you or a family member **without any prior warning** (see previous 'early warning' signals) at all, or without the slightest provocation on the other party's behalf, then this is also pretty serious, and you should have words with the rescue organisation who provided you with such a dog, with a view to returning it if so desired. Many dogs with habits like these can be **very troubled, psychologically**, due to genetic aspects of character, poor early socialisation and / or a pretty traumatic past and only you can decide - hopefully with the benefit of more professional guidance - whether you and the dog in question really have a chance of overcoming its fundamental problems.

Being bitten by one's own dog, in terms of how really 'serious' it is, or not, can be greatly governed by individual owner reaction, and the strength of the bite involved. Some owners, for instance, will not tolerate the slightest 'nip' from a dog under any circumstances. Others can be regularly nipped or bitten by their dog with seemingly little provocation and still adore it (the dog that is, not the biting!). If you want to love and keep a dog who could bite you at any time, this is your business, though sometimes - depending on the exact cause of the problem - much can be done to remedy such behaviour with professional help.

Should you not seek professional help, however, or should professional help not be able to satisfactorily change your dog's behaviour then, both legally and morally, you have a duty to ensure that your dog cannot become a threat to others, be these other dogs or people. To avoid this worrying possibility occurring, you may need to keep your dog restrained and / or muzzled at all times when it is out with you, or when any visitor comes to the house.

Although this may not be an ideal solution, it is the price owners generally have to pay for keeping a dog with such uncontrollable, or un-remedied, tendencies, which could be a danger to others.

Play biting

If you have an adult dog who **was never deterred from 'play-biting' when young**, you must react to it much like you would to a puppy who nips. Give out a loud yell the moment it so much as touches you with its teeth, and instantly walk away looking suitably offended. If the dog, apart from this annoying habit, is otherwise good-natured and co-operative, your continued disapproval and rejection of it whenever it uses its teeth should have beneficial effect. The problem is more serious if the dog **bites very hard** and will not release its hold instantly when you yell. In circumstances like these, it would be best to seek some additional behavioural advice, as remedies would depend on the individual nature of the dog.

'Working' or 'hunting' instincts

If you have a dog whose hunting / working reflexes - in terms of inappropriate 'nipping' - are easily triggered, you will often find this happening in the context of over-stimulation of some kind - e.g. 'rough and tumble' play, or the excitement of a 'chase' or 'tug and shake' game. A cessation of such games should help the problem.

Also be aware that dogs like these can be rapidly stimulated into nipping in scenarios where small children are running and screaming around, or they are being heavily patted and petted, or there is a general high level of noise and commotion. So bear this in mind. **It does not mean that the dogs in question are intrinsically 'bad'.** It just means that they can find it harder than other dogs to restrain natural 'working' or 'hunting' instincts when excited or pressurised in some way.

Fear and 'dominance'

As we have already highlighted in this book, **fearful or nervous dogs** can react aggressively or defensively in the face of a perceived threat. The main aim of their 'defensive' posturing, however, is to make you back off, or go away. Thus, it is only when you do not take this opportunity, or push them even further with increasingly threatening proximity, or with aggression of your own, that the dog could resort to biting as a 'last resort'. Once again, see **Fearfulness**, to keep this possibility in check.

In the case of **dominant-minded dogs**, biting can sometimes be a way they'll attempt to 'intimidate' or 'put down' others in a household whom they imagine to be inferior to them. Usually the biting will be a progression on from other lower key forms of aggressive intimidation - e.g. snarling, growling-which they have used with success, or with little adverse impact, in the past to get what they want - e.g. possession of a 'special' chair or the 'privilege' of going first out of a doorway. The more often they have been 'successful' with such behaviour, the more emboldened they may then feel to get even more 'assertive' with imagined 'inferiors'.

As previously highlighted in this book - see **'Dealing with stronger-willed dogs'** and **The Rules of Superiority**, last chapter - the key to this problem usually revolves around how you manage and relate to your dog on a day-to-day level. In other words, the more 'privileges' and general 'status' you allow it to secure effortlessly, or without challenge, then the more 'superior' it could consider itself in relation to you.

Do remember that 'inferior' behaviour in a human can look much the same to a dog as inferior behaviour in another dog. You do not get any extra automatic 'brownie points', in terms of status, to a dog, simply through being a different species. Thus if we want a dog to judge us as 'superior' to itself, then the only way we will do this is through acting towards it in a suitably 'superior' way. Little else will have the same effective impact on its behaviour.

C

Car travel problems

Many owners can find that their new dogs do not travel well in the car. They are either exceedingly restless, bark continuously - or bark at passing vehicles - or are actually physically sick.

Reasons for this in your rescue dog include:

•It is anticipating an exciting destination

•It has negative or frightening associations with cars or car travel

•It believes its barking is making other cars 'go away'

•It is seeking your attention

•It genuinely suffers from car sickness

What to do

Most dogs soon twig that car travel frequently means that they are going somewhere exciting or new for a walk or outing. Naturally this is a great treat for a dog, and the reason why it might get so worked up in the car, simply through anticipating the excitement to come.

Unfortunately, as with so many more aggravating forms of canine behaviour, this could have been nipped in the bud if former owners had simply stopped the car the moment the dog barked, each time the dog barked, until it realised that barking got it nowhere. So this is something you could try, even though progress initially may be slow, and it could take you half an hour to do a drive that normally takes five minutes.

It can however work in cases like these, though it is vital that you **always** stop the car when the dog barks - except please in the fast lane of a motorway or anywhere else remotely hazardous to others! - and never drive off again until the dog has stopped barking.

Alternatively, or as an additional measure, do **regular** short trips round the block, and sometimes further, at different times of day, with your dog in the car - and then come straight back home again, without the dog getting out of the car. Your dog may look baffled. How much fun was that? But eventually it should realise that trips out in the car won't always mean it is going somewhere exciting, so getting excited becomes a less appropriate response.

Do also remember to praise your dog and / or give it a treat for being quiet in the car, so that it begins to realise that this is the right thing to do. Do not **ever** shout at the dog to shut up when it is in an excited state, as it will simply think you are joining in with its joyful racket.

Frightening associations

Some dogs can develop **negative or frightening** associations with cars for a variety of reasons. In Chapter five we looked at how this could have happened because they were left in one during frightening circumstances - e.g. a thunderstorm - or because a car was the last thing they saw before previous owners abandoned them. Or perhaps the dog just got frightened by noises, or sudden movements, a car made while it was in one as a puppy.

If you suspect this might be the case with your dog - i.e. it is clearly incredibly reluctant to get into a car - **then do not keep forcing it into the car against its will,** as it may well be genuinely terrified, and your behaviour will only make it even more frightened. Instead, try these measures.

- **With your dog on a lead, walk past your car a couple of times.** If your dog does not react with any fear, reward it with a treat. If it does react with fear, move past the car from a distance the dog is happier with, then reward it for not showing fear.

- **Next, over the next day or so, try to get your dog nearer and nearer to the car without it showing fear.** Do this only in gradual steps, always reward the dog when it doesn't show fear and never force it to go nearer if it is reluctant to do so. Be patient and let the dog progress only when it is ready.

- **Once the dog is happy about going right up to the car, open both back doors of the car -** or front doors if you have no back doors. The dog needs to see that there is an immediate 'escape route' back out of the car should it want it.

- **Next, with the help of someone you know your dog likes and trusts, get your helper to stand by one open back - or front - door while you are at the other with the dog.** Ask the helper to call the dog through the car, perhaps with the aid of one of its favourite treats or toys, and make sure the helper is not too near the door. Make the whole procedure look and sound like an exciting game.

- **Eventually, with patience and persistence, your dog should shoot through from one side of the car to the other.** When it does so, praise it ecstatically, give it a treat and play a game with it. Leave it another day before you try more progress. If you have a car with a tailgate, also try getting the dog to go into the car and out through this rear exit, then back again - removing any dog grills, guards or cages for this purpose.

- **Repeat this exercise as a game, then eventually get into the car with the dog and encourage it to play with a toy and have a treat.** Close one of the doors. If the dog panics, let it out again immediately and repeat previous exercise. If not, continue to praise the dog and play with it in a light-hearted way, then close the other door. If the dog seems fine, praise it again. Then get out of the car with the dog.

- **Gradually prolong the time you spend playing with, and praising / rewarding the dog in the car until it is completely relaxed.** Next, with the dog in the car, turn on the engine and keep it running a few minutes. If all is well, praise the dog again and give it a treat. A few minutes later, drive literally around 25 yards. If the dog is fine, praise it well and have another game. Reverse back, praise the dog again if all is well, and then both get out of the car.

- **Over time, as long as you never push your dog when it is apprehensive, you should be able to increase the journey times with it, while it remains relaxed** - and eventually learns that a car takes it to exciting places and, just as importantly, back home again. Dogs who get car sick - see later - may also need this sort of 'remedial therapy' to overcome their 'bad associations' with cars.

If the above sounds painstaking, then this is because measures to overcome fearfulness of any kind in a dog usually are. They can only move on as fast, or as slowly, as the dog's ability to develop more confidence or trust. Equally, they may easily be ruined through impatience on an owner's behalf. The joy of having a dog you can happily take in the car, however, should certainly be worth all this earlier effort in the long run.

'Attacking' other cars

A dog **barking or snapping at other cars, while travelling in yours,** to make them 'go away', can literally drive owners to distraction. Dogs who do this will classically have their noses pressed up against the side windows of the car, in eager anticipation of the next 'victim'. They will get a 'high' from this exercise in the belief that their aggressive actions have 'seen off' other possible 'threats' - and yes, some may argue that they know human motorists whose behaviour behind the wheel is not so very different!

One of the most effective ways of dealing with this problem is to tether the dog down in the rear (if it is quite low) or floor of the car so that it cannot see out of the car windows. What it cannot see it cannot bark at. The dog should be allowed to shift position comfortably and easily while lying down, without being able to get its head level with the windows. **If you are** going on long journeys with a dog fixed in this position, then it's important to stop regularly to let it get out of the car and to stretch itself out properly.

You can secure a dog via a lead, or leads, attached to its ordinary collar or, preferably, a harness. You can then tie the lead or leads round a car seat, or you may have to fit some special attachments to the car interior to get the level of restraint right. Your dog may protest and generally gripe for some time about this curtailment of its fun, and it may be worth giving it something else - e.g. a chew toy or bone - for it to focus its immediate energies upon. Eventually, however, it should resign itself to less reactive - and vociferous - behaviour, given that the triggers for it have been removed. And car journeys with your dog may actually be pleasurable again.

An alternative strategy for dogs like this is to put them in a purpose-made travelling crate in the back of the car, which you can then cover over with a light blanket or sheet - but not something airtight like plastic or PVC. Whatever you choose to cover it with, ensure that the dog still has adequate ventilation while travelling, especially in hot weather, and keep checking that it is not **over-heating** in any way.

Attention seeking

Some dogs will bark in the car purely as an **attention-seeking** device. Maybe they don't like looking at the back of your head, as you appear to be 'ignoring' them, or in a past life they were allowed to sit in the front of the car, or on the back seat, and now you've placed them - entirely for their own safety - behind a grill in the rear and they don't like it. In such scenarios, it is likely that they will be looking at you for 'effect' when they whine or bark, rather than out of the window or anywhere else. Don't give them any 'effect'. Do not talk to them, shout at them or look at them or give them any attention at all when they are barking. Only talk to them, and praise them, when they are quiet. This may initially take nerves - and resolve - of steel quality, but stick with this strategy if you really want to solve the problem.

Car sickness

Some dogs genuinely do suffer from **car sickness**, and this can also be one of the reasons why they are reluctant to get into cars (see earlier). The measure of securing a dog down (as above), so that it cannot see out of windows, and thus feel more nauseous, could help the problem. This may not happen immediately, however, as sometimes just the prospect of feeling nauseous will actually **make** a dog nauseous. For longer journeys, or if this doesn't work, your vet could prescribe suitable medication to stop your dog feeling so sick.

Chasing - and 'predatory' behaviour

Over the years I have lost count of the number of owners who have told me that **their dog**

does not have any predatory instincts at all and 'loves the cat'. And then the next moment the dog is off down the street chasing runners or bikes (if **that** isn't a 'predatory' form of behaviour, what is?), or the owner is suddenly at his or her wits' end because their dog attacked some sheep in a field during a walk in the country **and they couldn't believe it would do that.**

Reasons for chasing or other predatory instincts in your dog include:

• **The fact that it is simply a *dog***

Dogs are programmed to be predatory animals; to track, chase, run down and kill other animals for food. As such, even though the strength of these ancient hunting drives or instincts can seem to vary greatly among different dogs today, it is usually safer to assume that most **are** capable of unleashing some sort of predatory behaviour, given the right circumstances or triggers, than to assume that they are not - because being wrong about this matter tends to have some pretty unpleasant consequences.

Predatory behaviour in some dogs, it must also be realised, is not just limited to animals like cats, sheep or rabbits - it can also be targeted upon other dogs or small children. And when this is the case, such dogs can be **highly dangerous to take anywhere without a muzzle.**

What to do

The urge to **chase** things - especially rapidly moving things at eye level - can be very powerful in many dogs, and particularly so in those breeds or types who have retained strong herding, guarding or hunting instincts - e.g. Collies, German shepherds, terriers, sight hounds (e.g. lurchers, greyhounds), Akitas, Dobermanns, Rottweilers. So this has to be accepted and then satisfactorily addressed as follows. Also be aware that some dogs with seemingly 'low' - or, if you like, 'dormant' - predatory instincts individually can be very different when teamed up with another dog, or other dogs, to 'hunt' collectively as a 'pack'.

Better control of natural instincts

Initially a dog's chasing can be fired by instinct, but then this behaviour soon becomes reinforced by some additional reward - e.g. the chase 'sees off' some potentially threatening person or dog, or just the act of chasing unleashes adrenaline and gives the dog a 'high'. Such rewards mean that the dog is increasingly motivated to chase again.

As long as a dog is allowed to chase things at will, it will never want to stop. And owners, even if quite unwittingly, can actually **'legitimise' their dogs' chase instincts even further** by giving them endless balls or other toys to tear after in the garden, or when out on walks. Quite rightly, a dog may not understand why you will positively **encourage** it to roar after some things, but get angry or whack it when it pursues other things, which - to its mind - are even more worthwhile to chase.

If you have a dog with incredibly strong chase instincts, then it's important to limit such 'pursuit and grab' games to a minimum, and to also work much harder on your overall control of the dog. In this respect, the most vital things you could teach it are an instant and reliable '**recall**' and '**emergency down**' on command (see Chapter six for advice on teaching this), and to generally focus readily on you when asked. During early days this is best done by keeping a special toy at hand - e.g. a tugging or squeaking device - that your dog **will only see when you are out** and which you know can instantly draw its attention from other distractions. When it turns its attention from chasing something else to you and the toy, play with it enthusiastically, praise it well and keep practising this exercise to get better and more reliable responses.

With the '**emergency down**', try to work up to a stage where you can throw a ball or favourite toy at some distance away from the dog and then make it drop down to the ground and stay there, immediately on command, when it is halfway in active pursuit of it, even if initially you will have to use a long lead or line to pull this off. Only after the dog has stayed down on command, and you have 'released' it from its 'down' command, can you reward it with its ball or toy and praise it well.

If you manage this, then congratulate yourself, because this incredibly useful 'tool of control' isn't always an easy thing to achieve. If you cannot manage this, or you have a dog whose will or instincts are too strong to be this efficiently controlled, keep it on a long lead **anywhere** where it might chase inappropriate things - e.g. cars, bikes, runners, trains. If you think your dog's chase instincts could well extend on to aggression towards other animals, children or smaller dogs, then **you must keep it muzzled** whenever it is out. And believe it or not, **this is all you need to do** to have a dog that doesn't chase or attack things, causing much grief all round in the process.

Chewing

Dogs chew things when they are puppies or young dogs because they find this a compulsive urge when new teeth arrive. They will chew because they are bored or anxious or stressed, or purely because chewing can be a rather enjoyable way to pass time, particularly if nature has given you some pretty effective teeth to chew with.

Dogs, all in all, do not tend to see chewing as a 'problem' - only owners do, when dogs chew rather inappropriate things like furnishings, furniture, floors, footwear or doors.

Reasons for this problem in your rescue dog include:

- It is a puppy or young dog with a compulsive urge to exercise its new teeth
- It was never taught, in puppyhood, the difference between items it was, and was not, allowed to chew
- It finds chewing the 'wrong' things a great way to get your attention
- It is anxious or frustrated about being confined and / or left alone

What to do

Owners of puppies and young dogs often seem to think it is inevitable that they will go through their homes like miniature chainsaws, wreaking havoc with those eager little teeth. But it is not. Any dog, of any age, can only chew what it is allowed to have access to, and for as long as it is allowed such access without being **stopped**.

Thus, vigilance and an immediate challenge to any 'wrong' actions are the keys to all early and successful behaviour 're-shaping' in dogs. In this vein, a most important lesson you can teach any puppy or young dog is the difference between what it can, and cannot chew. And this is where the puppy crate or 'indoor kennel' - see Chapter four for more details - really comes into its own. If your puppy or young dog is chewing something you do not want it to chew, then instantly say '**no!**' and gently encourage it into its puppy crate with something else - e.g. a hide chew or chew toy - that it is allowed to chew instead. Then praise it effusively while it chews.

If you do this instantly, consistently and with minimum preamble or fuss every time your puppy or young dog chews something it shouldn't, it should soon get the message about leaving other items of 'yours' alone.

Knowing no better

If on the other hand your puppy or young dog went off to chew things it shouldn't because you were not supervising it, and thus couldn't correct its behaviour at the right time, then it can't be blamed for not knowing any better. You can only correct a dog while it is actually **in the act** of chewing something it shouldn't. If you leave it even just seconds after it has destroyed something, it is unlikely to know what you are scolding it for, and your anger could distress it, rather than teach it anything valuable for the future.

If you do not have a suitable puppy crate or 'indoor kennel', you can put your dog in its bed with a suitable chew item, instead, whenever it starts gnawing at something it shouldn't, then again praise it while it chews the 'right thing'.

If you have an adult dog that you suspect was never taught these early lessons about chewing, then you can attempt to modify its behaviour in much the same way.

Attention seeking

It is important, however, not to make an exceptional fuss when your dog chews the 'wrong thing' in your presence, as it may rapidly learn that this is a brilliant way to get your attention. For more advice on dealing with behaviour along these lines, see the earlier **Attention-seeking behaviour** section.

Very many owners, however, will tend to find that most 'inappropriate' chewing occurs when they are out of the house. As such, it may often be part of other destructive things a dog will do to externalise its anxiety, frustration or boredom when left alone and / or confined somewhere. In which case, see relevant sections on **Separation Anxiety** and **Destructiveness** (below). There is also more advice on destructiveness in Chapter five.

D

Destructiveness

Destructiveness, as with **Separation Anxiety** (see later) is one of those behavioural issues which really tests and challenges the way we keep dogs today. At the heart of so many destructive episodes in modern domestic homes will lie unhappy dogs kept in circumstances which often worry or frustrate them. Dogs who are simply externalising, or reacting to, the misery, boredom, stress or fear caused by the solitude and confinement we have enforced upon them via our absence - however necessary we might view such absences to be.

Unfortunately, however, when owners come home to trashed fixtures and furnishings, or a dog that has lost 'toilet control', their first priority tends to be their own anger and upset, which will then be projected on to the dog, rather than a calmer appraisal of why the dog should have behaved in this way, plus a desire to put the dog more at ease.

Although this is perfectly understandable, such angry or hysterical reactions can simply make future destruction problems by the dog even worse. This is because, on top of the usual concerns it has about being left alone, it will then worry further about the prospect of an owner coming home in a bafflingly hostile state.

If you suspect that your dog's destructive episodes are basically fuelled by **Separation Anxiety**, see the relevant section in this chapter.

Other reasons for destructiveness in your rescue dog include:

•**It is frightened by something inside or near your house**

- It is bored and simply wants to 'let off steam'

- It has discovered that destructiveness gives it a 'high', and is thus a pretty rewarding 'habit'

What to do

Before we look at measures to address the above, it first needs to be understood that dogs, unlike us, **have little sense of the 'value' of the things they destroy.** They do not, as can fondly be imagined, 'deliberately' pick items to destroy that you treasure, or will cost a lot to replace, to 'annoy' you or to 'pay you back' for leaving them.

A notion that your dog is 'deliberately' picking things of value to you to destroy might make you feel better about getting angry with it. But ultimately this will be wasted emotional energy, because dogs simply pick what is nearest, or most 'logical' for them to direct their destructive urges upon, when such urges arise.

Fear and anxiety

Items with strong concentrations of an owner's scent may be common targets for dogs who are anxious or missing these owners badly (again, see **Separation Anxiety**). Carpets, door frames and doors out of rooms, or out of the house, may be targeted by dogs who either seek to reach their owners, or simply want to escape to somewhere better or 'safer' than where they happen to be confined. This is often because something nearby is **frightening** them.

Lots of things can frighten dogs when they are left alone, and often these things can develop more fearful associations in the dog's mind purely because it was alone when it heard or experienced them, and therefore felt more vulnerable.

'Frightening things' for a dog can range from noisy workmen outside or strangers passing in the street to the clunking and shuddering of a rackety fridge or heating system or even the answerphone suddenly kicking into action. And once a dog has attached a fear or 'anxiety' response to any of these things it will not be able to settle and may also be driven by an urge to get away from them.

How can you tell what your dog is frightened about when you are out? Well, there is a high chance it will also show a level of fear towards the same things while you are in the house. Watch your dog a bit more carefully. When certain sounds arise, does it suddenly look rather agitated and / or apprehensive, maybe getting up quickly from where it was lying and pacing around or whining to get out of the room if the door is shut? It may also look back and forth from you to the imagined source of the noise and back again to gauge your reaction. Behaviour like this could give you good clues to what it causing a problem for your dog.

Once you have established the possible cause of your dog's fear or anxiety, you can then look for ways to modify or overcome it. If noises outside are the problem, for instance, you can move your dog to a quieter part of the house, away from windows or the front door, and - as previously advised - leave a radio on, or television, to mask other sounds.

Similarly, you can move the dog away from objects - like noisy fridges or the answerphone - which disturb it, or try to build up more 'positive' associations with these objects. This will take a bit more effort, and will involve you giving the dog a 'reward' - e.g. a treat or favourite toy - each time these objects kick into action when you are home - but the timing **must** be right.

Never, for instance, reward your dog when it looks remotely worried by a noisy object, or it will imagine that it is actually being rewarded for showing fear. Instead, **reward it the instant the object makes a noise,** before it has had time to react fearfully, and reward it again each time it does not react to the noisy object in a fearful way. In the meantime, ignore any fearful reactions.

Boredom and frustration

Some dogs will get into destructive patterns of behaviour when left alone and / or confined simply because they are **frustrated** or **bored** by their circumstances. Then they can also find that such behaviour gives them an immediate 'high' which releases them from the discomfort of their frustrations and generally 'lets off steam'. Often these will be dogs with a need for high levels of mental stimulation, and a low tolerance of any form of enforced inactivity.

Owners viewing this as essentially 'bad' or 'aberrant' behaviour might like to consider what the consequences might be if they left any highly active or excitable young child locked up in a house or room, alone and unsupervised, for lengthy periods of time. Chances are, they'd be uglier still.

Because dogs most commonly destroy things when left alone, this in turn can lead owners to the erroneous belief that 'dogs **know** it is **wrong**, because they never do it while I'm around'. In truth, it's highly unlikely that dogs will destroy things, look remorsefully at the chaos they have caused and think, 'oh no, I'm going to be in **big trouble** when the boss comes back'. They can only focus on their immediate frustrations or anxieties - among which might be, is the owner actually coming back **at all?**

And if they tend not to destroy things when you're around then it's because your presence tends to make such anxious / frustrated feelings less likely. This apart, you are an inhibiting influence on their behaviour. Maybe in the past a dog has begun chewing or destroying something and instantly you will have told it to stop, and it has.

You cannot do this, however, if you are **not there**.

Let us imagine for a moment that a dog's urge to destroy things when suitably motivated can be as powerful as some people's desire to chew their nails when tense or apprehensive. If you have a strong urge to chew your nails but are in the presence of someone you know will heavily disapprove of such a habit, the chances are you will not do it. But this does not mean that you will **stop having future urges to chew your nails.** Or that you will not chew them again the moment you feel the need arise and you have the opportunity to do so without challenge or restraint.

As we earlier highlighted in Chapter five, destructiveness in dogs will persist as long as they have access to things they can destroy, and as long as they have reasons to want to destroy things. If you leave a dog with destructive tendencies alone in a car, for instance, for some time, and **do not confine it within a suitably sized and purpose-built travelling cage,** should you really be so surprised at the havoc it might wreak on the car's interior?

No 'quick fix' solution
People always seem to want a 'simple and quick fix' to destructiveness in dogs. Any behaviourist could tell you that the simplest and most foolproof answer to canine destructiveness is not to leave your dog regularly unsupervised and alone. Yet the 'simplest' answer is also the one which most owners tend to find least acceptable or realistic.

Unfortunately, few 'solutions' you pick for this problem, are going to be 'ideal' for both owners and dogs, due to their completely different needs and expectations of life. If owners stay home all the time with dogs, this might suit dogs but not owners. If dogs are put into indoor kennels, or confined in rooms or elsewhere where they can do little damage when owners are out, this may suit owners better but not necessarily dogs. On the other hand, if dogs are not allowed the option of destroying things, through such confinement, then they will also not have to face the resentment and fury such actions can trigger in their owners, and they will not be able to have the 'habit' of destructiveness reinforced through repetition and pure opportunity.

If we are going to confine dogs in some way, in order for them not to be destructive, then what ultimately matters is the length of time we confine them for, alone, and how well we mentally prepare them for the experience. Chapter four (**The puppy crate or 'indoor kennel'**) and Chapter five (**'Early Destructiveness'**) give advice on how to get dogs better used to such forms of confinement.

Getting used to separation
If you have a dog prone to destructive behaviour when left alone, then this in itself should tell you that its anxieties or natural energies are such that it could find any sudden lengthy confinement a trial. For this reason, start such dogs off with only very limited confinement -

e.g. **a minute or two at a time** in a room on its own while you are still in the house - as outlined in the **Separation Anxiety** Section.

If you eventually intend to leave such dogs alone and confined for more than two hours at a time, then do try to ensure that a neighbour, friend or 'sitter' drops in to check on them regularly, at set periods throughout the day and, even better, also lets them stretch their legs or go out for a run. This is particularly vital during early periods of separation, until the dog can make the transition into understanding that spells of isolation and confinement are just a 'normal' part of its daily routine, rather than some 'open ended' and inexplicable form of banishment that could be inflicted by owners at any time.

Also ensure that the dog has had plenty of exercise and mental stimulation - e.g. through training - before you go out, that a radio or television is left on in the background, and that the dog is also left with plenty of things to chew and play with - e.g. a special 'activity cube' stuffed full of treats, available from most pet stores.

Dogs who come to understand that periods of inactivity, solitude and confinement are merely a part of 'normal daily routine', interspersed with nicer things before, after and in between, will cope much better with the experience than those who have very lengthy confinement suddenly inflicted upon them for no apparent 'reason', and with no sense that it will only be a temporary state of affairs.

Often early destructive habits in rescue dogs will wane or disappear as they become far more settled and secure within their new environment. To help bring this more 'settled and secure' state of mind about, however, it is **vital** that you do not physically punish, scream at or otherwise frighten or distress the dog when you come home to find it has destroyed something. **It cannot** *know* **this is why you are angry.**

Instead, however hard it may be, take a deep breath, greet the dog casually, then place it immediately into the garden. Then come back inside and scream and / or have a stiff drink. I'd say punch a wall too, but this hurts. Tidy up the mess while you mutter all manner of expletives under your breath. When you feel calmer let the dog back in. You don't have to **like** it at this particular moment. You just have to not be mad with it. When you don't come home mad a dog's already got one less thing to worry about during the day, which can be a start, at least, to overcoming its problems.

Digging

Digging can be another part of the **destructive** behaviour - see above - that a dog will undertake while you are out. The dog, for example, might be trying to dig its way out of the room or place where it is confined, or trying to make itself a hole or 'den' it can crawl into to feel safer when it is frightened by something. If you suspect that digging in your dog is just a part of general

Destructiveness when you are out, or related to **Separation Anxiety**, see the relevant sections.

Other reasons for digging in your rescue dog include:

- It is just following its natural instincts

- It has stronger digging instincts than other breeds or types of dog (e.g. it is a hound or terrier type or breed)

- It is excited or just finds digging fun

- It is bored or generally under-stimulated

- If it is a bitch, digging - e.g. behind sofas, under tables or in corners of rooms - can be a classic part of 'nesting behaviour' female dogs will display when they are pregnant, or imagine they are, roughly within three months after a 'heat'.

What to do

Dogs in the wild will dig for a variety of useful and important reasons - to make themselves dens, for instance, or to unearth prey, or to bury food that they intend to eat later. The problem for most owners, however, tends not to be the fact that dogs like to dig, but that they will do so in inappropriate places - chief of which tends to be the garden.

Before tackling this problem, do be aware that when it comes to the urge to dig, dogs cannot naturally discriminate between the more cherished bits of your garden - e.g. lawns and exquisite planting arrangements - and any other bit of old ground. The splendours and wonders of the horticultural art are completely lost on them at any given time, and probably most particularly when they've got a deliciously pungent bone they want to ram a foot under your favourite lilies, scattering a good dozen crocus bulbs in the process.

Natural instincts

Do also be aware that if you do give your dog nice juicy bones to eat in the garden, the time will come when it may want to bury what's left of them in a flowerbed, or in the beautifully prepared area where you have just put some tender new seedlings. To avoid this scenario occurring, it therefore makes sense to remove the bone from the dog the moment it looks like it is about to happen.

Do **not**, however, just snatch the bone away from it, as not a lot of dogs will take kindly to such a gesture. Gestures like these can also make dogs more aggressively protective over items in future. Instead, walk casually out into the garden with a delicious treat, titbit, or toy you know your dog can't resist. Showing absolutely no interest in the bone whatever, lure your dog inside with the treat or toy, shut the door behind you, ask the dog to sit, then reward it with the treat and praise. Wait a minute or two before going back out into the garden by yourself - leaving the dog inside. Pick up the bone and put it in a plastic bag, then bring it inside and put it in the freezer or fridge for another time - or in the bin. Whatever seems most appropriate.

This way you have not only stopped your dog burying its bone in your garden - you have also avoided any possible confrontation with it in the process.

Digging 'aversion therapy'
Puppies usually dig up the garden because this is part of their exploration of the world - and their natural instincts - and also because they find it fun. Older dogs can also find it fun, or a way to **relieve boredom**, and some may feel more compelled to dig than others because they are of a breed or type in whom this instinct is particularly strong.

Most puppies could be stopped from digging in inappropriate parts of the garden via this simple measure. Get a hosepipe fitted to an inside tap with the external end trained on where you know the puppy is likely to dig but shouldn't. Wait until next time it tries to dig there, then turn the hose on full blast **once it is actually digging**.

It is **vital** that the puppy is actually digging when you turn the hose on, and that it **does not see you** when the hose goes on. This way, it will immediately associate the shock of the cold blast of water with its **actions**. If, on the other hand, the puppy sees you turn on the water, or sees you while it is on, it could associate the 'unpleasant consequence' with you, and not its actions. This may stop it digging when you are **around**, but not at other times when you are out or away or not supervising it.

Chances are your puppy will rush inside to 'tell' you about the dreadful thing that has just happened to it. If so, look suitably sympathetic and surprised. After all, it had nothing to do with you, did it? Or that's exactly what you want your puppy to think.

If it takes a bit longer to cure an older dog of digging in inappropriate parts of the garden with the same above measure, then this is because the dog is likely to have already found digging rewarding, no doubt in its past life. In other words, unlike your puppy, the dog has had sufficient time to associate digging with pleasure in its mind rather than to immediately discover that it has nasty consequences. To reverse this state of affairs, it obviously has to learn that **every time** it digs in certain parts, or any part, of your garden there are always unpleasant consequences and no good ones. And it may take quite a few consistent and persistent applications of the hose before it gets this message.

Special digging areas

If you feel that your dog really is an incorrigible digger, or that it needs some opportunity to unleash its digging urges and energies, an alternative would be to set up a **special digging area** in the garden. Mix some sand into the chosen spot, make it at least a couple of metres square and half a metre deep and fill it up with chews, toys or old bones. Thereafter, every time you see the dog digging elsewhere in the garden immediately bring it back to this proper place and praise it when it uses it.

Naturally, how much of a 'digging area' you can set aside for your dog will depend on the size of your garden. The drawback with this alternative is that your dog **can still fundamentally believe that digging in your garden is okay,** or won't have unpleasant consequences. This means it could occasionally forget - especially when you are not around to remind it - where it should, and should not, be digging. Or it might just prefer a more novel location for digging in.

Letting off steam

Some breeds and types of dog need far more physical and mental stimulation than others, and if they do not get it, digging can be a way to simply 'let off steam'. If you suspect this could be the case with your dog, do be aware that stopping it digging could mean it would then just channel its frustrations and surplus energies into some other activity or habit you find equally, or even more, annoying. So the answer to behaviour displayed by dogs like these is to give them more outlets for their physical and mental energies throughout the day. More advice on this in Chapters nine and ten.

Digging, particularly in areas that have triggered immediate and vociferous reactions from you in the past, can also become an **Attention-seeking** ploy for some dogs. For more advice, see the relevant section.

'Nesting' behaviour

As we mentioned at the beginning of this section, **bitches** can display some seemingly 'bizarre' digging behaviour - e.g. scratching and clawing under furniture or in room corners - when expecting puppies. If your bitch has not been spayed, a similar behaviour pattern can occur roughly within three months after a heat, even if she has not been mated. This is because, whether or not she has been mated, her hormone levels, influencing such behaviour, can be similar to those of a genuinely pregnant bitch.

This condition, especially when accompanied by the bitch producing milk, and 'nursing' toys, is usually termed as a **'pseudo'** or **'phantom' pregnancy** (see Chapter nine on **Health** additionally, and also the **Possessiveness** section). How bad or not the 'symptoms' are can vary from bitch to bitch and from one heat to another. Most symptoms can pass in the ensuing weeks after their onset, but more severe or distressing 'phantom pregnancy' cases sometimes need veterinary intervention to stop the bitch getting excessively distressed, frustrated or miserable. If you do not intend to breed from your bitch, spaying her would obviously save her the unpleasantness of this condition, as well as other serious problems also covered in Chapter nine.

Disobedience

'Disobedience' is a term commonly attributed to dogs who will not do what we ask, when we ask them to do it. In the last chapter, we touched on some possible reasons why this should occur in a training context. Now it's time to look at scenarios within the home where your dog's 'disobedience' might be giving you problems to see how similar they might.

Reasons why your rescue dog should be generally 'disobedient' at home include:

- **It is too anxious or stressed to concentrate on what you are asking it to do**
- **It does not understand what you want it to do**
- **It does not respect your authority or consider you 'high-ranking' enough to be obeyed**
- **It does not, or cannot, trust you**
- **It is getting 'conflicting' commands and signals within the home about what it should do**
- **It finds your approach frightening or threatening**

And we'll find that there is not really a vast amount of difference between disobedience in one context or another, is there? The point being that dogs who won't obey a person in the context of a home, where there are fewer distractions and less escape from an owner's more inhibiting proximity, aren't likely to do so anywhere else, and for similar reasons.

What to do

Frequently I have gone to homes where this sort of scenario is in action. The dog is racing around in an agitated and seemingly excitable state. The owner is shouting all manner of different things at the dog - 'come here!', 'don't do that!', 'behave yourself!' - while the dog disregards them and, if anything, appears to be getting even more 'badly behaved'.

At which point the owner will declare, 'See! He / she won't pay a blind bit of notice to anything I say or ask!' The owner is getting more and more tense and neurotic. The dog is getting more and more agitated as the owner gets more tense and neurotic about its apparent 'disobedience'. But most of all, what strikes you is that **nobody actually appears to be in charge.**

And usually the dog realises this more rapidly than the owner. So let us look at what has gone 'wrong', and also appreciate this scenario a bit more from the dog's point of view.

A calmer approach

First of all, the owner needs to **calm down** his or her general approach to the dog. Not just because a calm, if firm, approach will always carry more natural authority than an agitated, irritated or semi-hysterical one, but because this will help to calm the dog down, too. Especially if it is already carrying existing burdens of stress or anxiety. For more advice on dealing with Stress and Anxiety, see the next chapter, plus the earlier **Anxiety** section.

Better understanding and trust

Also realise that continually shouting at your dog or - even worse - using physical punishment towards it for not 'obeying' you, will not make it 'understand' you, or respond to you, any better. Here's why.

First of all, a dog needs to feel that what you are asking it to do must ultimately be in its best interests. It cannot feel this if it cannot trust you, and through acting aggressively towards your dog to get 'obedience', you are undermining this essential trust.

Second, if it is a strong-willed dog, it may feel increasingly resentful about your seeming 'hostility' and 'persecution' and may eventually want to retaliate against this approach.

Third, particularly if you own a rather sensitive or nervous dog, your aggressive actions will just make it get extremely stressed and uneasy. This in turn will make it more agitated and 'mentally fuddled' and thus less capable of 'taking in' what you want it to do.

And, come to that, are you sure that your dog actually **does** know what you want it to do? Again, appreciate the difference between aimlessly shouting at a dog and actually giving it a proper **command** it has been taught to understand.

Imagine for a moment that, to a dog, an owner is a bit like a radio he or she is trying to pick up intelligible 'signals' from. When you aimlessly shout or gabble at your dog this, to its ears, is the equivalent of all the 'white noise' or foreign babble we'd find unintelligible inbetween clearly recognisable 'stations'. A properly taught command to a dog, on the other hand, is a 'recognisable station'. Only when it hears this, delivered in the same consistent tone and fashion, does it understand what is being conveyed and what it should do in response.

Consistency of approach

Within many households, however, commands will not always be delivered in exactly the same tone and fashion by everyone. Some people may be calm and firm in their approach but others will be less clear, or will approach the dog in a manner it could find threatening or frightening.

This can make a dog less confident about what it should be doing, and give the impression that it is being 'disobedient' when it is actually just anxious or confused. Throughout this book - and in **The Rules of Superiority**, last chapter, especially - we have also made it clear how 'authority' must be conveyed to a dog on a consistent day-to-day basis to improve overall 'obedience', particularly if it has a naturally 'strong' or 'defiant' character.

'Disobedience' in a dog, ultimately, tends to happen when we cannot convey our authority or commands convincingly enough, or do not give a dog the opportunity to think clearly and act confidently in an atmosphere of calmness, security and 'order'. Hopefully through thinking hard about all the above considerations, you will begin to see what could be changed to make your dog more responsive to you.

A dog's right to independent action and thought

This apart, be aware that few dogs, like few children, **will necessarily be 'brilliantly behaved' a hundred per cent of the time,** as long as they have independent minds and the capacity to be distracted by aims or needs which conflict with our own. Sometimes just the sheer presumption that we should have 'perfect' dogs which never act independently or seek to defy our will can put unnecessary extra pressures on owners and their dogs alike.

If we never give dogs the chance to think or act independently, or to occasionally just be 'themselves', we can undermine their self-confidence or ability to use their own intelligence and initiative in positive ways. And this is important for their overall psychological health. At the end of the day, the most crucial thing is not that your dog is 'brilliantly behaved' a hundred per cent of the time, but that your dog understands the importance of doing what you ask, immediately, **when it matters.**

If, for instance, your dog will reliably and **immediately** do things like the following:

- Get down off furniture

- Come back to you

- Let go of anything it is holding

- Wait and stay while you go out of a door ahead of it

- Lie down or sit down and stay still or quiet

- Go downstairs / out of a room

The **moment** you ask it to, then this shows that your dog fundamentally respects your authority and is as 'obedient' as most owners could expect.

The rest of the time owners should maybe relax a bit more, get less neurotic about repressing or analysing every canine quirk or foible that seems less than 'ideal' - and just remember that dogs have a right to their own identities and space sometimes, without incessant checking, criticising or interference from us. And also that dog ownership is primarily supposed to be both enjoyable and **fun**.

'Dominant' behaviour

See last chapter, plus **Possessiveness** and **Aggression** sections.

F

Faeces eating - or Coprophagia

There are quite a few things dogs will do that we can find pretty distasteful. And maybe top of the list in this department is faeces eating or, to give it its more clinical term, **Coprophagia**. Whether our dog has developed a penchant for eating its own faeces, or those of other dogs - or cats - we'll find this truly disgusts us, regardless of the satisfaction it might appear to gain from it.

Reasons for Coprophagia in your rescue dog include:

- It is a puppy or growing young dog
- It is a habit it picked up in kennels through boredom, or while it was a stray and had to use its 'scavenging' instincts to the full
- It has worms, or some ailment giving it an excessive hunger
- There is a mineral deficiency in its diet
- It simply likes this habit and finds it rewarding
- It has turned this habit into an attention-seeking ploy

What to do

First of all, if your rescue animal is a puppy or young growing dog, understand that Coprophagia is often a way they'll ensure that maximum amounts of nutrients are taken into their bodies. In the wild, puppies and young dogs will often have tough competition for food as they grow, and will thus have to sharpen up their scavenging instincts to survive. At this age they will also be keener to 'experiment' with different food forms. In many puppies this habit can wane as they grow older, particularly if they are also taught to 'leave' undesirable things in the right way (see later).

Whether you have a puppy or older dog who indulges in this habit, try getting them wormed as a first resort, if this hasn't been done recently. While you are at the vet sorting this out, also mention the problem and discuss the possibility of other health ailments or dietary deficiencies causing it.

If these are ruled out you are left with the option that your dog simply finds eating faeces an enjoyable and / or rewarding thing to do for some reason, and thus we have to make it less so if we don't like it.

A rewarding habit

If your dog eats its own faeces, your vet can advise a range of dietary additives which might make them far less palatable. Courgette or pineapple added to a dog's food can also sometimes make its subsequent faeces appear less appetising. If your dog eats its own faeces, or those of other dogs when out, it can additionally be suggested by some that you immediately sprinkle the faeces with something horribly off-putting - e.g. Tabasco sauce, mustard - to deter it. However, the practical logistics of this operation, especially in public, for most owners - forever trying to race their dog their dog to a pile of poo with a sauce bottle in hand - can be testing, if not laughable. And as dogs aren't blessed with gourmet palates at the best of times, you could still find this doesn't work.

It could also be said, of course, that if selfish and anti-social dog owners did not leave their own animal's faeces lying around in popular walking areas, there would be far less around for your dog to consume.

This apart, the problem of trying to race any dog to a pile of poo - be it its own, or another animal's - is that you then trigger 'competitive' instincts in its mind. Yes, ghastly though it might be to contemplate, your dog could actually start to believe that you are trying to eat that poo **first**. Which means it could guzzle it down even faster the moment it sees you near.

Also, if you make an extraordinary fuss each time it eats faeces, it could also turn this activity from an erratic experimental act into a full-blown **attention-seeking** ploy.

Distraction, muzzling and the 'leave!' command

What then **can** you do, apart from recoil in horror? Well, at home, each time your dog has relieved itself in the garden, instantly distract it with something pleasurable - e.g. a delicious food treat, or toy. Call it into the house instantly with this, reward it with the treat or toy, praise it, then leave the dog inside while you remove its faeces. If you do this consistently enough, each time it relieves itself in the garden, the dog will then be anticipating you calling it in for something rewarding. Or at least, more rewarding than immediately eating its own faeces.

At times when you cannot see what your dog is doing outside, or you suspect it is going to eat faeces left by your other dog or dogs, you may have to use a basket-type muzzle on it to prevent this. See the end of the **Aggression** section for more details / advice on muzzles. This might also prevent your dog eating dogs' faeces while out if the habit seems fairly persistent and ingrained.

Another helpful exercise to teach a dog, to stop it eating inappropriate things, is the 'leave' one. To do this, begin in the garden with your dog on a lead, an empty food bowl ahead of you - though not the dog's normal one - and a delicious treat in your pocket or hand. Allow your dog to walk up to the bowl but, the moment it puts its head inside, say '**leave!**' firmly, and then '**come**' as it turns its head away.

Encourage the dog back to you enthusiastically. As there's nothing in the dish it should come back. When it does so, give it the delicious food treat and praise it well. Practise this three or four times or longer till you get a reliable and instant response. Then, put some chopped or grated carrot in the dish. Again, allow the dog up to the dish and call it back on the 'leave!' command. Then try the exercise off the lead until you can actually put something quite tasty in the dish and the dog will still come back, if only because what **you** have is even tastier.

Next, practise this exercise while out. Call the dog back to you with '**leave!**' when it is sniffing something unsavoury and reward it with something really tasty. From now on, when you go out with your dog, you must **always** have tasty treats in your pocket to reward it for leaving something you don't want it to touch, and for coming back to you instead.

The scavenging instinct

Many dogs who would not normally touch canine faeces seem to find feline faeces irresistible. This is because cat food tends to have higher protein levels and other ingredients dogs can find tasty or tempting. If this is the case with your dog, ensure it cannot have access to any cat litter trays, or keep them cleaned out religiously after each use. If it picks up feline faeces in the garden, try to remove these before it has the chance. Even if this means making a few unsavoury inspections round the garden while your dog stays inside.

The chances are you will not always be able to stop your dog eating faeces each time the opportunity occurs. And if not, try not to get too neurotic about it. Dogs, as born scavengers, have digestive systems capable of surviving - and, if necessary, expelling - a wide range of cringe - inducing 'nasties' with generally less impact on health than might be imagined. Needless to say, however, your dog's worming treatments and vaccinations should be kept up to date to ensure this. And if your dog looks remotely ill after consuming something unpleasant while out, do seek further veterinary advice.

Fearfulness

Dogs, as we have already outlined in Chapter four (see '**Puppyhood**') do not see the world around them quite as we do; in other words, full of stranger sights, sounds or experiences which usually have a 'rational' explanation. They either trust, or are led to believe, that something less familiar is really 'safe' or harmless, or they strongly sense instead that it is threatening. Grasping this basic principle is the key to understanding 'Fearfulness' in dogs.

It also needs to be understood that caution in a dog, when faced with something strange and / or potentially threatening is actually a pretty **logical** and **healthy** response, if not a vital tool of survival.

For most owners, however, it is not 'Fearfulness' in itself that tends to be the main problem, but the excessive reactive symptoms or side-effects dogs can display when strongly affected by it. Chief among these will be bouts of over-defensive **Aggression**, covered at the beginning of this chapter. This apart, owners can get upset when dogs run and hide the moment a stranger or visitor calls, or worry about dogs bolting, or getting into an incredibly agitated state, when they see particular things or hear particular noises.

Reasons for this problem in your rescue dog include:

- **It was poorly socialised as a puppy**
- **It is a naturally very sensitive or 'reactive' type of dog**
- **It has been genuinely harmed, or was severely frightened / threatened by, a certain looking object / person / dog**
- **It has consistently has its 'fearful reactions' in the past rewarded in some way**

What to do

First, if you own a rescue puppy, understand how much you can do to prevent or reduce this problem through correct early '**socialisation**' - as outlined in Chapter four (again, under '**Puppyhood**'). The Puppyhood section also explains in detail how and why dogs get to react to different things 'fearfully'.

Second, be aware that if your male dog's **aggression** is primarily fuelled by fear, rather than testosterone, then castration will have limited effect on its behaviour.

Third, appreciate that **certain individual dogs** - i.e. those with particularly sensitive / reactive temperaments or natures - can be more prone to 'fearful' behaviour than others. Dogs can 'learn' to react fearfully through parental example, or poor early socialisation, or a bad past experience, but they can also simply be **born** with such a tendency in place. Generally, this is because such a trait is an intrinsic part of their **inherited** behaviour. Chapter three explains more fully what can make dogs so different from each other in terms of character and temperament.

Once a bit more about the background of 'fearfulness' in dogs, and why it should occur, is understood, the next step is - what do you do about it?

To start with, you need to ascertain as accurately as possible what your dog is actually frightened of. Is it certain noises - e.g. a thunderstorm, or certain-looking dogs, objects or people or a whole mixture of these things? If it's a mixture, begin by selecting one particular 'fear stimulus' to get to work on. Once you have some success in 'improving' this, you can then move on to others.

Noises

Let us suppose that your dog has an acute fear of **thunderstorms or fireworks**. These are very common triggers of fear and anxiety in dogs because of their erratic and sudden onset and because the dog cannot possibly 'rationalise' in its mind what is causing the intermittent bangs and vibrations.

Owners of dogs with such fears are often recommended to get special 'noise tapes' that recreate the sounds of thunderstorms and fireworks. The idea of these is that you play them regularly in the background for your dog to get used to, only gradually increasing the volume according to how well the dog is coping with the noise.

They are certainly worth trying with your dog, if so desired, but the drawback of such tapes is that they cannot always recreate the entire atmosphere of a 'real' thunderstorm or firework display. The vibration levels, for instance, might not be quite so authentic. Similarly, as well as the loud rumbles and lightning flashes, dogs can also react adversely to sudden drops in atmospheric pressure that usually accompany a real thunderstorm.

Wrong responses

Unfortunately, owners can often make dogs' responses to such noises worse through cuddling them, or speaking to them in 'soothing' tones each time they react fearfully. Naturally, in doing this, we are trying to 'reassure' a dog that all is well - but instead we are simply '**rewarding**' it for a fear response, making it believe this reaction is most 'appropriate' in the circumstances. Or it could believe that we are actually coming to it for greater reassurance ourselves.

When you get a rescue dog, there's a chance that its fear responses to things like thunderstorms or any other similar banging / cracking noises will have been rewarded many times in the past. Either through the intervention of owners 'soothing' it, or because it was able to 'bolt' away from such noises somewhere, and thus immediately feel a bit more at ease. This is what makes the problem harder to tackle than in a puppy.

If your new dog is afraid of any noise at home, the best thing you and anyone else in your household can do, as outlined below, is to completely ignore it and carry on nonchalantly with what you are doing.

'Comfort' dens

It may initially help for your noise-sensitive dog to have a special enclosed 'comfort den' it can run to whenever it feels worried by loud sounds at home. This can be anywhere where it feels safely 'closed in' (e.g. under a bed or small table, or behind the settee) as a dog's desire to get into such a tight and enclosed spot when frightened is instinctive. In its mind it is fleeing to a 'den' where it feels more protected from the worrying things that are happening around it 'outside'.

Should your dog run to this 'den' when frightened by noise, however, do not give it any attention at all. Do not talk to it, look at it and certainly **do not attempt to drag it back out again, as this will only make matters worse.** Even if it is rooted under a table or behind furniture, the chances are it will still regularly be looking at you to gauge your own reactions. Always remain nonchalant. Eat a snack or start playing with something in a carefree and totally unbothered manner in front of your dog, because - as we have previously mentioned - eating and playing are two things dogs find very hard to do when they are anxious.

Providing your dog is **always** ignored for its 'fearful' reactions in this way, and everybody else in the household continues to happily disregard any fireworks / thunderstorms etc. going on around them, it should eventually get the message that maybe its own reactions are not appropriate. In which case, reward the dog for any attempt it makes to be more confident - e.g. coming out of its 'den'. The second it shows fear again, ignore it again. Stick to this strategy consistently and, hopefully, you should begin to see real progress in its response to noise.

Be aware, however, that any progress you make in this area will **immediately be undermined if just one person gives the dog's fears attention**, or suddenly runs over to hug it while it is still worried. So try to avoid this happening at all costs.

Noises outside

If you're out with your dog any time when thunderstorms, fireworks or any other distressing noises are likely, then keep your dog on a long lead. It may panic and try to 'tow' you home. If so, resist. Do not say anything to the dog. Just meander on in your own time, looking extremely relaxed, and maybe make quite a few stops to look at things which appear to be far more interesting and important than the behaviour of your dog.

If your dog suddenly 'bolts' off the lead, do not shout at it, as you could just make it more afraid. If you cannot get someone to apprehend the dog it may eventually come back to you if you keep calm and it is somewhere unfamiliar. If it actually makes its way home, do not just walk into the house with it, as this will have **rewarded** its reactions. Instead, simply walk straight round the block with it again immediately, ignoring any panicky behaviour and only come home when it has moderately calmed down.

If it digs its heels in and won't budge, don't tug it or try to force it along or touch it at all. Instead just wait with your back turned to it, looking up the street. After a minute or so, call it to you gently. **Do not put any urgency or pressure into your voice.** You may wait quite some time before it finally moves forward to you a couple of steps. If it does so, praise it well and encourage it a bit further - totally ignoring any fearful or nervous behaviour. Then try another couple of steps, praise it, and so on until you can get quite a way up the street and your dog seems calmer. As soon as it is calmer, turn back for home.

If it immediately tries to 'tow' you back at this point, stop, and repeat the entire exercise, until the dog learns that only a 'calmer' approach is going to get it home. **If you don't do this, then all your earlier hard work and persistence will have been wasted, and you'll be back to square one - rewarding the dog for being afraid.** If you're in the middle of a thunderstorm then you might get pretty wet before real progress is made. But what valuable progress it will be.

People coming to your home

Some dogs may react fearfully to other people - and strangers in particular - because they cannot be sure that they do not wish them harm. Sometimes a dog can begin with a fear of one particular-looking person who caused it real fear or harm in the past, and then this fear becomes 'generalised' and projected on to a range of other people later on.

> *Note - before we move on to some common 'fear-reducing' techniques to make dogs more at ease with people, be aware that any canine fear involving aggression towards people is always something that should be tackled with professional guidance and help, as it is so easy to time or handle things 'wrong'. This apart, you must always ensure that any visitors you 'use' to help your dog with its 'fear aggression' are willing participantswilling participants who are well aware of its nature, and what the risks of encountering such a dog could be. Never leave them 'in the dark' about how your dog could potentially react to them, or use children for 'fear reduction' exercises in dogs without the most expert professional supervision. Do not use very young children - i.e. under ten - at all. And if you have the slightest doubts about your dog's possible reactions to people, put it in a muzzle before it meets them.*

> *Remember - always put safety first.*

Reducing fear about people

If your dog reacts fearfully to any stranger or visitor who comes to your house - e.g. it looks tentative and nervous, or attempts to hide - then be aware that you can easily make the problem escalate into defensive aggression if you try to 'force' the dog to be 'friendly'. In other words, if you deny it an 'escape route' or attempt to push it into a proximity with the visitor that the dog will find highly threatening.

One of the best ways to introduce such fearful dogs to visitors is not in the doorway, or while they are standing up - and thus looking more threatening - but in the lounge. Get your visitor to sit down in a chair before you engineer an introduction between him or her and the dog, as this approach is, potentially, a lot less 'confrontational'.

When the dog comes into the room, it is very important that the visitor does not make eye contact with it and, if anything, ignores its presence. If you fear that your dog really could react in a dangerously aggressive way at this point, **or at any point, remember - as previously outlined - to fit it with a muzzle.** Your dog may keep some distance from the visitor initially but if it eventually settles down and does not react, praise it well.

If your dog does not have a muzzle on, get your visitor to then drop one of the dog's favourite treats on the floor a little way away from his or her chair. If it has a muzzle on, you may have to be sure that your dog won't react aggressively, through repeated exposure to visitors in the above context, without incident, before you can move on to this step.

It will help greatly if the visitor you choose for this initial sort of exercise has no fear of dogs. Canine fear also seems to be triggered by men most and women least. If your dog is frightened of all visitors or new people start off, therefore, by just using women in this initial exercise, then older men, then younger ones. If your dog is just frightened of men, start with older men rather than younger ones. And the dog has always got to approach them when it is ready and on its own terms.

Steady progress

Once the visitor has dropped the treat and the dog takes it - it may well be quite suspicious at first - praise it well. Then get your visitor to drop treats nearer to herself or himself, while still avoiding eye contact. If the dog continues to take the closer treats without reacting in any way towards the visitor, again praise it well. If the dog growls or snaps at the visitor at any time, make it instantly go and lie down in the corner of the room and ignore it for a while before repeating the exercise again. **Don't say anything further to the dog, or interact with it in any way that could inadvertently 'reward' its 'bad' behaviour with your attention.**

Do remember, as has been constantly emphasised in this book (**The Rules of Superiority**, last chapter, and elsewhere) that 'authoritative' owner leadership can be a vital additional asset in many fear-related problems. This is because a dog who feels essentially 'well protected' will often have less need to react so 'defensively' in an owner's presence, and a dog who respects its owner will be more likely to take it own 'behavioural cue' from him or her in a range of different circumstances.

If all goes well in this exercise with the 'closer' treats then next, get your visitor to stand up **very slowly** with his or her back or side to the dog (again, with eye contact avoided, and no touching of the dog by the visitor) and drop another treat. If the dog takes it without reacting in any nervous or aggressive way, praise it well. Then get your visitor to sit down again.

Following this, everybody should ignore the dog for a while and carry on their conversation. The chances are that the dog's initial fear will now be moving to curiosity, plus a desire to prompt this potentially 'harmless' person into dealing out another nice treat. At this point the dog might feel bold enough to approach the visitor and sniff the **back** of his or her hand. Make sure the visitor has got another treat in that hand and that he or she then drops it slowly from their hand for the dog. Then keep ignoring the dog until it continues to return to the visitor for treats of its own accord.

If this goes well, the point could come when the visitor is actually able to stroke the dog on its shoulder - but **never** pat it on the head or neck, as this can be highly frightening or threatening to many dogs. Again, however, eye contact should be avoided and this should definitely not be tried if the dog curls its lip or looks like it could retaliate aggressively in any way - in which case, it goes back in the corner.

When measures like the above are properly executed, many fearful dogs are able to overcome, or greatly modify, aggressive reactions to strangers or visitors in the home. However, how successful or not they will be can depend on how regularly and consistently you perform the above steps, and how much professional back-up you have to get them exactly right. It will also depend on how strong, or ingrained, your dogs' fears about people might be.

If you have a dog with potentially **very aggressive, or unreliable / unpredictable reactions** towards visitors in the home, then it is highly recommended that you first get the dog assessed by a suitably qualified / experienced behaviourist before undertaking any of the above exercises. This is because you need to be sure that the dog's behaviour really is purely down to **'fear'**, rather than any other factors - including those with a mainly genetic origin.

Rewarding fear aggression

As we have outlined earlier in this book under the **Aggression** section, dogs who react aggressively towards other people, or dogs, often tend to do so because they imagine they could represent a 'threat' to them in some way. However, once this strategy has had success or been rewarded - i.e. the 'threat' goes away, or the owner takes the dog away from the 'threat' - then it can so easily become a 'habit'.

In other words, if a nervous dog has repeatedly found that through looking 'hostile' other people and dogs will 'disappear', that suits it down to the ground - and where is its motivation to behave in any other way?

And sometimes the more success a dog has with this strategy, the more 'exaggerated' its defensive behaviour can become, in the sure past knowledge that it always works and is not challenged. Hence the tendency for dogs to often 'lunge', in a greatly over-blown or theatrical manner, at passers-by when they are on a lead. Sometimes, too, fearful dogs will feel 'bolder' on a lead that secures them to their owners.

Wrong handling

Unfortunately if owners put check, or 'choke' chains on such dogs, or haul them back to heel on the lead in an aggressive manner, when they 'go for' other people or dogs, then they usually make the problem **even worse**. This is because the dog can then easily associate the instant pain or discomfort it experiences from this with passers-by and not its own actions. Which means it feels even more 'defensive' about them. Similarly if you shout at the dog, it could easily think you are merely 'backing it up' in its responses or 'legitimising' its fears - in other words, it's as if you were saying, **"look - there's another one! Have a go at it!"**

The tragedy about this problem, as highlighted before, is not just how easily it can be worsened by owners, even if unintentionally, but also how often it will not be spotted and addressed in its very earliest stages, when there's always the best chance of remedying it or preventing it from becoming too ingrained or 'compulsive'.

Once the habit has become 'compulsive', then a dog won't even bother to 'evaluate threat' before reacting to it. In other words, the dog has gained such belief in, and dependence on, this 'defensive strategy' that whether it is being approached by a man, woman or child, or a dog or a bitch, it will react in exactly the same way, in a virtually knee-jerk fashion.

The strategy, all in all, has become the only way it knows how to relate to, and cope with, the worrying outside world around it.

Fear aggression towards other dogs

Remedying the problem of 'fear aggression' towards **other dogs** can involve a lot of dedication and perseverance on an owner's behalf, depending on the strength of the dog's fears and how 'compulsive' its defensive behaviour has become. **It is also another problem where the use of professional help or back up is advised.** First owners will have to take the 'reward' factor away from their dog's behaviour, then they will have to try convince it that other dogs really aren't so constantly full of 'threat' as it might have imagined.

To do this, you are going to have to recruit some willing 'volunteers' to help you in your mission, plus employ the services of some pretty friendly dogs and their owners. Starting out on some pretty 'neutral' territory - i.e. not at home, or somewhere fairly enclosed or very familiar, or anywhere more likely to trigger 'defensive' responses in your dog - put it on a long and slack lead. I'd also recommend for inveterate 'lungers' the application of a Halti or Gentle Leader 'headcollar' - type device mentioned in the last chapter. **Note - if you have even the vaguest suspicion that your dog could actually attack another person or dog during this exercise, then you must put it in a muzzle.**

Next, get one of your 'volunteer' pairs - a friendly dog and its owner whom yours doesn't know, or know very well - to walk repeatedly **past** your dog at a distance, but n**ot directly towards it,** which can be a lot more threatening. Ensure that the two dogs in question do not make eye contact as they pass - do this by bringing your dog's head round to face you by calling it or possibly distracting it with a treat or toy. Different dogs can vary in the length of their own personal 'critical distance' - in other words, the distance at which the dog will feel obliged to react defensively when another approaches. Some dogs with highly fearful tendencies, and in whom defensive behaviour patterns have become a compulsive habit, can often start reacting to strangers, dogs etc. from a fairly long way away.

Again, like 'lunging' theatrically, this sort of exaggerated display of defensiveness can be a measure of their real fear, or simply the result of a dog who has become over-reliant on one strategy for coping in a 'frightening' world. If it only has one strategy for coping, then it always has to work, and it is this 'urgency' for it to work that can lead to defensive reactions bordering on 'over-kill', or from further and further distances away.

Once your volunteer dog and owner have walked past your dog a few times, you will discover the distance at which your dog will start reacting defensively. And it will no doubt be expecting the 'strange' dog and owner, as a result, to go away. But they do not. Instead, they keep walking by at a distance the dog can just about cope with. And if the dog, on a slack lead, and with the owner staying calm and quiet does not, as a result, react in any way it should be praised and - should it not be wearing a muzzle - rewarded with a treat. If it does ever react defensively during this exercise, then it should be **ignored**.

From this first point of encounter, the 'strange' dog / owner will then attempt to walk nearer and nearer - but still past, rather than at, your dog - in very gradual stages, and still not have the dog react. If it does react, the stranger and dog still won't go away and the dog will not be rewarded or praised. A good dog trainer or behaviourist could also show you how to 'distract' your dog's focus off the 'stranger' in situations like this, with the use of 'clicker' or 'disc' devices.

If you have the ability to redirect your dog's focus on to you in a situation that could otherwise appear quite threatening or worrying for the dog, then this will be a very helpful additional measure to use in the future.

Slow progress

Do not attempt to push this exercise too far in early days. Progress only as and when your dog seems able to cope with each stage of proximity. If your dog becomes extremely agitated and will not calm down when the 'strange' dog and owner get quite near, then get them to increase their distance just a bit further away from your dog, and when it copes with that, end on this good note for the day, before trying more progress another day.

If you keep up this exercise every day, with a variety of different people and good-natured dogs, and always end each day on a good note, and with a little bit more progress, you should eventually get to the stage where the 'volunteer' dog and owner can actually come up pretty close to yours and pass without a reaction.

The ideal scenario is when you can finally get a strange dog to come right up to yours without it reacting. But even if you can get your dog to pass strangers or dogs without reacting, this in itself can be good enough for most owners.

Don't blow it

Once you get to this stage, however, don't then 'blow it' by immediately foisting every new person or dog you see on your dog to 'test' or 'improve' its progress. This could actually have a **reverse effect**. It could find such 'saturation' unnerving, and may then resort to its old 'nastier' instincts under pressure. Remember, too, that the slower and more carefully you do things, the longer the effects are likely to last.

Fearful dogs are never likely to be the 'life and soul of the party', and it can be unfair to expect them to be. But if you can just get them to accept the passing of most people or dogs, when out, without much reaction, and get them to actually **like** just a few special people they've developed good associations with, then do congratulate yourself for achieving something that is often quite a challenge, but is always exceptionally worthwhile when it works.

Objects and situations

Dogs can possess, or develop, 'phobias' about certain objects either because they look or sound obviously 'threatening' - e.g. a loud vibrating truck - or because they 'associate' them with bad past experiences, or because they have encountered them at a stage in their lives when the most 'logical' reaction to something 'weird' or 'unfamiliar' would be fear.

To give just one example of the latter case. My own Border collie, Ilona, saw and encountered horses extremely frequently during her early puppyhood and thus has never perceived them as being remotely unusual or worrying. One day, however, when she was about a year old, she saw her first donkey and bolted in absolute **terror**. Despite the fact that a donkey does not look so very different to a horse through most eyes, donkeys had not become 'programmed' into her mind as pretty 'normal' or 'safe' things at a critical stage in her life, and thus she reacted with appropriate - and to her mind, highly logical - caution and fear.

To get Ilona's fear of donkeys most effectively reversed, I had to immediately go somewhere where I knew donkeys would be. I then walked nonchalantly back and forth past donkeys with Ilona until we were both bored stiff with them, and it was also clear to her that donkeys were not going to do anything spectacularly worrying or indeed, particularly interesting. The moment Ilona looked less worried about these stranger-looking animals, she got her favourite toy to play with. After roughly half an hour, donkeys weren't much of a problem any more.

The above exercise works much like a rider getting immediately back into the saddle after a fall off a horse - in the sense that, the longer you leave re-facing what frightened you, the deeper your fear is likely to get, and the stronger you are likely to resist facing the source of that fear again in future.

If your dog has developed a phobia about some new object or sight, and **it really matters to you that you should change this,** then the quicker you address it and try to reverse it, through immediately building happier or more positive associations with the original fear trigger, the more successful you are likely to be. If, however, you allow the phobia to become more ingrained, through repeatedly letting your dog avoid the source of the fear, then it can take much longer to overcome later, in slower and more painstaking steps of progress.

Fear about situations and places

Many dogs get fearful about certain **situations** - e.g. getting in the car, going to the vet's, entering certain houses - because unpleasant associations have become attached to them. E.g. they were car sick (see **Car travel problems**), or they hated having injections or pills put down their throats or because when they last went to a certain house a resident dog or cat attacked them, or a door slammed on their foot. How important it will be to change this state of affairs will depend on how often you will need to put your dog into situations like this which it doesn't like, and how violently it tends to respond to them, in terms of fear. Sometimes strong fears for one particular situation or scenario, if not rapidly addressed or reversed, can soon become more generalised and affect the dog's whole quality of life.

The vet's surgery can be quite a unique 'fear' situation, in terms of its limited potential to ever look convincingly 'harmless' to many dogs. This is because you may not go there more than once or twice a year with your dog, and each time you do it may be hard to avoid your dog having some rather unpleasant or undignified experience, however essential this may be to its welfare. Dogs soon cotton on to this simple connection between location and unpleasant experience, which is why so often you're on to a loser trying to convince them that vets are a good place to be. Even if you took your dog ten times to the vet just for a lovely fuss and tasty treat, and only once for an injection, the chances are it's the injection the dog would still remember most.

On the other hand, if there are places or situations that your dog doesn't like, but which you must for some reason expose it to regularly, it makes sense to persevere with a fear reduction programme, such as those already outlined. Especially if you know that the 'nasty' event which triggered a dog's initial fear about a place or situation won't be repeated, making it easier to replace its earlier 'negative associations' with more continually 'positive' ones.

If you don't do this then you may find that your dog's fears about certain objects, places or situations just get stronger and stronger, simply through being able to repeatedly avoid them when so desired. Similarly your social opportunities with your dog could soon dwindle, as it then starts to dictate to you a rapidly growing list of places or items that it doesn't want to encounter.

Last points

All in all, **fearfulness** about anything, in any dog, requires an owner to primarily appreciate the strength and 'legitimacy' of a dog's fears about something. Dogs cannot know what we know about the world, and must therefore base their own evaluations of 'harmlessness' on trust, experience or example. If dogs cannot trust that something is safe, then we have to give them a 'logical' reason to believe differently, and generally find ways to show them when their fears are inappropriate or misplaced.

This might take time, effort and great dedication in some cases. But ultimately it's also about the only approach that is ever going to work.

J

Jumping Up

Adult dogs who jump up on people generally do so because they were not deterred from this habit when they were puppies.

Other reasons for this in your rescue dog include:

- It uses jumping up as an attention-seeking ploy

- It is merely an outgoing and exuberant young dog

What to do

To teach puppies not to jump up, see relevant advice under '**Puppyhood**' in Chapter four. For dealing with **Attention-seeking behaviour**, see relevant section. Many dogs can abandon, or greatly reduce, their 'jumping up' habit as they get older, because it is basically a pretty juvenile activity. It also has a specific natural function. So often people can imagine that puppies or young dogs jump up to lick their faces because 'they want to be friendly and give us a kiss'.

It can look like, and is, a classic bit of 'ingratiating' behaviour, but such youngsters are just as likely to be hoping, on an instinctive level, that you might bring up a tasty bit of spare dinner. This is because in the wild, youngsters in a pack will jump up to lick the muzzles of adult dogs returning from a hunt to stimulate them into regurgitating food. If you prefer to think that dogs are 'kissing' you, however, I'm sure this doesn't bother them unduly.

If jumping up persists as the dog gets older, then this is usually because it has remained a rewarding habit, in that it rapidly gains attention. Dogs can also be given constantly conflicting signals about the 'rights' or 'wrongs' of this behaviour. Unfortunately, down one stretch of street three passers-by might positively encourage your dog to jump up through excessively petting it and thinking it friendly and cute when it does so, whereas the fourth might recoil in horror and offence.

Often the size of this problem for owners can be related to the size of their dog. A hulking great Mastiff or Great Dane jumping up on you, for instance, is likely to elicit far more unfavourable - if not horizontal! - reactions than a tinier terrier.

It is this inconsistency of reaction from other people, inside or outside your house, that can undermine your own attempts to teach a dog that jumping up is 'wrong'. This is why it is routinely advocated that you should tell any person you meet to **always** ignore your dog immediately when it jumps up, and only give it attention when it stays down on the ground. Either that, or they should turn their back on it until it gets down.

This type of strategy is always the best one. The snag about it, however, is that other people might not always remember to employ it - or they will simply ignore your requests to ignore a jumping up dog, as it were.

So instead, this is what you can do. You can teach your dog to stop and come to you whenever people approach, sit **immediately** on command, and not budge until you say so, then reward it profusely for doing so. This way, when people come to the house, or when you see other people approaching when you're out, you can have this handy command 'option' at your disposal.

Eventually your dog will realise that when people approach it will get this command, and it will then be well rewarded for obeying it. And as long as it can be relied upon to obey this command whenever you make it, the next step will be up to you. If you're faced with non-dog friendly people, the dog will have to stay down on the ground at home, or move on without greeting them if out. If you've got people, on the other hand, who love your friendly young enthusiastically greeting them, why not instead then simply release your dog from its sit and let them all enjoy each other's company?

Ultimately, the only thing that matters is that **you** aictate the terms of your dog's greeting behaviour - **not** your dog. You're also giving the dog far clearer guidelines about what it should do when it encounters people.

M

Mail problems

Many owners can get highly irritated or disturbed by dogs who will 'trash' their mail in the hall, leap up at the letterbox indoors and bark, or generally make mail deliveries a pretty dreaded - if not precarious - experience.

Reasons why your rescue dog does this include:

- It is frightened by this avalanche of 'strange stuff' coming into the home, particularly if it is alone when this occurs.
- It is defending your home from this 'intrusion'.
- It is bored and frustrated and this gives it something active to do.
- It is part of your dog's general 'vendetta' with 'imagined intruders' like the postman or other delivery people, who always have the wonderful, ego-boosting habit of going away when it barks or launches a 'defence'. Remember it has no idea that the postman, leaflet delivery person etc. were going to go away again anyway. It just thinks it has *made* them do so with its actions.

What to do

There are several possibilities, but here is the one that is usually the simplest. Go to a hardware or good DIY store. Purchase a sturdy wood or wire mesh box to put under your letterbox and hold any mail delivered inside. Better still, get a nice big outdoor mailbox. And that's it!

Mounting behaviour

Unfortunately, when many dogs have an urge to do something, 'social decency' doesn't come into the equation. Whether it comes to sex, eating, or just having a good instant punch - up with another dog they don't much like the look of, dog behaviour and social embarrassment just do not seem to go together. For this reason, we will frequently find ourselves getting embarrassed on our dog's behalf - and rarely is this more likely than when it insists on having 'sex' with cushions or visitors' legs or other people's dogs in the park.

Reasons for this in your rescue dog include:

- **It is sexually frustrated / sexually 'experimenting'**

- **It is trying to signify its 'dominance' over another dog of either sex**

- **It is trying to get your attention**

What to do

First, be aware that dogs, much like any other species, grow up with instincts and urges to reproduce. And with such instincts will, not so surprisingly, also come the desire to 'practise' sexual functions. Sometimes puppies will 'experiment' frequently with mounting behaviour even before they reach puberty, when hormonal surges can then increase their sexual drives. Similarly be aware that **bitches**, as well as dogs, can engage in mounting behaviour for any of the above outlined reasons.

Owners often believe that the immediate 'answer' to dogs, as opposed to bitches, who will routinely mount other dogs, visitors or furniture, is to have them castrated. If this subsequently makes too little difference, however, then this may be because the dog has already had ample time to find mounting behaviour **rewarding** in some way. In other words, the drastic reduction of hormone levels in the dog won't necessarily stop it from remembering, or still imagining, that mounting is a good thing to do.

Wrong reactions

From the outset, it has to be understood that mounting is a 'natural' thing for many dogs to do, but more often than not the behaviour will be perpetuated, or worsened, by an owner's reaction to it. It is pretty hard to ignore a dog who is making lewd overtures to the sofa in front of visitors, or obscenely gripping their legs. And, as a result, many dogs can quickly discover that the way to get masses of instant attention is to promptly go and mount something. If you suspect this could be the case with your dog, then you need to immediately take the 'attention' reward of mounting away. For more advice on how to do this, see the relevant **Attention-seeking behaviour** section.

Alternatively, try **distracting** the dog with something else - e.g. a toy or treat - the instant it looks like it is about to engage in mounting behaviour. It is very important, however, to distract the dog before mounting takes place in earnest, and only to give the dog its reward **after** it has come over to you and **done something else** to deserve it - e.g. a sit, or a lie down. Otherwise you will simply be rewarding it for its mounting behaviour!

If you suspect that your dog might have naturally high sexual drives, or is getting increasingly frustrated on this front, then castration might have some helpful effect, and you can discuss this with your vet. Do not, however, believe the old wives' tale that allowing your male dog to mate will 'cure' it of its frustration, because if anything, this is likely to make it even worse.

N

Noise Phobias

See **Fearfulness** section.

O

Over-attachment to an Owner

See **Separation Anxiety** section.

P

Possessiveness - 'guarding' food, bed, toys etc

How strongly motivated a dog might be to possessively, or aggressively, 'guard' resources it considers of importance to itself - e.g. its food bowl, bed, toys, the car - can depend on a variety of factors.

Reasons for this problem in your rescue dog include:

- It is a dog with naturally high 'defensive' reactions
- It has a high notion of its own 'status'
- Such responses have been very 'effective' or 'rewarding' in the past
- Past treatment has made it believe such behaviour is 'necessary'

What to do

First let us look at the **food** or **food bowl** scenario, and see how easily owners can make a dog's possessiveness over food worse simply through not understanding it. For a start, dogs are not born with the notion that they should invariably have generous and superb 'table manners'. They are born with the instinct that food is a precious resource.

In the wild, meals for dogs will be highly competitive activities. If you watched any wild dog pack taking apart a 'kill', you'd see a frenzy of animals all trying to get what they could, as fast as they could - usually in order of 'rank' - and 'seeing off' other rivals for the food with aggression if necessary. Principally because dogs who don't eat don't survive.

The presentation of regular meals in bowls from owners might have changed the way most dogs get their food today, **but not necessarily the age-old instincts they will have about protecting it once they get it.**

Protecting food

If a dog growls or lifts its lip when someone hovers around its food bowl, then usually on some instinctive level it is seeing that person as a potential rival for its meal. The chances of this happening can often be greater if the dog sees itself as pretty 'superior' within the household, or if it has a naturally more reactive / defensive type of personality. Once this 'protective' instinct displays itself, it is not so difficult to reverse it, through following a procedure outlined a little later.

However, rather than following this practical procedure, owners instead can get extremely heated about their dog's reaction around its food bowl. They will either, as a result, snatch the food away as 'punishment', or retaliate with aggression towards the dog. It's usually at this point that the problem dramatically escalates.

It escalates because, previously, the dog only had an 'instinct' that its food might be under threat, which was never actually 'proven' in reality. By snatching your dog's food bowl away, or physically or verbally abusing it by its bowl, **it now knows for sure** that people around its food bowl pose a real threat. Which means that next time it is going to react even **more** defensively to protect a vital resource - and also, possibly, itself.

Why anyone should see snatching a food bowl away from a dog as any sort of 'solution' to this problem is totally baffling. And one wonders how most people would feel if they were hungry and kept sitting down to a welcome meal, only to have it rapidly removed each time to 'teach them something'. Chances are, by the second or third time this happened, what they would have been 'taught' is to stick their hands down pretty firmly on the plate and to react to the 'food snatcher' in a suitably defensive way.

Whether you have a particularly dominant-minded dog, a dog with a highly 'defensive' nature, one who has found 'food guarding' rewarding in the past, because it has made people go away, or one who has been forced into believing aggressive 'food guarding' is necessary, due to the actions of its owners, the solution lies in **making a dog realise that its defensive reactions are unnecessary.**

Minimising food 'guarding reactions'

In a moment we are going to look at a procedure to help reduce a dog's 'guarding reactions' around food. Before we do so, however, be aware that is **yet another problem where professional back up is strictly advised** to keep any risk of danger to a minimum.

If your dog's reactions to anyone near its bowl are likely be extreme or unpredictable, then ensure that the dog is restrained on a lead during this exercise. If tied up, it should have enough room to pick up any food placed below it on the floor, but not enough to be able to leap up, or sideways, to attack anyone nearby.

If your dog will 'guard' its bowl even before there is any food placed in it, **do not use its bowl for this exercise.** Use a different dish or place food below it on the floor instead.

Here is now what you should do:

• The next mealtime, get your dog's empty food bowl and put it on the floor - unless (see above) you are using a different dish, or simply the floor for this exercise.

• If you use the dog's empty bowl or another dish, it might look suitably 'baffled' - but it also has nothing, as yet, to 'guard'.

• Ask your dog to **sit** and **wait**, unless it is secured too tightly on a lead to bring its head up to do this - in which case, ask it to **lie down** and **wait** instead. When it obeys the appropriate command, drop one small dog biscuit or tiny piece of meat from your hand into its dish, or on to the floor and move away while it eats. Make sure your hand is kept well away from the dog's head or mouth.

• Repeat this exercise three or four times until your dog is getting the message that

a) it must do what you say before it gets anything to eat and

b) you are there to put food **into** its bowl and **not** to take it away

- Once it has started to get this message, next, try dropping a biscuit or scrap into your dog's dish, or in front of it on the floor, and staying nearer to it this time while it eats.

- Is there a hint of any sort of defensive or aggressive reaction? If so, promptly **walk out of the kitchen and refuse to give your dog any more food.**

- Try again fifteen minutes later. If the dog is still looking defensive about you being near its dish again, walk away immediately it does this. If it does this more than three or four times, do not give it any more food until the next mealtime, when you'll try this exercise again.

- Eventually your dog will make the discovery that your presence at its dish, as well as its own co-operation with your commands, means the arrival, rather than removal, of food. If, however, it behaves in any sort of aggressive way around its dish or the feeding area, off you go and, with you going, also goes the food.

- Once you are having a consistent measure of success with this exercise - i.e. you have been continually feeding the dog for days this way without any aggressive reaction shown by it - get everyone else in your household to feed your dog in the same way - piece by piece, as long as a 'civilised' reaction is maintained. **Do not, however, use children for this exercise without the strictest supervision, and until you are absolutely sure that the dog will not react to them adversely.** Then only later, when you are feeling increasingly confident about the success of this procedure, can you also get visitors to feed the dog in this way, too.

- As time goes by - and as long as your dog continues to accept your presence around food, or its bowl, with no hint of aggression - you may be able to gradually increase the amounts you put into your dog's food bowl, or in front of it, at one time, and even 'mash' the food in the bowl around with your hands in front of the dog without it reacting in any kind of defensive way. If so, that is a sign of real progress.

Caution

Please do use **utmost caution** with this exercise, however, and only progress from one stage to another very **gradually**. It may be some while, for instance, before you can risk feeding your dog while it is not tied up, and you may need professional advice to tell you when this point may have come, if you cannot easily, or safely, judge for yourself. This exercise will involve your dog having to redefine possibly deep-rooted and instinctive former reactions to your presence around its food, and this cannot be achieved overnight. Similarly, by rushing the stages of this exercise before your dog is fully ready to change these former attitudes / reactions, you risk not only dangerous behaviour, but also the reversal of any progress already made.

*Note - if your dog is a particularly **strong willed or dominant-minded** character, then the best way forward may be to not feed it regularly from bowls on the floor at all. Make it 'earn' every item of its daily food ration from you, piecemeal, by doing something for you first - e.g. 'sit', 'down' or retrieve - instead. This gives the dog the message that only cooperation with your authority - or the authority of others around it - gets it food. And it no longer has anything in front of it to 'guard' from anyone else.*

Dogs and cars

Dogs can become aggressive in cars for a variety of reasons. In the **Car travel problems** section we looked at dogs who imagine, while you are driving, that their aggressive behaviour towards other cars / passers - by etc. is actually 'making them go away'. And this can give them a real 'buzz'. Now let us look at why dogs should get aggressive while the car is stationary and they are left inside it. The first reason is, they are confined in a restricted space. This instinctively makes them feel more vulnerable when strangers approach, and thus can trigger highly defensive reactions and responses.

Alternatively, they might just be 'guarding' the car as a resource or prized bit of territory. In the main, most dog owners won't find this a problem unless the dog actually **starts to try to prevent either themselves, or invited passengers**, getting into the car with aggressive overtures. Or if it turns snappy or particularly nasty when owners attempt to remove the dog from the car.

Heightened status

Unless fearfulness is at the root of the behaviour somewhere (in which case see relevant section) problems like these usually stem from the dog's over-heightened sense of its own 'status' - and therefore its belief that it is entitled to challenge you or others over ownership / access rights to the car. Similarly it is within its rights to resist your attempts to remove it from its 'territory'. They can also escalate if you start to get into frantic tussles with the dog to remove it, or physically punish it or threaten it for its aggressive stance.

In the short-term, the way to avoid the dog actually attacking yourself or other car passengers - should you believe this is possible - is to **muzzle** it while it is in the car, and to thereafter totally ignore any aggressive posturing. When you get home, do not try to force the dog out of the car, but instead try to 'distract' it out with a favourite toy - or by looking like you are all about to rush off somewhere important. **Do not get drawn into any all-out confrontations.**

In the long term, you may have to view this problem as a symptom of a dog who probably does not sufficiently accept or respect your authority over itself. And if, in general, you have problems getting such a dog to immediately do what you ask, when you ask it, this is even more likely to be the case. In order to remedy this state of affairs, your whole relationship with the dog may have to be redefined, as outlined under **The Rules of Superiority** and **Dealing with 'stronger-willed' dogs** in the last chapter.

Dogs and beds

Dogs may 'guard' their beds because they are a 'core' bit of personal territory, or a prized resource, or they may associate their beds with some increased level of vulnerability. They go there when they are about to sleep, or have in the past gone there when they felt 'under the weather' or wanted to retreat from pressures or activities elsewhere in the house.

Where you put a dog's bed can be relevant. If, for instance, you stick it in a kitchen or hallway where there are constant levels of noise, activity, and people generally to-ing and fro-ing in a rushed and rackety state, then this can make some dogs feel stressed and therefore more 'defensive' when it comes to protecting their own precious little bit of 'personal space'.

Respecting a dog's need for peace

Sadly, too many households do not appreciate a dog's right to have some quiet, comfortable spot of its own to retreat to, and never be disturbed, when it needs to for some reason. When we do not allow a dog this basic right to retreat somewhere peacefully and alone, without children jumping on it, or exposing it to a constant barrage of surrounding noise, physical interference and activity, we are actually depriving it of a 'safety valve' of vital importance to its overall psychological well-being.

If we always put dogs' beds in relatively quiet places, and always accepted that a dog's retreat to its bed was a 'signal' that it wanted peace to sleep, or just to psychologically or physically 'regroup', undisturbed, then what a difference this might make to the mental health of many dogs today. If no one ever disturbs you or troubles you when you're on your bed, you can also have rather less need to 'defend' it.

The fact that dogs will often rush to their beds when worried or apprehensive also underlines the measure of 'security' they can attach to them. So if you undermine a dog's essential faith in the security value of its own bed, you can also undermine its entire sense of security, full stop. After all, if its cherished bed can't protect it from being harassed or threatened within a household, what can?

Apart from the measures of putting your dog's bed somewhere relatively quiet, away from the main commotion centres of the household, and allowing it to retreat there when it wants to, undisturbed, also ensure that the dog always comes to you off its bed when necessary, rather than the other way around. By asking the dog come to you off its bed - providing it is not unwell, or has had sufficient time to rest - **rather than you going to the dog on its bed,** you are not just establishing your authority. You are also ensuring that the dog's bed remains a 'secure' spot. It has made the decision to come to you, rather than had itself 'forced' out of somewhere where it felt safe.

Similarly, if you need to groom your dog, cut its nails, brush its teeth or do any other manner of essential things to it that it might not really welcome or like, **do not do this while it is on or in its bed**. Likewise, never shout at it or threaten it or frighten it in any way when it is in its bed. All of these things will give a dog a reason to believe that an approach to its bed by someone means something unpleasant could happen within its prized 'safety spot'. This in turn will give it a reason to feel more 'defensive'.

Reducing 'defensiveness' about beds

A way to further reduce a dog's 'defensiveness' about its bed is to get all members of your household to occasionally drop a tasty treat on to it as they pass by, without actually looking at the dog or saying anything to it. If this is done repeatedly by your household members and also other visitors, the dog should soon come to realise that people passing or approaching its bed can be a pretty positive or rewarding event.

Not all dogs will 'guard' beds because they feel defensive about them and / or want other people to leave them in peace. Some **dominant-minded dogs**, or dogs who have been able to gain too high a notion of their own real 'status', will guard them much as they will 'guard' sofas, or doorways or anything else they might regard as a 'status symbol' others would be well-advised to keep their hands off.

In other words, the bed tends to be just one of a catalogue of things the dog thinks its 'status' gives it a right to 'own' and defend from 'lesser rivals'. Some may advise that you should regularly sit in the beds of dogs like this to 'show them who's boss'. I wouldn't. Not only can it be a pretty uncomfortable and smelly experience, but it's also ultimately pointless if, in the meantime, your dog is snoozing contentedly up on the sofa instead. The higher the sleeping area, the more 'status' dogs tend to attach to it. So if your dog is sitting guarding the sofa, while you are crouching in cramped and obvious discomfort on the floor, I'm not sure it will deduce that you have the 'superior' deal.

Basically, your dog is simply guarding what it has been allowed to guard, or have access to to guard in the first place. So this must change. In future, it must not be allowed on to furniture, or into rooms where it might be likely to challenge you over 'access'. Additionally, the whole way the dog regards its own status, in relation to that of others within the household, must be altered and redefined. Whatever your dog 'guards', including its bed, must be systematically taken away from it until it learns better respect for an owner's authority (for more advice on achieving this, see once again **The Rules of Superiority** and **Dealing with strong-willed dogs** in the last chapter).

The **exception** to the above will be its **food**. Food possession problems should be dealt with as earlier outlined. Whatever privilege you intend to withdraw from a dog to reduce its status, however, **do not do this in a way that might invite conflict or confrontation, as this can be highly dangerous.** In other words, **do not make removing 'items of privilege' from the dog an obvious personal challenge or tussle.** Remove them instead when it is not looking or not around, or simply close doors into rooms where these items are kept.

The fewer 'items of privilege' your dog has access to, the more it might reconsider its own 'real' status, in comparison to yours, and the less it will certainly have to 'guard' from you. As and when your dog shows better general respect for you, you can reintroduce its bed, only removing it again as or when it still gets aggressive about it. Do, however, put the bed each time in a fairly 'lowly' place - e.g. a far corner of a back room downstairs - and also somewhere where people aren't constantly going past, making its 'guarding' instincts stronger. Dogs like these should not be allowed upstairs, into bedrooms, or on to beds, to sleep - as they may subsequently want to guard such 'privileged' areas or items from owners.

Dogs and toys

Dogs, thankfully, don't tend to have anything like the amount of possessions the average human can clock up over the years. Because of this, it is perhaps not so surprising that what they do have regular access to, or consider their 'own', can take on far greater significance for them than it can for us. A classic example of this being toys.

Dogs who become 'possessive' about toys often do so because, as puppies, they were never taught a proper 'off' command by owners, requiring them to immediately let go of whatever they were holding when asked. As a result, games with owners soon turned into 'tugs-of-war', with the dog then discovering that the more aggressively it tugged, pulled, or kept hold of things, the more likely it was to 'win' them and keep possession of them.

The problem could subsequently have been worsened when the owner, disgruntled about 'losing' the game to the dog, then went to try and forcibly remove the 'disputed' item from its mouth, or got aggressive with the dog to regain control of it. This in turn led the dog to feel wary or defensive about items it was holding when an owner approached.

If you don't want a dog to be possessive about toys, then here are your options:

- **Teach it a suitable 'off' command and make 'possessiveness' over toys far less appropriate or rewarding**

- **Don't get it any toys**

As you can see, one is a lot simpler than the other. For many owners, however, engaging their dogs in play, with toys, is looked upon as an important exercise for 'bonding' as well as an undeniable form of pleasure - potentially - for owners and dogs alike. So they might prefer, instead, to perfect a command that will make their dog let go of whatever they are holding.

Off!

How quickly and effectively you can get an 'off' command across to a dog can depend on how 'protective' it feels about items in its possession, or how 'anxious' it feels about any approach from others to remove them. It is vital that dogs with possessive tendencies towards toys are not allowed free access to them. In other words, toys should not be readily available to them, in a box, or left around the house, as this could lead to the dog believing that it 'owns' them, or that the issue of who actually owns them is open to dispute.

Instead, the dog needs to learn that **you** own **all** toys in the house. So games only start when you bring out your toys, and likewise they must end when you want them back. The rest of the time you keep 'your' toys hidden somewhere out of sight.

To teach your dog to 'leave' or get 'off' a toy, follow this procedure:

- **Get some delicious treats or titbits in your hand and let the dog know you have them.**

- **Throw a fairly 'lowly' play object on the floor - e.g. nothing wonderfully squeaky or fluffy or 'tug-able', which to dogs can simulate 'prey' items, or something the dog has been highly 'possessive' about in the past. Try something like a plastic flowerpot or yoghurt carton, or a cardboard tube from the inside of a kitchen roll.**

- **Your dog should instinctively go up to sniff the 'new' item. At the exact moment it does this say '*off!*' in a calm but firm voice and encourage the dog back to you immediately for a treat. If it comes back quickly without the item, also give it lots of praise.**

- **Repeat this exercise three or four times daily over the next few days. If all continues to go well, then put down something like a ball or rubber ring in front of the dog - do not *throw* it, just put it on the floor. As the dog goes to grab it, again say 'off!' and if it leaves it while you pick it up, again give it a delicious treat and praise it well.**

- **If, on the other hand, it grabs it and runs off with it, do not follow it. Simply get out an even better toy and appear to be playing with it. This will give the dog the message that its own item has little 'status' or 'worth' compared to yours. Its interest may then shift to trying to get your toy - which will require it dropping what it already has.**

• When it looks on the verge of dropping the ball or ring it took, say 'off!' and call it to you. When it comes, again give it a treat and praise it well - but do not give it your toy. Instead, give it back its ball or ring and let it keep it for a while. After three or four minutes, get fairly near the dog, without looking at it or touching it and say '*off!*' again. If it leaves the ball immediately and lets you pick it up, then instantly give it your better toy as a reward, together with much praise.

• Only when your dog has shown better and better responses to leaving things you ask it to, and letting you pick them up, should you gradually 'up' the 'value' of the toys or treats you give it in exchange. The dog can then calculate that every time it lets go of one toy, it stands a chance of being given something better.

• Whatever toy your dog ends up with, however, it must not be allowed to keep it for as long as it likes. The last toy, like the first one, must be given up on command when you want it. You can then reward your dog with a treat and praise it, and put all your toys away until next time.

• Eventually, you should not have to reward your dog every time it relinquishes a toy on command, as this will begin to smack of 'bribery'. Once your dog has got the message about what it should do when you say 'off', it should do it out of respect for your authority, and out of a realisation that all toys ultimately belong to *you.*

• If at any time it continues to show aggressiveness towards you over items or toys in its possession, then this could be because you are trying to 'force the issue' - i.e. trying to coerce or pressurise the dog too heavily into letting go of things, rather than waiting for it to relinquish them of its own accord. The more effort and fuss you make about trying to get things back off a dog, the more 'defensive' it could feel, or the more 'prized' it could imagine its 'possessed' item to be. If things get too 'heated', then you will have to keep starting this exercise from scratch, and not move on to another step until the dog's behaviour improves and is generally more reliable.

Ultimately you want to get to the stage where the dog will happily let go of anything on command, and allow you to take it - if only, initially, because it believes this action will gain it a reward more 'valuable' than keeping possession of its existing item.

Because this exercise rules out any form of 'confrontation', it should work particularly well with dogs whose 'possessive' reactions over toys stem principally from a fear that they will have these toys forcibly or aggressively removed from them. If there are never any confrontations over toys, then there will be less and less need to feel 'defensive' about them.

This apart, be aware that **bitches** can be particularly 'protective' about certain toys when entering a 'pseudo pregnancy' phase within months after a heat. This can be classic, hormonally-induced 'nurturing' behaviour and should pass when hormone levels return more to normal. For more details on this phenomenon, see Chapter nine on **Health** and also the **Digging** section.

Also see the **Stealing things** section, for dogs who have this habit, whether or not they will then become highly possessive about items - or 'trophies '- they have run off with.

R

Restlessness

See **Anxiety** section, and also the next chapter.

S

Scent-marking

Owners can readily conclude that any male dog with a tendency to 'cock its leg' around the house must be doing so purely to 'mark territory', when this isn't strictly true. It should also be realised that **bitches** will often 'scent mark' territory, too. More on scent marking in a moment, but for now realise there can be other reasons why dogs might not be 'reliable' with their toilet habits indoors.

Other reasons for this problem in the house with your rescue dog include:

- •**It got into this 'habit' in kennels, or elsewhere, whenever it felt insecure or stressed**
- •**It has never been properly 'toilet-trained'**

What to do
First, understand that the quantity of urine a dog leaves behind can be fairly significant. A dog, for instance, who leaves lots of small 'sprays' around in different places is a dog who is 'scent-marking'. A dog who leaves just one big flood is generally a dog who could not get out in time to properly relieve itself, or was not fully aware of the place where it **should** have been relieving itself. It could also be one with some sort of medical complaint requiring it to pass urine more frequently, so this might be checked out by your vet.

In some dogs, and often those who have spent some time in kennels, regular - and sometimes even quite obsessive 'scent-marking' - can be more fuelled by **anxiety** than hormones. In other words, scent marking has been adapted into an anxiety or stress-reducing exercise, employed whenever the dog feels insecure or under pressure. If this is the case **then neutering might not necessarily 'cure' the dog's behaviour,** whereas a reduction in its overall stress / anxiety levels might.

When a new rescue dog comes to your house remember that, if it had previous weeks or months in kennels, with no one making clear to it where it should or shouldn't relieve itself, then it is likely to need some **'re-training'** on this front.

Once older dogs have had ample time and opportunity in the past to urinate anywhere, however, there is a chance that they may still have the odd 'forgetful' moment for some while after you rehome them. This is especially so if the apparent 'scent-marking' is partly fuelled, or entirely fuelled, by anxiety of some kind - e.g. when you are out. As with destructiveness, owners can imagine that a dog 'scent-marking' only while they are not around indicates some sort of 'deliberate' attempt to 'get back at them'. In truth, their absence might just be a prime trigger for the behaviour. For more advice on this sort of behaviour see both the **Anxiety** and **Destructiveness** sections.

Sometimes 'scent marking' problems will be worse if you own more than one dog - especially of the same sex - and this thus turns into a 'competitive activity'. In such cases, establishing a proper hierarchy between dogs can help (see **Rescue dogs and other pets,** last chapter).

Also **be careful to thoroughly clean any soiled areas with something that will not keep attracting dogs back to the same spot to urinate** - e.g. biological washing powder followed by surgical spirit, as outlined under **Toilet training** in Chapter four. If your dog remains a persistent offender on this front, it might be safer to restrict it to a special area, room or crate while you are out, or cannot supervise it, which will be easy to clean should 'accidents' occur. Also see the **'Toileting problems'** section later.

Separation anxiety

Earlier on, in the **Destructiveness** section and others, we have looked at how an owner's absence can trigger a range of behaviour - i.e. barking, 'trashing' things, loss of 'toilet control' - related to the amount of frustration, boredom, fear or general anxiety it feels while alone. Some dogs will react badly when owners are out because they do not like to be confined, or are frustrated or bored by a total lack of stimulation or purpose. Some dogs react badly because they are frightened by something when they are left alone, and therefore feel more vulnerable. Others simply suffer from **'separation anxiety'** - which, in essence, means they find the simple absence of their owners highly traumatic.

If 'separation anxiety' has become an increasing problem among dogs today, then it's basically because human lifestyles have changed considerably in recent years, whereas dogs' natural expectations of life have stayed much the same. More and more households can now have both principal members out at work for much of the day, rather than just one, as tended to be the case in days gone by.

Similarly, many more dogs are being owned by single people, or single principal household members. This means there is often no one left to look after the dog should they have to go out. The end result of all the above is a lot more dogs spending longer and longer periods on their own. And not all dogs can cope with this as well as others.

Reasons why your rescue dog should suffer badly from 'separation anxiety' include:

• **It has become over-attached to you**

• **Past owners left it too long, too often, on its own**

• **It fears abandonment**

What to do

First, appreciate better why your dog should get so 'panicky' while you are out. Dogs are highly sociable animals whose own levels of security can greatly hinge on being part of a 'pack'. Even if that 'pack' is merely one other person. Being part of a pack is a key to a dog's survival in the wild. And while your dog is sitting confined in an empty kitchen or hallway, it might be haunted by this simple, stark reality. Hence the strength of its anxieties.

If you have not trained your dog (see later) to view your absences as a predictable and regular part of daily routine, you also have to ask yourself, how can it actually **know** how long you will be and when if ever, you **will** be coming back? All of which can make it view its predicament as increasingly desperate.

Also remember that many rescue dogs might have been left alone for very long periods, and in pretty unhappy circumstances, in past lives. Thus, when you go out of the house your dog may think this is all going to happen again. Remember, too, that a past experience of being totally 'abandoned' by a former 'pack' - when it went into rescue - may have left the dog with **deep-rooted insecurities about an owner's absence.**

Over-attachment

This apart, it can be very easy to let a rescue dog become over-attached to you, or overly dependent on your constant presence. Remember, as far as your rescue dog is concerned, you might be the greatest thing, or greatest source of security, it has ever had in its life, which is why it doesn't want to let you out of its sight.

How can you stop a dog becoming over-attached to you? Well first, be aware of some of the more obvious symptoms of over-attachment, such as a dog who insists on following you everywhere in the house, from room to room. You might initially think (as mentioned in '**Early destructiveness**', Chapter five), that this is actually quite an 'endearing' or 'flattering' habit - whereas it's actually pretty **unhealthy** behaviour to see in any dog who is destined, at some time, to be left on its own.

Apart from continually following owners from room to room, dogs who become over-attached to their owners can have the following in common:

- **They'll have constant access to their owners when they are home, and are able to 'demand' attention from them whenever desired**

- **If the dog is left with someone else while the owner leaves the room and shuts the door, it will immediately start to whine or get panicky - either trying to follow the owner, or else constantly staring at the door the owner left by, oblivious to any other distraction**

Also, if dogs like these actually destroy items when the owner is out, these are frequently doors or doorways the owner left by, or items with a high concentration of the owners' scent.

Dogs who are over-attached to their owners have to be taught, primarily, that they cannot have access to their owner's attention / presence all the time, whenever they desire it. To get this message across, you have got to start ignoring many of your dog's daily 'attention' overtures towards you - e.g. for a reassuring pat, or a game or for a 'greeting' when you come home.

At first this may be very hard. You and your dog might have quickly built up quite an intense bond and you'll be worried about it viewing your disinterested response as 'rejection'. If you really want to help your dog with its separation anxiety problems, however, then you **must** persevere with putting more 'emotional distance' between yourself and the dog.

Increasing owner / dog 'distance'

Once your dog is beginning to get used to the idea of you ignoring it occasionally, next start doing all the things you'd normally do before leaving the house - e.g. lock doors, pick up car or house keys, put on a coat. Your dog, no doubt, will quickly start to look anxious about these 'leaving cues', but totally ignore it. Then immediately put the keys back, take off the coat, unlock doors etc. and carry on your normal household routine.

Go through this ritual a few times a day without ever leaving the house and your dog should start to look a little less anxious each time.

From this point, start your usual key-collecting door-locking routine and then totally ignore your dog, however much it pesters you for attention, **for a good five minutes afterwards.** Then build this up in stages to around an hour. This way your dog will begin to realise that key-collecting, door-locking etc. means it is going to be devoid of attention for some time, so it may as well settle down.

The next stage is to try and get your dog to settle in another room, while you shut the door on it - or, to begin with, you can use baby gates or child gates to put some room distance between you, while the dog can still see you.

Perform the early separation operations very casually. Do not speak to the dog. Just walk out of the room, shut the door or baby gate and leave your dog for around 20 seconds. Then walk back into the room to your dog just as casually. Do not 'greet' the dog or give it any attention. Simply carry on with what you were doing before you went out of the room. Then, over the next few days, go out of the room for 30 seconds, then a minute, then five minutes, then ten, leaving the dog behind - **never paying it any attention either when you leave or come back to the room.**

Repeat this exercise, until you can leave your dog for up to 30 minutes or an hour without it reacting adversely. You are now beginning to psychologically equip a dog far more for the experience of being left alone when you go out. In the best scenario, providing you regularly keep the above exercise up while you are at home, and **never give your dog any attention either just before you actually leave the house, or immediately when you come home,** your dog may be able to cope tolerably with an hour or two on its own.

When you do come home, as stated, leave it a good minute or two before you call your dog to you to give it attention, rather than have the dog come up and demand immediate attention from you. It might also be a good idea to **get your dog used to sleeping downstairs at night,** on its own, rather than in your room, if this is currently the case, using the same gradual 'separation' techniques outlined as above if need be. This should further its acceptance that separation from you, at regular intervals, is quite 'normal'.

If you need to leave your dog for longer than an hour or two each day, and suspect that it might be destructive through anxiety while you are out, then see the Destructiveness section for how to get a dog better used to being confined or kennelled during the day.

Stealing things

Some dogs may steal food off kitchen tables or surfaces while owners are not looking, others may take owners' personal items, run off triumphantly with them and then refuse to give them back.

Reasons for such habits in your rescue dog include:

- In the case of stealing food, it is simply 'scavenging' and has found the practice highly rewarding.

- In the case of stealing and running off with 'trophy' items, the dog may be trying to get your attention, or viewing such behaviour as an indication of its 'high' status.

What to do

Not all dogs have the 'manners' to wait until they are properly fed. Some are, as they say, greater devotees of the 'see-food' diet - as in, see food, take it and eat it whenever possible, in true canine scavenging tradition.

This might make you mad but, unfortunately, all a dog learns from being told off or punished by owners for taking food is not to take it **while they are around, or watching.** In other words, it might prefer to slip that joint or cake off the side while you're all looking at TV or up in bed.

Being furious with a dog for stealing food is understandable but, in reality, also pretty pointless. After all, you left food around, and the dog didn't necessarily know that it was yours. All it could see was an opportunity to employ a pretty logical instinct, so that is what it did.

Booby traps

Not leaving any food around that your dog could take is the most obvious answer to this problem. Another is to set up an effective '**booby trap**'. To do this, get a tasty and fairly large piece of meat. Tie one piece of string round the meat. Then tie a series of five or six clean and empty tin cans in rows round the central piece of string on the meat, but do not let your dog see you do this.

Leave the meat poking temptingly over the kitchen side, or table, for your dog to see later. Go into another room with your dog. Wait for the dog to go out of the room and into the kitchen for the meat and ... "**ker-assh!**". Your dog will fly back out of the kitchen in panic mode.

There is a high chance it won't steal things off that side or table again, especially if you keep leaving the same trap around every so often to check if it will still risk taking the 'bait'. This is because it has associated its **own** action of taking food off the kitchen side, or table, with horrible consequences, and not with **you**, because you weren't around at the time.

Some dogs, however, might not be so easily deterred. They might even get a taste for grabbing food to the accompaniment of a high decibel tin pile-up. In which case, keep food out of their grasp at all times.

Do also be incredibly careful not to leave chocolate, or cocoa powder anywhere in the house where a persistent dog thief might be able to get it, as they contain a chemical - theobromine - which can be lethal to dogs, or at best make them very ill, if consumed in anything but the smallest of quantities.

Stealing 'trophies'

Many owners may notice that when they give their dog a bone or fairly large and prized treat, it will take it in its mouth and then trot off with it with a triumphant flourish, tail in the air. Its body language is basically saying, "look at **me**, see what **I've got**". Immediately it feels pretty important and pleased with itself, and it marches off away with the 'prize' or 'trophy', instinctively, to try to avoid anyone else getting it.

Once we can grasp why this behaviour gives a dog a 'high', as well as a degree of heightened self-importance, we can better understand why some dogs might not want to wait until their owners give them a 'prize'. They'd rather just go and 'steal' one instead - tearing off with things like socks, shoes, clothes, or anything else that takes their fancy as a suitable "look at me" item.

Some dogs can just do this to gain attention from owners, quickly realising the sort of items that are likely to get you roused when taken. If you suspect this is the case, and they are never aggressive when you remove such items from them, all you need to do is this. Go over to your dog the moment it takes something - without saying a **word**, or looking at all fussed - and **gently** remove it. Once it has let go, praise it well.

It can also help greatly to train dogs to '**retrieve**' all manner of different household objects - e.g. cloths, brushes, shoes - for you on command. If you consistently reward and massively praise your dog for bringing things to you, and then letting go of them, it will realise that this can get it far more attention than just running off with items you will immediately take back.

Don't tussle

Whatever item your dog takes, it is vital **not to make removal of it any sort of forceful or aggressive tussle.** This may make a dog increasingly defensive, or could make it actually swallow the item in dispute. It might also give it the notion that the object it holds is far more 'valuable' than it really is, and thus requires greater 'protection'.

If your dog steals something and will not give it back, or looks pretty aggressive towards you when you try to get it back, and the item stolen is particularly **valuable** to you, then you could try doing what another dog would do in these circumstances - start a 'false commotion'. Rush out very suddenly into the garden, calling your dog urgently and making loud 'shushing' noises as if you were attempting to scare something away. Few dogs, unless intensely nervous, can resist wanting to pile into a 'commotion' of this kind.

Chances are your dog will rush out after you without the stolen item and charge off up the garden in full cry. At which point you deftly nip back into the house, shut the door, and retrieve your stolen item - then hide it away somewhere. Then let your dog back in, and don't pay it much attention. This way, you've got your 'stolen' item back without any confrontation - and if your dog didn't **see** you take its 'trophy' it can't know you've 'stolen' it back.

Status problems

Naturally, this is a ruse you can only use a limited number of times before your dog 'gets wise' to it. In the meantime, if bouts of stealing and aggressively guarding items continue, you might have to ask yourself what is it about the dog, or your relationship with it, that is making it behave in this way. If the dog is acting in this way due to high notions of its own status in the household, then the whole way you interact and live with it may have to be changed (see **'Dealing with stronger-willed dogs'** and **The Rules of Superiority**, last chapter).

Also, if the dog's stealing of 'trophies' is status-related, you might notice a marked tendency for it to only steal things belonging to less authoritative or 'lesser-ranking' (to the dog's mind) members of the household.

If the dog is being highly 'defensive' over stolen items because it fears you are going to be aggressive with it, then never try to remove such items from the dog. Instead, present it with something better - like a favourite toy or treat. Use these to lure the dog out into the garden or into another room, then shut the door behind you. When it comes to get the toy or treat, praise it heavily and really make a big fuss. Then go back inside and get your 'stolen' item. Eventually your dog will realise you are never going to forcibly remove an item from it which, in the end, will greatly reduce its need to be so 'defensive'.

Submissive behaviour

Dogs with fairly 'submissive' natures are not generally viewed to be a real 'problem' by owners as, if anything, such natures can tend to make them more obedient or 'eager to please'. When dogs show excessively submissive traits, however - such as crawling towards owners on their stomachs in 'greeting' and possibly urinating at the same time - then this can seem somewhat worrying or distressing or both owners and their visitors.

Reasons for this 'problem' in your rescue dog include:

- **It is a puppy or very young dog**

- **It is an exceptionally 'submissive' dog by nature**

- **It has been badly treated or 'bullied' by an owner in its past life**

What to do

First, understand that many puppies and very young dogs can grow out of this highly 'appeasing' sort of behaviour as they grow in both confidence and size.

Second, appreciate that some dogs just have exceptionally submissive natures. They could have been born this way, or equally learned early on that exaggerated submissive postures were the most effective way to keep themselves out of conflict or trouble - much like 'fearful' dogs soon learn that 'exaggerated' defensive reactions can achieve much the same aim.

Sadly, another explanation for such behaviour is that your dog could have been very badly treated or intimidated by a past owner. If this is the case you might find that its approach towards other dogs is far less 'over the top' appeasing than it is towards other people. This is because people, rather than dogs, have given it a **need** to react in this exceptionally submissive way, if only through a self-protective instinct. **Naturally** highly submissive dogs, on the other hand, tend to be rather 'over the top' in their appeasing reactions towards dogs, people and possibly even your cat alike.

Building self-confidence

Whether your dog is highly submissive by nature, or has learned to be this way towards people, a most important priority is the improvement of its general self-confidence. In other words, much as you have to 'manipulate' a more dominant dog's self-confidence downwards, in a highly submissive dog you have to put this process into reverse.

Dogs who are, or who have become, highly submissive are unlikely to ever become massively confident or 'fearless' characters, no matter what you do. But their owners can give them sufficiently more confidence to approach people in a less 'appeasing' way.

It is very important that dogs like these are never **shouted** at or threatened by people in any circumstances. It's also important that they are **always rewarded more for confident, rather than less confident, approaches towards people.**

If you have a dog like this, then initially when you greet it, always do so crouching on your haunches and turning your head away to avoid direct eye contact - all in all, far more 'inviting' and less possibly confrontational body language for any dog. If your dog comes towards you without crawling on its stomach, or looking highly submissive at this approach, then praise it effusively and give it a treat. If, instead, it starts crawling towards you on its stomach, **then immediately get up and walk away, ignoring it.** Go and sit down somewhere for five or six minutes, still ignoring it. Then try this exercise again.

If your dog is exceptionally submissive, the only way it might come to you when you call it, without crawling, is if you lie down or sit on the floor with your back to it. If it comes to you at this approach, without crawling, or any other excessively 'ingratiating' behaviour, then praise it heavily. Then move on to the haunches approach. If both these approaches work in getting your dog to come to you without excessive 'fawning' behaviour, only then move on to greeting your dog while standing up.

It would also help to get all visitors to your home, or people met while out, to greet your dog in these less confrontational ways - though a few will naturally baulk at having to lie down! Give them all treats that they can hand your dog should it come to them with a degree of confidence. It is important, however, that the dog always **approaches these people in its own time,** rather than have them suddenly 'flood' it unnervingly with their attentions.

Bit by bit, your dog should discover that approaching people in a more confident way tends to be pretty rewarding, and that - in the case of past ill treatment - maybe people aren't so bad, or so in constant need of 'appeasing', after all.

How you handle and train dogs like these on a day-to-day basis can also be very crucial. For more details and advice about this, see **'Shyer or more submissive dogs'** in the last chapter.

T

Toileting problems

Earlier on in this chapter we have looked at **Scent-marking** around the home, and also why some dogs' 'toilet habits' could be less reliable than others, especially if they have spent time in kennels or were never correctly 'trained' as puppies where to relieve themselves. Additionally, fouling or urinating in the home could be part and parcel of general **Separation anxiety,** or just basic **Anxiety** in itself - in which case, see relevant sections.

Other reasons for 'toileting' problems in your rescue dog include:

- It has some digestive upset, malfunction or infection

- Bitches can occasionally 'forget themselves' when 'hormonally challenged - i.e. during the 'heat' or 'pseudo pregnancy' phases of their cycle

- Spayed bitches can sometimes suffer from urinary incontinence

- Older dogs cannot always 'hold on' as long as they could when they were younger when they have a need to relieve themselves - or else simply get 'forgetful' or 'disorientated'

What to do

In the case of suspected medical problems, consult your vet to get these properly diagnosed and treated - or else ruled out. If a dog is excessively incontinent in any way, it might be sensible to put special covers over areas where it sleeps, or to confine it to areas of the house where its 'accidents' will have less traumatic impact, or will be a lot easier to clean up. Apart from this, simply be **patient**. The chances are your dog simply cannot help what it is doing, and is certainly not doing it to deliberately annoy you. If you feel unsure that you have really got to the root cause of your dog's 'accidents' around the home, do call in **professional advice** as, age and medical conditions aside, there can be lots of other different reasons - or combinations of reasons - for this problem.

Before we close this chapter, here are some last important points to consider about 'behavioural problems - or, as I see it, behaviour in dogs which we'd prefer to change:

• **First,** never expect to cure any 'problem' in a dog **overnight**. Your success in remedying any canine problem is usually dependent on the amount of time, effort and commitment you are prepared to put into the 'mission'. Succeeding in this 'mission', however, can be an intensely rewarding experience for all concerned

• **Second**, although there are a range of **drugs** and **deterrent devices** around today to help treat a variety of 'behavioural problems', these should not be viewed as substitutes for proper behavioural modification programmes. **Conventional drugs** should be used with veterinary guidance and only when this is **absolutely vital** for the dog's well-being or welfare - **not** just as a 'tool of convenience' for the owner. You could also consider **homeopathic remedies** (see back of book) if preferred. If **deterrent devices** aren't used in **precise contexts**, and with **precise timing**, they can also sometimes do more harm than good - which is why you should only use them with professional behavioural supervision. This apart, not all behaviourists today will agree on the ethics, or ultimate efficacy, of using devices like electric 'shock collars' on dogs, whatever their 'problem', and you're entitled to feel the same, should devices like this be 'recommended'

• **Third,** rewards - in the form of 'titbits' or 'treats' - feature heavily in this chapter, when it comes to trying to 're-shape' a dog's behaviour. If you're going to use a lot of treats, then make sure they're as 'healthy' as possible, and also that **you make these part of your dog's daily food allowance,** rather than regular 'extras'. Otherwise you are going to end up with one fat dog! Some dogs, of course, will respond better to games and toys as 'rewards' than food, so always bear this in mind.

Chapter Eight

How To Have A Happy Dog. Canine (and Human!) Stress. Understanding What It Takes to Make Your Dog Secure And Content. Respecting Why Dogs Get Anxious, Insecure And Afraid

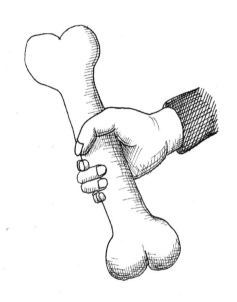

They say that happy people are seldom found in the clinics of 'shrinks'. Equally, people who lead pretty stress-free and fulfilled lives tend to be rarer visitors to doctors' surgeries.

Much the same can apply to dogs. When dogs are fundamentally unhappy, frustrated, stressed or just put under too much overall pressure in their lives, then not only are they likely to have more 'behavioural problems' - they are also more likely to get ill.

Over past decades, people have gradually begun to realise that dogs really aren't 'unfeeling' creatures, immune to the impact of unhappy or uncomfortable experiences. They can get stressed, anxious, frightened and insecure much as we can, when given suitable reasons, and what we do to them, or expose them to, is destined to have some resultant psychological effect, be this short or long term.

Because dogs cannot talk to us, explain to us what they need, or tell us when they are insecure or unhappy, this makes it too easy for us to misunderstand them, and instead dismiss their symptoms of stress, frustration or unhappiness as merely 'bad' or 'problem' behaviour. Similarly, day after day, dogs will find themselves scolded or punished for behaviour we might not like, but which is entirely 'logical' or natural for them as a species.

The only way you could ever fully understand how hard life can be for dogs in the modern human world, under total human control, would be to become a dog for one day. It would be an eye-opener to say the least. Failing that, you can just try harder to appreciate what it takes to make dogs happy or more secure.

How to have a happy dog

How would you define a 'happy' dog? In essence, I'd say it is one who feels fundamentally 'safe' or 'secure' within its living environment, one who 'understands' its life and what is required of it at any given time, and one who finds its basic needs as a dog - be these physical or psychological - met or respected whenever possible.

Nobody can give a dog exactly what it wants or needs a hundred per cent of the time. No person can have what he or she wants or needs a hundred per cent of the time. But what we can do is better understand factors that might significantly contribute to dogs being happy or unhappy.

Dogs tend to be happiest when:

- They are part of a 'pack' and know their 'place' in that pack
- They have security, and 'order' in their lives - e.g. strong leadership and set daily routines
- They have regular mental stimulation, outings and physical exercise
- They have undisturbed rest and peace when they need it
- They have a healthy diet
- They have consistent commands whose meaning they understand
- They know that 'no' *always* means no and never 'maybe'
- They are *always* praised for good behaviour
- They are only ever scolded or challenged over 'bad' behaviour the instant it occurs, so they'll understand why - and after the quick reprimand, no 'simmering resentment' is harboured by owners towards the dog
- They are *never* physically punished or shouted at unnecessarily
- They are never deliberately put into situations by owners which make them feel threatened, persecuted or betrayed
- They have ample and regular freedom of action to use their brains and initiative and just be dogs doing what dogs like to do
- They are not constantly criticised for smallest misdemeanours or simple quirks of 'natural' dog behaviour
- They have total faith in their owner's desire to protect their welfare

As humans, we actually have the unique ability to make dogs happier than they might be in the wild, because we can take away many of the daily survival struggles and stresses which would dominate their lives in this natural state. We can also be kinder to, and build greater confidence in, more naturally 'lower-ranking' / highly submissive dogs who might otherwise, in the wild, have led lives of constant persecution from their peers.

It is important to understand the difference, however, between a life for a dog that we might consider ideal for it, and one that it might have preferred for itself, if given the choice. Lots of dogs, for instance, may well be happier running free on the streets than being lengthily confined alone, or in an over-repressed manner, in our 'ideal' human home, however great their resident toybox or the meal they get at night. Similarly, canine pets who are continually pampered and indulged like children, or clipped and prinked like ornaments, might happily swap all this in a flash to be charging freely across muddy fields or down rabbit holes like proper dogs.

If dogs are fundamentally frustrated, insecure or unhappy, then they may not be able to tell you, but they can do lots of rather unpleasant things - e.g. snap, bark, destroy things, consistently disobey owners - which will get the message across in other ways.

Dogs tend to be unhappiest when:

- They cannot trust or respect their owners or have 'faith' in their leadership
- They are constantly punished for reasons they do not understand
- They are frequently hit, shouted at or generally treated harshly
- They are frightened of owners, or think them 'weak', and thus feel insecure as a result
- There is no reassuring 'consistency' in their lives - e.g. about when they are fed / walked / are able to relieve themselves / how long they will be left alone
- They do not get enough mental and / or physical stimulation daily
- They're not really clear about where they stand in their household 'pack'
- They're being harassed by children or being picked on by other dogs
- They're rarely able to use their own initiative, or act independently in any way without instant criticism from owners
- They cannot get peace when they need it
- They are in some sort of continual pain or discomfort
- They are constantly surrounded by high levels of human upheaval / neurosis which troubles them, but which they also do not understand

Sometimes we can make dogs unhappy without ever realising it, simply through not fully understanding or appreciating the impact our behaviour can have on their minds.

Some people might deduce from all the above that making dogs feel secure - and therefore fundamentally happier - seems hard work, or rather complicated. Read through the previous lists again, however, and you will see that the task does not require a dramatic dismantling of your whole lifestyle. More often than not it simply means altering or reconsidering some previous approaches or attitudes towards dogs that you never thought to question or reassess - until that is, you suddenly had a dog with 'problems' that you didn't like.

Canine (and Human!) Stress: understanding what it takes to make your dog secure and content

The modern world most of us live in is pretty different to the one our ancestors knew. It is also a lot more stressful. This is because we are born with most of the same natural needs and instincts our ancestors had, but have less and less chance to have them fulfilled.

We were designed as a species to live in proper 'communities', to work the land, hunt and gather food and to generally be able to build things, create things and watch things grow. We were not designed to hurl up and down motorways in tin boxes at rapid speed, to work in soulless offices or on production lines where we never see the true 'material' fruits of our labours, or reside in communities where we barely know our neighbours, or have little connection to their lives.

Can it really be a coincidence that with all these 'artificial' modern demands and pressures, and deteriorations of 'basic natural needs' has come an unprecedented explosion in human stress and 'behavioural disorders'? And also the increasingly widespread use of sedative and anti-depressant drugs.

Now let's look at dogs. Dogs are also increasingly having to live in environments totally at odds with their instinctive needs as a species. Worse than that, no one can actually explain to dogs **why** their environment is so at odds with their needs. And what do you know? Dogs are also 'stressing-out' in record numbers, and having 'behavioural problems' and apparently now needing sedatives and anti-depressant drugs just to 'cope' with everyday life.

There seems to be, as they say, an awful lot of it about.

Unfortunately stressed-out people tend to have stressed-out dogs. It might seem an obvious point to make, but it is still one many owners can fail to appreciate or acknowledge, when their dog suddenly starts to 'play up' or 'act weirdly'.

I have not got all the answers to human stress - who has? - but what I do know is that if you are a stressed-out person with a stressed-out dog, **it's a good idea to sort the dog out first.** That way you will at least have one less thing to get stressed-out about. Your dog will also be in a better position to be a comforting companion, rather than just an additional source of annoyance. Humans are also in a far better position to deal with and control canine stress, than the other way around.

Making dogs secure

Sometimes it's helpful to imagine, just for one moment, what it can be like to be the average pet dog in an average domestic home. 'Pack members' are continually coming and going and leaving you alone. You do not know why, or where they are going. If you're a rescue dog, you might also wonder if they will ever be coming back at all.

Maybe you are hungry sometimes, but you can't just go and hunt something or scavenge around dustbins. You've got to wait until an owner says you can eat. Maybe there are times when you really need to go to the toilet, but there's no one around to let you out. You may be thirsty but your owner has forgotten to fill up your bowl with enough water. You may be bored, but you have no company, and you cannot go out anywhere until your owner says so.

When you do go out your owner often yanks you around by the collar on your neck in a most painful or uncomfortable manner, and shouts at you for reasons you completely fail to understand. When you come back and have had your meal, maybe you just want some peace and quiet, but people keep pestering you to do other things and continually jump all over your bed.

Stressful or what? Would **you** like a life like this? And if not, don't you think the wonder is how many domestic dogs **don't**, rather than do, go a bit round the bend when faced with regimes like this, day in and day out?

Dogs can be incredibly adaptable animals, but what we also have to understand is that we afford them few essential **freedoms**. They cannot choose who owns them. They cannot escape or control much of what happens in their lives. They are at the mercy of our transient, inconsistent and often totally incomprehensible whims and emotions, 24 hours a day.

If we're going to have a dog sacrifice its freedom for us, and always do what we ask when we ask it, then rather than take this privilege for granted, why not instead make a dog feel that what we offer in return is a pretty good deal? We can do this - as previously outlined - through making dogs always feel secure under our protection and leadership. By giving them the feeling that as long as they are with us they will always be safe, their basic welfare needs will always be met, and their trust won't be betrayed.

Shouting at dogs

Many people will shout at, and / or casually whack their dogs all the time. They do it so often, so automatically and in so many different contexts that they don't even stop to consider **why** they are doing it, or whether it is actually having any impact at all.

It is pretty unpleasant and stressful for dogs to be shouted at or whacked all the time, particularly if they are quite sensitive individuals. Most owners who do this will also hardly ever get the timing right between the behaviour in the dog that they didn't like and the accompanying 'reprimand' for it. Which means that many dogs simply have **no idea** why their owners are continually shouting at them, or whacking them. This in turn - as previously outlined - can make them pretty insecure.

Very soon you will also devalue the currency of a shout or whack. The dog will eventually realise that shouting and whacking just appear to be a part of your everyday rather hostile approach to it - and beyond that, these assaults seem to have no other reason or purpose. Additionally, if somebody shouted at you day and night, you could soon start to feel pretty hostile yourself.

So what exactly are you achieving by doing it - other than steadily undermining your dog's trust in you, and making it potentially more uneasy and aggressive into the bargain? There may always be odd times when we really do need to shout at a dog - e.g. when it's in danger running off somewhere, or when it has done something truly bad. But if we never generally shout at our dog, and we get the timing absolutely right on these occasions, then this is likely to have real and fairly immediate impact. It won't have much impact if we are always shouting at our dog.

This apart, most dogs do have pretty acute and sensitive hearing. There is no evidence to suggest that a dog screamed at in a mega-decibel tone from five paces will comprehend what you're saying any better than it would in a raised whisper. If anything it will be less likely to listen because it imagines you are persecuting it for a totally unknown reason - rather than simply asking it to do something for you.

How to stop your stress becoming your dog's problem

If you are ever feeling particularly stressed or neurotic about something, try to get into the firm habit of **never taking it out on your dog.** Even if your dog's behaviour has made you feel more stressed or neurotic. Yes, it might seem far easier said than done, but dogs simply cannot understand hostile reactions towards them triggered by **what you feel,** rather than **what they have actually done.** It just makes them feel tense, insecure - and therefore, probably a lot more neurotic themselves.

So instead, when a tricky moment strikes, count to ten, walk straight into the garden or another room from your dog and close the door. Then scream your head off, if desired, and kick cushions or flowerpots around if necessary. Designer 'punch-bags' are also pretty trendy these days - and quieter - should you want to avail yourself of one for this exercise. Or you could keep a plank of wood to hammer nails into - but maybe not in the house.

However you 'let rip', make sure you come back to your dog in a much better frame of mind and give it a good pat. Long-term, it's much better and healthier for your dog to believe that you have occasionally baffling habits than to feel you are regularly angry with it for no apparent reason. You might also like to explain these little 'steam releasing' habits to your neighbours. Just in case they get worried.

Also remember that **emotional self-control** and **calmness** are key qualities of convincing **authority** and **leadership**. Most people find it hard to have faith in the 'leadership' of people who are forever getting into a semi-hysterical or agitated state - and so do most dogs. So please bear this in mind.

Respecting why dogs get anxious, insecure and afraid

Most of our traditional relationships with animals have been constructed on the basis that our needs will always be more important than - or superior to - theirs. Over centuries this attitude has become so ingrained and automatic that we rarely seem to question it, or consider what a toll this can often take on the psychological health of the dogs we so intimately share our lives with.

It can be very easy, and convenient, to consistently ignore the 'viewpoint' or 'basic rights' of an animal that cannot speak, or which has no power to simply walk away from us when we make it unhappy, insecure or afraid. But if we want to do that then we also have to accept that ultimately this will generate some pretty negative consequences for us, too - i.e., in the case of dogs, an animal whose behaviour can become increasingly worrying or annoying to live with.

When dogs are given reasons by us, or others, to feel anxiety, insecurity or fear and we do not respect the validity of these feelings, or disregard the need for them to be suitably addressed when they occur, then 'little' problems or worries in dogs can rapidly turn into far bigger ones. The **Fearfulness** section in the last chapter gave classic examples of this.

Respecting fears

People cannot always be expected to put a dog's need or feelings 'first', but what they can do is understand when their expectations or demands of a dog's behaviour are unreasonable, given a dog's own anxieties at the time. Owners will routinely say, for instance, that their dog 'gets so worked up over **nothing**', when one of the virtual miracles about dogs is the range of new experiences or people they seem capable of getting used to in human society today, without adverse reaction. Remember that dogs have to **trust** - rather than know - that all the strange new things they keep experiencing are 'safe' or harmless when their instincts may be telling them otherwise.

All in all, the continual 'leaps of faith' we expect dogs to make about baffling or threatening looking features within the human environment can be like us being expected to believe that things like Martian spaceships, three-headed mermaids or flying elephants appearing daily on our streets aren't worthy of too much concern.

Fear of the unknown or 'inexplicable'

To take another example. Most people are afraid of ghosts, or the possibility of encountering them. They are afraid of them because they **cannot 'rationalise' them**. They do not know what causes them, where they come from and whether or not they may wish them harm. Most people faced with a ghost will therefore want to run, because they deduce that this is the most 'logical' and 'self-preservatory' thing to do.

Such reactions will work on a purely **instinctive** level. They also mirror exactly how your dog feels, and why it can react as it does, in the face of something equally startling and inexplicable, which represents its own equivalent of a 'ghost'. It suddenly doesn't look so 'daft' or illogical, does it?

Dogs get anxious, insecure and afraid basically when they can't make sense of the world around them, can't avoid or control situations that they find upsetting or threatening, and can't be sure that their owners will always have their best interests at heart. Anxiety, insecurity and fear are all things that can have a severe impact on a dog's behaviour and overall quality of life, plus the confidence it needs to happily face the world.

Many rescue dogs can arrive suffering from one or all of these feelings to some degree. Do make allowances for this. Don't take it for granted that your dog can always see the world, and its own personal circumstances in quite the same way that you do. It may need time, patience, understanding and reassurance before it can truly feel 'safe' with you. Give it these considerations and give it that time and it's unlikely that you will ever regret it.

Chapter Nine

All You Need To Know About Your Dog's Health. To Neuter Or Not To Neuter? Everyday Grooming And Health Maintenance. Understanding Genetic Disorders, Health Danger Signs And When To Call In A Vet. What Should You Feed Your Dog? Beware The Perils Of Obesity. What Is 'The Right Amount Of Exercise' For Your Dog?

Considering some of their less savoury habits, dogs in the main tend to be pretty healthy creatures. Modern advances in diet and veterinary care are also affording them to chance to live longer lives in better condition.

This being said, however, there are always things we can do to improve our dogs' chances of maintaining good health, through better care, knowledge or vigilance.

Worming and vaccinations

More obvious health priorities for dogs include the need for them to be regularly **wormed** and **vaccinated**. It is usually recommended that adult dogs are wormed every six months, but if they are in areas or conditions carrying particularly high risks of worm infection, this may have to be done more often.

How often a dog should be vaccinated against major diseases - i.e. **Canine Infectious Hepatitis, Parvovirus, Leptospirosis and Distemper** - has become more controversial. There are many now, for instance, who believe that annual 'booster' vaccinations for all these things in 'one dose' is not only unnecessary, but can have a harmful effect on a dog's immune system. For this reason, some vets will now take blood tests annually to see whether your dog's resistance to different diseases really does need a 'top up' or whether its existing antibodies or 'immune defences' from previous vaccinations are already sufficient. You might prefer this option. Alternatively you might want to consider a range of **homeopathic vaccines** now available (see back of book for more details).

Dogs, muck and more common illnesses

Although protection against life-threatening diseases like the above - especially for younger dogs or puppies - is vital, dogs' habits of trawling the ground (or each other!) with their noses and occasionally eating rancid or revolting-looking bits of muck can expose them to a wide range of bacteria or viruses. This in turn can lead to bouts of digestive upset or illnesses like **Kennel Cough**. The latter is usually distinguished by a recurring cough that sounds very much like the dog has got something stuck in its throat. If symptoms accompanying any of these ailments are lengthy and / or very severe, then veterinary advice and / or treatment should be sought. Dogs with persistent diarrhoea and vomiting, and who cannot keep fluid down, can run a dangerous risk of dehydrating - and this is a particular worry in small puppies.

This apart, try not to get too neurotic about your dog's habits or occasional short-lived health upsets acquired as a result of them. Not only can you not protect your dog from the wealth of bacteria and viruses in its environment, but it is also vital for your dog to get regularly exposed to them in order to develop a strong immune system.

If your dog has constantly recurring bouts of diarrhoea or loose motions that are often jelly-like or full of mucus, but is otherwise fairly bright and eats well, then it may be a colitis sufferer. **Colitis** is generally characterised by recurring inflammation in the lower part of the dog's gut and can sometimes become a chronic condition. It is not always known why certain individual dogs, or breeds, are more prone to it than others, but measures to help relieve, if not cure it, can include a switch to a blander - or hypo-allergenic - diet, more roughage in the diet, doses of 'pro-biotics' (which increase the number of 'healthy' bacteria in the gut) and other special drugs available from your vet.

To neuter or not to neuter?

To neuter, or not to neuter, a dog or bitch seems to be an issue few owners can look at dispassionately. Many rescue dogs might have already had this operation done - in which case, you are saved any further agonising.

If not, it appears that men in particular - and some male vets, come to that! - are more ready to baulk at the idea of having a dog castrated. Principally, it is argued, because they 'over-identify' with the dog's predicament. They can also accuse women of being too keen to 'administer the snip', as if there were always some element of gender vindictiveness involved. In truth, this is a daft bit of nonsense, as most women tend to be as keen to get their bitches spayed as their dogs neutered for the same simple reason - to avoid litters of unwanted puppies being born, or to spare their dogs - and themselves - the less pleasant effects of caninereproductive hormones.

Owners of male dogs will often argue that "it should be up to owners of bitches to get them spayed". Owners of bitches, on the other hand, might argue that "dogs should be 'done' because it is a far simpler operation". But really what should be at issue is this. Do you intend to breed from your dog - bearing in mind how many unwanted dogs there already are in the world? And if not, are you aware how many health problems in both male dogs and bitches could be avoided through having them neutered?

I've known some truly lovely bitches who would still be around today if they had been neutered when they were young. Instead, because they were not, they died of **Pyometra** (see **Health danger signs and**

emergencies later) or mammary cancer in older age. I've also known older entire male dogs with testicular cancer or unpleasant prostate problems for similar reasons.

And these are things you need to bear in mind when making your decision. Entire male dogs are also much more likely to get into fights, run off roaming, and suffer from recurring sexual frustration. Bitches who come on heat will not only have to be kept away from other dogs for up to three weeks or more, twice a year, they can also suffer distressing **'phantom pregnancies'**, within months after them. In this condition they can blow up with milk, mope around obsessively guarding soft toys and try to dig enormous holes in the floor. Personally, I cannot see why all this is worth going through continually, for yourself and your dog alike, unless you intend to breed from it.

Practical concerns

The agonising owners may go through over neutering tends not to be shared by the dogs themselves, who seem able to recover from such operations without trauma counselling - or indeed, any indication that they are aware of what has happened to them. Dogs, unlike owners, also do not mourn for puppies they have never had.

Neutering operations, however, are not always drawback-free. Many neutered dogs or bitches may have to have their food cut back as they might otherwise put on weight more readily - though this isn't always the case. Some bitches can also suffer from a degree of urinary incontinence after spaying, which can be helped with veterinary treatment.

With bitches, the earlier you spay them - i.e. before a first or second heat - the higher the protection they will have against mammary tumours, which are a major killer today of older female dogs who were either not spayed, or not spayed early enough, to prevent them occurring. With male dogs, you might want to wait until the dog has reached full physical maturity before considering castration.

Sometimes spaying a bitch can make it a bit more aggressive, particularly if it was already this way inclined. And castration cannot 'remove' behaviour traits in male dogs that are caused by factors other than levels of testosterone.

Whatever you decide to do, make decisions on the basis of what's best for your animal's overall welfare, rather than in simple response to your own emotional feelings, prejudices or philosophies about genders or reproductive systems.

Everyday grooming and health maintenance

One of the best 'health checks' you can give your dog is during a regular daily grooming session. Grooming with a brush or comb from head to foot, to clean dirt off, remove knots or tangles and get oils spread through the coat is good for your dog's hair and skin and can also be accompanied by a thorough search over it's body to detect any potential problems.

We'll now outline how you should do this.

Noses

Start with your dog's **nose**. Is there a discharge of any kind that could suggest an infection or some foreign body - e.g. a grass seed - stuck up a nostril? This could be the case if it has also been doing a lot of sneezing or - in the case of an infection - coughing. If you suspect a foreign body you may need to get your vet to remove it, possibly under anaesthetic if it has gone far up the nose. If your dog seems fairly bright, active and eats well despite a possible infection, it may soon recover without further help. If not, or its symptoms get distinctly worse, it may require anti-biotic treatment from your vet.

Dogs can be prone to a range of **tumours** affecting the nose. Some will be benign but others could be malignant cancers. If you see any new lump of swelling occurring on or inside your dog's nose, get your vet to check it out at once. As with all cancers, the quicker they are spotted in earlier stages, the better the prognosis can be for recovery after treatment.

If your dog has **pink pigment** patches on or around its nose, these should not be exposed too regularly to strong sunlight, as they could be more vulnerable to burning or skin cancer. Keep an eye on these patches regularly to check they aren't burning or changing in any way. Sunscreen creams might not be practical, because it can be extremely hard to keep these on a dog's nose without it licking them off.

Mouths and teeth

Next, look inside your dog's **mouth**. Yes, it's often not a pretty sight. Some rescue dogs can be intensely 'hand-shy', or will strongly resist their mouths being handled or approached, so do be patient in achieving this aim. It is very important that you know **how to open a dog's mouth properly**. Do not just walk up to the dog head on, stick your fingers between its teeth and try to wrench its mouth open, as you could frighten the dog and risk getting bitten.

As it is so important to know how to perform this procedure properly and safely, and the only way to be absolutely sure is to have a graphic demonstration carried out in front of you, please ask your vet or a veterinary nurse to do this for you - or anyone else you know with suitable experience of dogs.

Do not get into a tussle with your dog over its mouth, as this could simply make matters worse. Just aim for a little bit more gentle progress every day until it finally accepts your interest in its mouth as more of a baffling, rather than threatening, phenomenon. Keep giving it masses of praise each time it stays still.

When you do look into its mouth, and at its lips, again, look for any **strange swellings** or lumps that might need to be checked out, any **broken** or **chipped teeth**, or any gum inflammations. Broken or chipped teeth can be a source of great discomfort or pain to dogs, which can be avoided if they are removed. If there's a lot of inflammation around one tooth, your dog may have an abscess under it, which will again be very painful and should have treatment.

Unfortunately, many owners can have very little interest or curiosity about what is happening in their dogs' mouths - until, perhaps, these mouths start smelling like sewers, or the dog is so miserable with pain that it can't eat. This is very sad. By keeping our dogs' teeth regularly inspected, cleaned and free of tartar, not only will they be nicer to have around in close proximity - they will also be far happier when they are freed from sources of permanent or recurring pain. Some dogs who have had long-term dental problems solved can literally take on 'new leases of life'.

Health risks from bad teeth

Such routine inspection and cleaning is also a way to prevent gum disease, which now affects a startling 85 per cent of pet dogs and cats. Gum disease not only causes animals to lose teeth - it can also **lead to more serious health risks** as toxins released into the blood stream from the gums start to affect the heart or kidneys.

Cleaning a dog's teeth isn't always an easy exercise but, like anything else, it gets easier the more often you do it, and once your dog accepts this is going to keep happening on a regular basis, and the quieter it is, the quicker it will be over. Over and above getting your dog's teeth initially scaled and polished by the vet, should they be in quite a bad state when you first get your dog, get yourself some proper dog toothpaste and a canine toothbrush.

Failing this, a special baby's toothbrush from the chemist, plus a warm dilute solution of sodium bicarbonate, will do the trick. Brush one or two of your dog's teeth very gently to begin with. If it struggles, don't be discouraged. Just try to get one more tooth brushed each day, until you can do the whole mouth without a kafuffle. Once you've finished, give your dog tons of praise and have a good game with it to cheer it up and forget about the horrors of dental attention.

Ears and eyes

Next, check your dog's eyes and eyelids. Do you see any strange 'droops' or growths on the eyelids, which might need checking out? Are the eye whites red, suggesting some possible infection, injury or irritation? - Particularly if there is also an accompanying sticky discharge.

If so, try bathing the eye in dilute saline solution a couple of time a day. If there's no immediate improvement, or the dog seems in real pain, you might need additional treatment from your vet.

Eye infections - due to irritation or injury - can sometimes be serious, and those that are allowed to progress too far unchecked may sometimes cause lasting damage. Also be aware that intensely red eyes with a discharge can sometimes be a sign of other illnesses causing high toxicity within the blood - e.g. **Pyometra** (see **Health danger signs and emergencies** later).

Ears can be common sources of infection for dogs, and some particular breeds - or crosses of them - might suffer from ear problems more than others. Springer and Cocker spaniels, retrievers and poodles, for instance, seem particularly prone. This can either be due to the narrower shape of their ear canals or - in the case of poodles - the amount of hair growing inside the ears.

Dogs who continually scratch at or shake one or both ears may have a painful infection, or some foreign body like a grass seed stuck inside the ear canal. You may also be aware of a particularly foul smell that occurs when ears are infected. For such infections or foreign bodies, it's best to get veterinary attention. First, because you usually cannot reach the source of irritation or infection yourself and second, because you can sometimes make matters worse through trying. Remember **never** to **poke anything further down a dog's ear than you can see.** An anaesthetic and an anti-biotic ointment may also be needed to solve the problem.

Your dog alternatively might have **ear mites.** These parasites are usually an enormous source of irritation, and their presence is usually accompanied by excessive amounts of brown wax produced in the dog's ears. However, an ointment from your vet should soon be able to eradicate them.

If a big swelling suddenly erupts on your dog's **outer ear** (or ear flap) it could be a **haematoma.** This blood-filled swelling is caused by a rupture of blood vessels in the ear cartilage, often if the ear has had a knock, or due to the intense scratching by a dog when it has had an ear irritation or infection. If you do not get this swelling properly drained and treated by a vet, the eventual result could be a bent or misshapen ear. This is because, once the swelling eventually bursts, the subsequent healing process can often bend or pull the ear out of its natural position.

Feet, paws and nails

Pick up each of your dog's **feet** individually and look at the pads. Do they look **dry and cracked?** If so, they might benefit from being regularly treated with a special paw wax available from pet stores. Olive oil rubbed regularly into the pads can also help. If you're going to do this, however, a word of advice - apply the paw wax or oil just before you take your dog out for a walk or feed it, or play a game with it. Otherwise it is likely to rush round the house trying to lick it all off.

Next, look between your dogs' paw pads and toes. Can you see any **sharp stones, hard bits of mud or grass seeds** stuck there? If so, remove them, as they could lead to soreness through rubbing. Grass seeds with pointed ends - or awns - can also migrate well into dogs' limbs, bodies and ears (as mentioned earlier) and cause serious infection and pain. So if you have been out walking with your dog anywhere where such grass seeds are around, do check it out all over afterwards from head to tail and pick out any that you can see.

Can you see any **strange lumps** on the feet or between the pads? These can also be a possible site for tumours, so get them checked out.

Next, **claws** or 'toenails'. Do they need cutting? Dogs' nails wear down according to how much use they get on hard surfaces. To tell if your dog's nails are too long, look closely at them all while the dog is standing on a smooth flat surface. Can you see any gap at all between its nails and the floor? If so, then maybe only the front inside 'dew claws' will need cutting. If not, you may need to trim any nail which is touching the floor, or which looks obviously long.

Many owners can get queasy about cutting their dogs' nails because they fear they will cut into a quick and cause distressing bleeding. This can be more likely with black nails because, unlike white ones, you cannot easily see the pink quick, or 'live' bit of the nail, inside. If you really dread this procedure, then get your vet to do it.

If not, this is what you should do. Get the sharpest pair of **proper dog nail clippers** you can find, plus a decent **emery board.** Also get a **silver nitrate pencil** from your vet, which will quickly cauterise any nail quick you inadvertently nick and stop it bleeding.

Once you have got these things together in one place, get your dog. If you suspect it might go for you, because it is frightened or worried, you may need to apply a muzzle, but do not apply this in a sudden or aggressive way. Alternatively, you can tie a ribbon of gauze gently but firmly round your dog's nose so it cannot open its mouth.

If you've got a fairly small or medium-sized dog, this procedure is often best done with the dog turned on its back and placed on your lap, so you can really get a good look at the nails and quicks. If your dog's nails are very long, do not try to cut too much off at once. Just snip a small bit off the end, then do the same again a week later once the quicks have retreated a bit. Once you have cut a bit of nail off, next file the end down some more with the emery board and 'round' it off to give a smooth finish. This will also ensure that the dogs' nails don't have rough edges which could badly scratch someone afterwards, and will stop them fraying.

Work your way methodically round the nails and dew claws to see which most need doing, and try to get this whole procedure finished as quickly as possible to avoid overly distressing your dog.

The more often you cut and file your dog's nails, the more it will get used to it and the better shape they will be in - but do not forget the aforementioned dew claws on the insides of the dog's front legs, which do not get any wear. Some owners can forget, and as a result these will sometimes curl right round as they grow, digging into the dog's leg, and causing it immense pain.

Body and coat

While you are grooming your dog, can you see any evidence of fleas? To detect their presence do the following. Put a damp bit of kitchen towel under your dog while you groom it. If black specs land on the kitchen towel while you groom, then turn a brownish red when moistened - this, sadly, is **flea dirt**. So get a suitable treatment for these from your vet.

As you go methodically through the coat, parting hair, can you also see any other parasites, such as **ticks**? These can sometimes look like small grey warts which grow and grow in size as they fill up with blood. You can kill these with flea spray, or smother them in Vaseline until they suffocate and fall off. Never try to pull a tick off forcibly as it will leave mouthparts behind, which can cause a subsequent infection. Instead, gently twist it off with a pair of tweezers once it is dead.

Mange in dogs can be quite a problem in some areas. Bald itchy patches round the ears, nose, head or tail area can be a sign of this. If your dog is intensely itchy in places and losing hair as a result, it might be worth your vet doing a skin scraping to test if mange mites are present. He or she can then give your dog a suitable treatment for them.

Lastly, have another good feel all over your dog's body. Are there any unusual bumps, lumps or swellings you can feel anywhere? Is so again, get them checked out.

All the above checks can take minutes to do each day. But if, as a result, you have been able to find a possible source or cause of pain, discomfort, disease or illness in your dog, or get some potentially serious problem spotted in its earliest stages, it has to be worth it. Remember, dogs cannot monitor their own health for themselves, which is why it's down to us to do it for them.

Understanding genetic disorders

Earlier on in this book, in Chapter Three, we looked at how a dog's individual temperament or character could be influenced by its genes. And much the same could be said about a dog's health or level of physical robustness.

A staggering array of different genetic disorders can be found among domestic dogs today, and pedigree dogs in particular. Commoner ones include joint malformations like **hip dysplasia**, which causes discomfort and lameness in back legs, to eye deformities, deafness, blood disorders, heart problems and ailments involving the digestive system.

The above, sadly, give an indication of what happens when mankind interferes with timeless laws of nature. Nature requires two basic things for optimum health in a species. One is a fairly large and diverse gene pool to minimise the replication of hereditary defects. The other is that only the strongest and fittest animals survive to breed and carry on their 'robust' genes.

If, however, as in the case of pedigree breeding, you want dogs that basically look much like each other and conform to a 'fashionable' or 'uniform' look, you have to pick them from a much narrower gene pool. It would also be easy to see these favoured looks, when selecting breeding stock, as a greater priority to yourself - and others - than how well the animal might survive in a natural state.

Hence the chance for more and more of these dogs to suffer from genetic disorders, or less than perfect levels of physical robustness. Further, it is no surprise that the more popular an individual pedigree breed becomes, the more likely genetic 'defects' are to occur in it - because you're continually having to produce more and more dogs from the same limited gene pool to meet demand.

How much overall damage has been caused to dog health as a result of human interference in canine genetics over the past century or more, has become a highly emotive issue today. To be fair to modern breeders, however, many of them today are simply inheriting problems originated by past generations. Other more conscientious breeders are also doing all they can to minimise or eradicate genetic disorders within their own particular pedigree varieties.

You might see all the above as a perfect argument for getting a rescued mongrel or 'crossbred' dog instead of a pedigree one. If so, be aware that just as many pedigree dogs can be extremely healthy, not **all** crossbreeds will be free of any health defects or problems. The health status of any kind of dog you rescue can't always be guaranteed, even if in the main mongrels are often deemed to be 'healthier specimens' than pedigree ones, particularly those belonging to highly popular breeds, or more 'exotic' breeds with very limited gene pools.

How can I know more about genetic disorders?

You may never have a problem with any sort of 'genetic' disorder in your rescue dog. If you get a pedigree variety, however, or a cross of two distinct pedigree varieties, it might be worth trying to establish which sort of disorders are known in these breeds. Many breed specific books on the market today can give you an indication of what they could suffer from. Alternatively, you could ask advice from your vet or an experienced breeder (see **Advice** section at the end of this book). The point of this exercise is not to give yourself unnecessary fears, but to be a bit more knowledgeable. This apart, how well or badly your dog might cope with a genetic disorder can often depend on how quickly the problem is diagnosed and treated.

Health danger signs - when to call in a vet

When you have a new dog in the house, and particularly if you don't feel extremely knowledgeable about dogs, it can be easy to panic when they suddenly go off their food or appear listless and ill.

Sometimes rescue dogs can be a bit under the weather, get digestive upsets or coughs during early days in a new home because of the general upheaval involved and the challenge of a completely new environment - much like people can get colds or stomach problems the minute they go away on holiday or move.

Because of the worries we can have about a new dog's health, it can help to have a better idea of what symptoms or ailments represent true canine **danger signs,** or **health emergencies** requiring urgent treatment from a vet. Some basic or more common ones are now listed below.

<u>Problem 1</u>: **Your dog suddenly collapses**

If your dog is also foaming at the mouth, having convulsions, appears weak and uncoordinated and was vomiting or attempting to vomit prior to collapse, it might have been **poisoned.**

Apart from taking it immediately to the vet, try your best to establish what toxic substance the dog may have eaten or drunk, as your vet could well have an antidote for it to speed recovery. Not all dogs will have the same symptoms when poisoned, depending on what they consumed - some, for instance, may just suddenly become excitable or depressed. Watch out for any of these symptoms should you suspect your dog has had access to anything toxic - e.g. slug pellets, rat poison, paint. Also be immensely careful not to leave lying around **anything that could be toxic to your dog** - slug pellets being a typical example, but also **cocoa powder or boxes of chocolates.** From **human drugs** and **medicines** to **bleach** or other **household cleaners,** there are so many toxic things a curious dog could lick, chew or swallow in the average home and you must be conscious of this at all times.

Epilepsy

Other reasons for sudden collapse include **epilepsy.** If your dog's eyes flutter violently after collapse, it chomps its jaws, 'paddles' its front paws and seems totally 'absent' mentally, or unaware of your presence, it could well be having a fit. It may also lose bowel or bladder control.

If you suspect your dog is 'fitting', keep it quiet and warm. Turn off any loud noises and close the curtains. Put a cushion or blanket under its head to avoid it injuring its head on the floor during convulsions. Do not touch the dog. The fit should pass eventually, and the dog will appear to 'return to normal'. Although highly distressing for owners, epileptic attacks in dogs can range considerably in how often or how violently they occur. If these attacks start to happen frequently in your dog, consult your vet about possible drug therapy for the condition, or the likelihood that it might have a brain tumour or other illness causing the convulsions.

Traffic accident

Your dog's collapse might have been due to a **traffic accident**, if it had been out in the road. Over and above possibly sustaining internal injuries, your dog is likely to be suffering from severe shock. This means it needs **urgent veterinary treatment**. Do not lift your dog up because it might have neck or spine injuries. Instead, with help, try to slide it gently on to a big board or on to a blanket. If you suspect, in its fear or pain, that the dog might be aggressive, then try to tie its mouth shut with something soft and comfortable - e.g. a tie or long thin sock. Do not make this improvised 'muzzle' too tight, and it may be best not to put it on at all if the dog is very weak and having obvious trouble breathing.

Once you have slid the dog onto a board or blanket, get it out to your car - or hopefully some other kind volunteer's car if you don't have one - and place it on the back seat, moving it out of position as little as possible. If you can, also phone ahead to the vet to let him or her know that you are on your way with an emergency case.

Vestibular syndrome or 'stroke'

If you have an older dog, it might have collapsed due to **vestibular syndrome** or a 'stroke'. It may also have a pronounced head tilt, seem 'giddy', and its eyes might be moving back and forward rapidly from side to side - a syndrome known as **'nystagmus'**.

Keep the dog warm and quiet, and on one level - e.g. nowhere where it can fall down steps or stairs. Dogs can often make a good recovery from such attacks - depending on their severity - over ensuing days, though steroid treatment from a vet often helps this. If your dog is vomiting excessively and lengthily due to the nausea caused by an attack like this, and cannot keep even water down, it could run a risk of dehydrating without veterinary intervention.

Heart problems

Another possibility, should your dog collapse without many of these other symptoms, is that it might have a **heart problem**. It could have a heart murmur, or a heart valve or artery defect, or blood might not be getting pumped quickly enough to its brain, particularly on exertion, for other reasons. Problems like these can often be greatly helped by surgery or medication, so do consult your vet about this as soon as possible.

<u>Problem 2:</u> **Your dog has been suffering lengthy and violent vomiting and diarrhoea**

Your dog may have a severe intestinal infection or other dangerous illness if not properly vaccinated.

If your dog's vaccinations have been kept up to date then some of the more life-threatening diseases like **Parvovirus** or **Leptospirosis** will generally be ruled out. If not, be aware that these illnesses pose a real danger to your dog, particularly if it is very young. With **prompt and intensive treatment**, your vet may be able to save your dog, but some lasting damage from either of these illnesses may remain.

If your dog has got a severe gastric or intestinal infection, rather than above illnesses, but has not been able to keep fluid down of any kind for a sustained period - e.g. three hours or more - then it could become seriously ill through dehydration and shock if not taken to your vet and put on a drip. Obviously the more fluid your dog is losing, through vomiting and diarrhoea, the greater this risk can be. Your vet could also provide anti-biotic treatment, plus treatment to alleviate vomiting and diarrhoea.

If you suspect your dog's symptoms could be due to **poisoning**, see previous section.

<u>Problem 3:</u> **Your dog becomes excessively agitated and restless, pants, and keeps retching like it wants to be sick**

If your dog also keeps looking round at its sides, or you can feel its abdomen is very 'tight' or appearing to 'distend', then it could well have **gastric bloat**.

This really is a truly **dire** veterinary emergency. So much so that if even half an hour passes between the onset of symptoms in a dog, and its arrival at the vet, it can still be too late to save it.

Basically, what is happening is that gas is building up in the dog's stomach which it cannot pass up or down. This causes immense discomfort and distress and explains the dog's attempts to be sick, in order to get rid if the 'discomfort source'. As a result of this gas build-up, the stomach swells and swells to the extent where it can actually revolve or twist round. This twisting or '**torsion**' carries the real danger, because it can start to cut off the blood supply to surrounding tissues and circulatory systems, sometimes with fatal effect.

Bigger dogs, especially from deep-chested breeds, can be particularly prone to this condition. Should you suspect it has arisen in your dog, do not delay. **Get your dog to the vet immediately,** if possible phoning the surgery before you leave, to warn of the arrival of this emergency.

Your dog's recovery will depend on how much gas can be removed from the stomach to prevent it twisting, or, failing that, how quickly the stomach can be returned to its normal position before sufficient harm has been done to internal tissues and organs.

Once this problem has occurred in a dog there is often a danger of it recurring after the first survived bout. For this reason, care must be taken over the feeding routines of such dogs. For more details and advice on this, see the **Appetite** section in the last chapter.

If you suspect the abovementioned symptoms might involve **poisoning** rather than bloat, see **Problem 1.**

<u>Problem 4:</u> **Fairly soon after a heat, your unspayed bitch seems incredibly listless, off her food or nauseous. She also seems to be drinking a lot**

It is possible that she has **Pyometra** - a womb infection common in bitches who have not been spayed. If she also has red eyes with a discharge, and a purulent discharge from her vagina or vulva, this is even more likely.

Your dog needs **urgent veterinary attention**. If she is not given immediate attention for this condition then she could die from the toxicity, dehydration and shock caused as the infection spreads through the body.

If you can see a purulent discharge coming from your dog's vulva, this is usually called '**open** Pyometra'. The prognosis for the dog can be better in such cases, because she is able to expel a lot of toxic matter from the womb. In other cases of '**closed** Pyometra', the cervix restricts the exit of such matter, so the bitch is likely to be even more ill.

Your bitch might need anti-biotics and fluid therapy as well as an ovarohysterectomy (the removal of womb and ovaries) to safeguard her chances of recovery, and to prevent this condition from recurring again.

Over and above these common health emergencies, it's also a good idea to get prompt veterinary attention for the following:

- Any eye injury

- Any paw or pad injury

- Any throat obstruction

- Any suspected broken limbs

- Any infected or broken teeth

- Any deep open cut

- Any dog who has not passed a bowel motion for several days - particularly young dogs who might have swallowed some indigestible object

- Any dog who starts wheezing excessively or shows increasing intolerance to exercise

- Any active dog who suddenly becomes very listless - rather than just 'under the weather'

- Anything that really worries you

What should you feed your dog?

There is a massive range of different commercial dog foods around today; tinned, complete dry food, semi-moist nuggets and so on. And then there are different theories about what sort of 'natural' diet really suits a dog best - e.g. raw bones and vegetables, cooked meat and pasta. No wonder dog owners get confused, and keep worrying about whether they are giving their dog 'the right thing'.

In the main, the 'right' diet is the one your dog thrives well on - and also happens to like. The most superbly - balanced wonder food in the world is not much good for your dog if it doesn't like it.

This apart, it is often said that dogs have few discerning powers when it comes to food, and therefore will quite happily eat the same thing day in, day out. This might be true of dogs who will hoover up anything left in their bowl - or anyone else's bowl for that matter - in seconds. But elsewhere owners might discover that they have 'fussier' eaters, or dogs who much prefer to eat **anything** other than what's put in their dishes.

Fussy eaters

The trouble with this is that owners will then start endlessly switching brands of food around, or adding extra 'tasty' ingredients, to 'tempt them'. So the dogs not only become fussier still, but their diets also become less balanced. A diet of sausages and digestive biscuits, for instance, might be one that your dog adores, but unfortunately it is not providing it with the essential balance of nutrients it needs to stay healthy.

My own feeling is that most dogs appreciate a bit of variety in terms of taste and texture. It seems sad to me that dogs can actually go through their whole lives never experiencing a delicious bit of proper meat, fish or offal, scrambled eggs or a milky bowl of porridge. Human beings don't always eat what they should eat in exactly the right balance all the time, but still manage to get by.

Certainly, properly balanced commercial complete foods for dogs are a boon, and can form the basic mainstay of a good canine diet. But if you occasionally deviate from this with freshly cooked food - e.g., meat or fish with pasta, a sprinkling of wheatgerm or porridge oats and a few cooked vegetables - I'm sure your dog would appreciate it.

Puppies and older dogs need specific care over their diets. The former because they are growing rapidly and the latter because they may need a specific food regime (or 'prescription diet') that takes into account lower activity levels, or conditions affecting the kidneys or heart. For this reason, get professional advice about what to feed dogs in these age groups if you are unsure yourself.

Limit treats

Ultimately what matters is that the food you feed your dog is **healthy** and **suits its digestive system.** In other words, it does **not cause digestive upset,** or **other problems like itchy skin.** Also keep treats to an **absolute minimum.** Treats are not treats if they're available too often. And once you've put a healthy food programme together for your dog - be this complete food, or a balance of complete food and different varieties of fresh food - and know the amounts your dog can eat without putting on weight, then **stick to it** and do not keep chopping and changing around or adding 'tempting extras'.

This is how you get a fussy eater. If your dog won't eat a meal, take it away after fifteen minutes and do not give it another meal until the next proper mealtime. And do not feed your dog snacks or treats instead. When it's hungry enough, and there are no other options, it will eat what you give it. All in all, whatever else they may try to tell you with their crafty, begging eyes, dogs are always healthier, and better off, eating food **designed for dogs.**

Beware the perils of obesity

Obesity is reaching epidemic proportions among domestic dogs (and cats, for that matter). It's happening because they are eating too much of the wrong things - or too much full stop - and not taking enough exercise. The same might be said for us in the Western world, as human obesity has reached the same record levels for much the same reasons.

As outlined earlier in Chapter four, inactive people who eat too much can tend to have dogs stuck in a similar situation. Such people may also be too quick to get the 'treats' jar down for dogs who have not earned treats or simply do not need them, and may feed their dogs a wide range of unsuitable snacks or foods which do not suit their digestive systems, make them fat and harm their teeth.

The greatest gift you can give any dog is the chance to live as long and as healthy a life as possible. By contrast, you take that chance away when you allow it to get fat and inactive, and make it vulnerable to a whole range of unpleasant ailments, **such as diabetes, heart problems, breathing problems, arthritis and painful joint calluses.**

Many owners can get quite touchy about the fact that they have overweight dogs. They take any remark about it as personal criticism, or they feel guilty about causing this state of affairs - and therefore get more defensive. They say all the treats are their way of 'showing love', or they can't resist their dog's 'begging eyes'. In truth, this tends to be mere self-justification for feelings or needs they will indulge in themselves through the dog. And the dog only does what it does because it is allowed or encouraged to do it.

If you want to be kind to your dog, don't let it get fat. If it does get fat, cut back its food and steadily increase its exercise accordingly to get it back into shape. Most vets can now give you advice about how to do this properly. If for some reason you can't be too active, get a friend, volunteer or local dog walker to help you out with your dog's exercise. Local pet stores and vets often keep details of people prepared to walk dogs for others.

All this may be hard, but so is being a fat dog, especially one that didn't have to be that way. Vets' surgeries are full of inactive and obese dogs on the verge of being 'loved to death'. Please don't let your dog become another one. Give it that chance of a longer, healthier and happier life.

What is 'the right amount of exercise' for your dog?

Exercise is not just vital for your dog's physical health - it's vital for its psychological health, too. Dogs who rarely go out, or don't go out often enough for long enough, can lack social confidence. This is because they do not have sufficient exposure to a wide range of new people, dogs or experiences in order to take them more readily in their stride, and generally hone their 'social skills'.

Dogs who are confined and kept inactive for too long are also more likely to develop more vices or problems within the home through under-stimulation, boredom or frustration. Much like horses will display a range of 'stable vices' - e.g. weaving endlessly back and forward, or biting and chewing their stable doors and fittings - when kept too long in their boxes. And the more naturally active the dog breed, the more likely it is that unused energy will be channelled into less suitable or more destructive pursuits.

Too **much** exercise, on the other hand, or too much exercise of the wrong kind, can be potentially damaging for dogs of certain ages or breeds, or for dogs who are basically less fit. So let us look at how the **mental stimulation / physical exercise balance** should be tailored for dogs according to their age, breed or condition.

Puppies

Young puppies - e.g. up to six months old - primarily have a need for **mental stimulation** through play with others and exploration of the world around them. This develops their co-ordination and cognitive skills, their initiative and appreciation of danger. Post-vaccinations, young puppies also need frequent forays out to encounter new people, dogs, sights, sounds etc. and generally develop their social skills.

What they do not need is vast amounts of intensive exercise involving jumping down off high surfaces, or jumping and twisting and landing awkwardly, or having to brake at speed and suddenly turn around - e.g. when they 'over-run' a toy they were chasing. Nor do they need very long walks. All these things can harm growing joints or put them under severe strain - particularly so with puppies from larger breeds. Some larger breeds' skeletons are not completely 'set' or formed until they are two years old or more, and are thus more vulnerable to strain or harm for a **longer period.**

A maximum of two or three steady walks, mainly on the lead, of no more than 15-20 minutes at a time, and with plenty of rest inbetween, is adequate for most puppies under six months old. From then on, step up the length of walks only gradually if the puppy is coping well.

Do not allow young puppies to **jump out of the back of the car** and on to the ground, or off other high places, until they are at least **nine** or **ten** months old, if not more. If they're allowed to do this day in day out it can severely jar their joints. Instead, carry them down out of the car or off high surfaces or walls. If you have a very big puppy, let it ease itself down slowly with your help, instead of carrying it, if carrying it is a problem for you.

Juveniles and working breeds

Young adult dogs, or juveniles, are obviously going to need more exercise than very young, or much older ones. Likewise, dogs from **active or 'working breeds'** - i.e. dogs bred to have high levels of energy and stamina - are also going to require a lot more than the occasional trot round the block.

Be aware, however, that simply **throwing balls about** for such energetic dogs does not make them fit or count as **'proper exercise'**. Dogs only get fit by covering increasingly long distances at a steady speed and not by just charging around after items you throw.

Endless ball throwing is too often 'lazy' exercise for owners who do not want to walk very far. If you genuinely cannot walk very far, you might think such exercise is better than none. However, if your dog is not already quite fit before it begins all these chase and retrieve tasks, it will be at greater risk of injuring itself during the course of them.

This apart, far from 'wearing a dog out', endless throw and chase exercises can get many of them intensely over-stimulated or over-excited. This means that when they stop them, or come home after them, they can be even more manic and boisterous, rather than 'more tired'.

Dogs from energetic breeds - e.g. **Springer spaniels, Border collies, Dalmatians, Boxers, Dobermanns, lurchers, many hounds and terriers and crosses of all these varieties** - tend only to get properly 'tired' with sufficient regular distance work. Others from some working breeds will only truly 'calm down' when physical distance work is balanced with adequate **mental stimulation**, both inside and out of the home.

Usually these are dogs whose original or natural work involved high levels of mental concentration and use of initiative to 'solve problems'. Border collies and other herding breeds are classic examples of this. Dogs like these have such a high desire to use their brains that if you do not fulfil this need they will find other outlets for their mental energies that could be more destructive or annoying.

A daily programme

If I were to devise a daily programme of physical / mental exercise to suit adult dogs like this, and keep them on a relatively 'even keel', it would be roughly along these lines:

- **A minimum of two separate hour-long walks a day, morning and evening. The exercise should be free-running and mostly off the lead - except near roads or other hazards.**

- **Throughout the walks, stop roughly every 15 or 20 minutes and give your dog some training exercises to do - e.g. basic heelwork, sit and stay, retrieve items back to you. Also get the dog, a few times, to find a hidden ball, treat or other object through its own initiative, exploration and sense of smell.**

- Keep these training sessions short - i.e. no more than four or five minutes at a time. Every time your dog does something right, or well, give it a thrilling run around with its ball or other throw toy. By this stage its joints should be warmed up. If you have a dog you are trying to discourage from chasing things, in general, have a game with its tug toy instead.

- Continue your walk, and then repeat all this 15 or 20 minutes later.

- End your walk with mental work - e.g. a down and stay for a minute or two, plus a couple of searches for a hidden object. This time do not get out the throw or tug toy. Instead get your dog to sit quietly for a moment or two while you stroke it gently, praise it and generally 'wind it down'. Make your way home at a quiet, steady pace.

Naturally the 'exertion' content of this programme would have to be modified for much older, very young or generally less fit dogs. The benefit of programmes like this is that they constantly challenge a dog's mind as well as its body, keeping it more 'balanced' mentally. They will also improve its overall training. By keeping training sessions short and always succeeded by thrilling games with a toy, your dog will also associate training with fun and generally having a good time with you.

Your active juvenile or young adult dog could additionally benefit from taking up a pursuit like **Flyball, Agility, Working Trials or Obedience** (see next chapter) to keep it mentally as well as physically active long-term.

Other 'puzzles' and mental pursuits

Dogs with high needs for mental stimulation can also be more 'wound down' at home with **exercises that challenge their brains.** These could involve looking for hidden food or toys in the house or garden, or getting a ball out of a sealed box with just a big enough gap in it to let the ball out. Or getting a treat out through the neck of a big empty plastic water bottle.

My own Border collie gets quite exhausted doing **'object differentiation'** exercises. These involve putting three familiar objects - e.g. a ball, activity cube and squeaky toy - around four or five feet in front of her and getting her to pick and retrieve the right one, on command, for a reward. The objects are well spaced out, and called for in a different order each time to keep her guessing.

With time and ingenuity you can devise many different 'puzzles' along these lines. If your dog was born with a first-class brain, why not let it use it to the full?

Middle-aged dogs

Dogs who are middle-aged may still be able to cope with a degree of steady distance work, unless they are particularly unfit or overweight - in which case, distance should only be increased very gradually as and when they are able to tolerate it.

Unless you have a very fit middle-aged dog, too much ball-chasing or excessive jumping / twisting exercises can take a toll on older joints and muscles - particularly if you do not give the dog's joints and muscles sufficient time to 'warm up' (i.e. with distance work) before commencing such exertions. Generally I would not advise intense bouts of exercise involving jumping / twisting and suddenly 'braking' for anything but the fittest and leanest of dogs.

As long as there are no physical reasons - e.g. heart problems, arthritis, other joint complaints - making lengthy walking a trial for them, steady distance work will keep a middle-aged dog fit. And the fitter it keeps in middle age, the more likely it is to stay healthier and in better overall shape when it gets older. Do not imagine that just because your dog is middle-aged it has to suddenly 'take things easy'. The time to 'take things easy' is only as and when your dog seems less able to cope with the exercise you are giving it.

In middle age your dog will still benefit from adequate amounts of **mental stimulation**, particularly if it is of a breed or type - previously mentioned - with a high need to use its brain. Even if it isn't, as outlined below, the older a dog gets, the more mental stimulation it needs, rather than less, to stay happy.

Older dogs

Owners of older dogs - and particularly owners who have had these dogs since they were young - **do not always realise when they are pushing their dogs too far** in terms of exercise. Maybe it's because they find it hard to accept that their dog is getting old, or because they fail to see the signs of a dog pushing itself to near exhaustion to keep up with them.

If there is one thing I would implore owners of any dog not to do - and owners of older dogs in particular - it is to subject them to any form of 'forced exercise'. Whether this means making a dog run after you, or alongside you, on a bike, or expecting an older dog to accompany you on a hearty four mile jog or run, just because it did this happily when it was younger.

Day in, day out, you can see this sort of thing happening - owners selfishly 'doing their own thing' while some gasping animal is struggling desperately to catch them up. This sort of regime can be **absolute torture** for many dogs. As pack animals with total dependence on you, dogs can be more likely to collapse dead, or with total exhaustion, rather than allow themselves to get left behind. Older dogs and / or less fit dogs need you to go at their pace rather than the other way around, so please give them that basic consideration.

Psychological stimulation

In the main, as dogs get older they tend to benefit more from three or four pretty short walks or 'potters' each day, rather than one or two very long ones. These walks, moreover, are important for their psychological as well as physical health, in terms of the general stimulation they can provide.

Because their faculties are often fading, and they cannot be as active as they once were, **mental stimulation** becomes even more vital for dogs when they get older. New toys, new sights, experiences and smells - all these things are crucial to keep an older dog happier and more alert. By contrast, an older brain that is never regularly stimulated and challenged is more likely to go into quicker and steeper decline.

Do not let your old dog 'rot away' through being mentally bored to death. Keep it involved in all your household activities - even simple little errands out in the car - and give it plenty of trips out to new or interesting places, even if these trips don't last long. The difference between a dog kept 'mentally young' and one allowed to 'rot' in old age can really be quite remarkable in terms of overall health and morale.

Please note that all the above advice on exercise **can only be a basic guide.** If you have any concerns at all about how well your own individual dog can tolerate different levels of exercise, do consult your vet. Also consult him or her should your dog ever show a sudden intolerance - e.g. wheezing, breathlessness - to exercise when out, or if your dog displays repeated lameness or discomfort of any kind after exercise.

This apart, now that we have covered basics about health and exercise, let us move on - in the next chapter - to all the more fun things you can do, activity-wise, with your rescue dog.

Chapter Ten

What Can I Do With My Dog? Agility To Flyball, Obedience Competitions To 'Fun' Dog Shows - The Wealth Of Sociable And Enjoyable Activities You And Your Rescue Dog Can Get Involved In

Early days with rescue dogs, as highlighted before in this book, are all about 'bonding'. They are less about placing unnecessary demands on a new dog in a new home, and more about establishing the trust and mutual respect that are vital foundations for any good relationship.

In Chapter six we looked at how important it was to get this 'good relationship' in place before beginning formal training, and also at how this might be achieved. Now let us suppose that you are ready to 'move on' with your dog. You feel you have 'bonded' to quite a degree and would like to know what more - apart from going to training classes - you and your dog could do together to have fun, or make new friends, be these canine or human.

Dogs and owners are fortunate today to have a wealth of different activities they can take part in - be this competitively, or just for fun. At the back of this book we will tell you who to contact to find out more about individual activities. For now though, let us look at these different activities in more detail. Beginning with:

Agility

Most people get into **Agility** through their local dog training club. Lots of these clubs will either organise Agility classes and events themselves, or will know somebody else in your area who does if they do not.

Increasing numbers of Agility clubs are now cropping up across the country, because the activity can be such fun for owners and their dogs alike. Basically Agility is a sort of 'show jumping' and 'assault' course for dogs, with owners acting as their 'guides'. Naturally the quicker and more accurately the two of you can complete the laid out course of obstacles, against the clock, the more likely it is that you will win.

Obstacles include hurdles (much like horse show jumps - only a maximum of 2ft 6 in high), collapsible tunnels, hoops, 'weaving poles', see-saws and 'A' frames. The latter are basically steep two-sided ramps that your dog must go up and down.

When Agility is done well it can look incredibly easy. But do not be fooled. It can take years for top Agility competitors to train their dogs to a high standard in the sport. This apart, the quality of a dog's relationship with its owner, and ability to interpret his or her directions at speed, can be severely put to the test. The sport not only calls for fit dogs - it calls for fit owners as well. Because of the physical demands of Agility on dogs, and the strain the activity could put on younger dogs' joints, usually they have to be over 18 months old to take part.

The more you study or take part in Agility, the more you will realise how much it calls for good basic levels of obedience from dogs, and anticipation of owners' commands, as well as fitness and athleticism. There is no point in having the fastest and most athletic dog in the ring if it overshoots obstacles or misses proper 'contact points' at the bottom of them - because you will only lose marks.

If you have a very active, agile dog, however, and one who'd love the challenge of something like this, why not give it a go? Even if you never get that far up the competition ladder, at least you can still have a great time and meet a lot of other owners and dogs.

Flyball

Many people move on to **Flyball** from Agility, again via a local training club. Flyball is essentially a relay event. Teams of dogs, one after the other, must clear a series of hurdles ending with a flyball box. This box has a special pedal that the dogs must push to release a ball. Once it is released they must catch and it come back home over the hurdles with the ball in their mouths. Naturally the team who completes all this properly in the fastest time wins.

Again, as with Agility, levels of overall fitness and obedience in your dog will have to be worked on before you can do well in Flyball. At any dog show, however, the event is a massive crowd - puller, because of the fun everybody seems to be having - the crowd in particular when some dog inevitably goes off course, or decides that the quickest way home is not over hurdles.

Obedience

Obedience, in essence, highlights not only your level of control over your dog, but also how well you are able to communicate with it. In other words - as with Agility and many other canine / human pursuits - it shows how well you and your dog can work together as a team.

For most people, Obedience as a pursuit tends to begin at local dog training classes. They start with teaching their dogs basic exercises - like sit, down and recall - and then progress on to increasingly more ambitious things, as well as greater accuracy and reliability in their dogs' responses to commands. The beauty of Obedience is that you can do it competitively, or just at home and in training classes and the results, if it's taught well, can be the same - i.e. a well-trained dog who is a delight to own.

At its highest competitive level, Obedience - in terms of accuracy and elegance - can be rather like 'dressage' for dogs, as handlers display faultless heelwork, or can command their dogs into a variety of different positions from some distance away.

It takes years of dedication and skill, however, to get a dog to top Championship (Class C) level in Obedience. And your sights may be set a little lower - maybe on a less formal competition at an Exemption Dog Show in your area (see later), to illustrate things you and your dog have learned together in training classes.

More and more local 'fun' dog shows are putting on Obedience competition classes now, and these often attract big entries. Within these classes, you will typically have to display accurate heelwork - sometimes both on and off the lead - plus good recalls, sit-stays and down-stays and retrieve work. All your 'sits' and 'finishes' of exercises will also have to pretty precise and straight or you will lose marks.

Needless to say, within a competitive situation, all this can be much harder to achieve faultlessly than it sounds. Owners naturally get nervous, and there can many surrounding distractions, all of which might make dogs react less reliably than in training. As with all such things, however, practise makes perfect - and you could soon find yourself getting quite addicted to the pursuit.

Should it be of interest, The Kennel Club also run something called **The Good Citizen Dog Test Scheme**. This comprises a series of progressively more difficult tests - bronze, silver and gold - designed to illustrate how well owners can handle and control their dogs. Exercises range from basic recall and 'stays' to more complex obedience tasks. The bronze test should be passable for many pet owners, with a bit of prior work and training - and if you do complete it successfully you will get an official certificate and rosette. You will also feel a great sense of achievement. More details on this scheme at the end of the book.

Exemption or 'fun' dog shows

The 'fun' in **Exemption Dog Shows** stems from them being far less formal events than others run merely for pedigree dogs by The Kennel Club. As such, they are 'exempt' from many of the normal formalities and restrictions governing KC-run shows, including the stipulation that your dog has to be a registered pedigree to take part.

With the exception of distinct 'breed classes' at Exemption Shows, your dog can take part in all other classes at these events even if it isn't a pedigree variety. Among these other classes will be popular 'novelty' ones - e.g. the dog in best condition, the prettiest bitch, or even the 'dog with the waggiest tail' or 'most appealing eyes'. Most Exemption Shows also have special 'rescued or rehomed' classes, giving you a chance to tell your dog's story and put it into the spotlight. Many can also give you your first taste of working your dog in a fairly informal Obedience competition.

All in all, apart from raising money for charity, these shows can be a wonderful day out. And many owners find that once they go to one or two of them locally and actually win something - however minor - they become absolutely hooked. As with all competitive events listed in this chapter, we'll be giving you details of where to find 'fun' dog shows at the end of this book in the **Advice** section.

Working trials

Working Trials are often judged to be about the toughest test of owner / dog competence, training and communication. They take part in open country, over one day or several days and consist of owners and dogs attempting to achieve progressively difficult 'stakes' - or levels of expertise in terms of training and performance. Each 'stake' consists of exercises in Control, Agility and Nosework which get steadily more difficult as you move up from one to another.

You begin with the **Companion Dog stake (CD)**, then progress on to **Utility Dog (UD)**, then **Working Dog (WD)**, then **Tracking Dog (TD)** and finally **Patrol Dog (PD)**.

Needless to say, the level of skill required for these events can only be achieved through prior formal training elsewhere, usually beginning with a local training club before approaching your nearest Working Trials Society for more guidance (see back of book). They are definitely not events for complete novices in terms of dog training. But if you're truly ambitious about what you and your dog might achieve together, why not go along to a few Working Trials to see what might be required?

Other events and considerations

Do be aware that if you **do not own a pedigree dog registered with The Kennel Club**, it will have to be put on to **The Kennel Club's Working Trial and Obedience Register** to take part in many of the competitive events previously outlined - unless these events, like 'fun' shows, are run at a very informal level.

Apart from all these widespread competitive activities for dogs, there are often other things like **sponsored dog walks**, **dog training workshops** and general **canine fun days** being organised around the country throughout the year. For more details on all of the above, see the end of this book.

Last points on competition

A last word of advice on this whole 'competition' subject might not go amiss. So often when things go wrong between owners and dogs in competition classes the dogs get blamed. It is, however, **nearly always** the owner or handler's fault in some way. Either commands weren't made clear enough, or weren't taught with enough accuracy and enjoyment, or the owner was confusing the dog or impeding its movement in some way. **Or maybe the dog just didn't like the pressures or atmosphere of competitions, full stop.**

Do bear this in mind. Also bear in mind that the moment you start looking to blame your dog for something that went wrong in a competition, rather than take full - or at least joint - responsibility for it, you stop being a **team**, and become something else that will never work together quite so well.

Chapter Eleven

*And Finally - Last Thoughts On Rescue Dogs, Plus
Where To Go For Further Advice*

(with apologies to E.H.Shepard)

Throughout this book I hope you have found advice that has been of help to you, or which has better explained behaviour in your dog that was worrying you or giving you problems. Rescue dogs, at times, can be pretty difficult animals to live with. Not just because - like all dogs - they'll have inherently different habits or priorities to us, which can clash head on with our own desires, but also because they will often carry 'mental scars' which need time to heal, or they will not have been taught the essential 'right' things at the right period in their lives.

In dealing with such dogs, however, it shouldn't be forgotten how difficult they can also find living with us at such close quarters. With rescue dogs, as with all dogs, when we fail to accept their right to be 'different', or have 'problems', and continually try to thwart, repress or punish behaviour in them which they find natural or instinctive as a species, then this makes for very insecure, frustrated or unhappy animals.

The secret of living in greater harmony with any dog is to understand more about what makes it 'tick' and to recognise what its behaviour is trying to tell you about its feelings. A lot of rescue dogs can spend months or years of their lives trying to express fear, insecurity, stress or unhappiness through their behaviour, only to have these 'symptoms' disregarded or punished as a 'nuisance' by former owners. Again, long-term, this can cause damage which will take time and patience to overcome or reverse.

Not all rescue dogs will be 'victims' whose problems will only be solved through greater sympathy and indulgence, and through believing this some owners can rapidly find themselves 'out of their depth' - especially when they apply the wrong approach to the wrong dog. Some dogs in rescue only ended up there not because they were 'misunderstood', but because their characters and / or overall behaviour were just too forceful or wayward for previous owners to deal with. Dogs like this often need levels of firm and consistent handling and control that not everyone finds it easy to accomplish, especially if they are not very experienced with dogs.

Not all rescue dogs will have 'problems'. Or sometimes what one owner may deem to be a 'problem' in a rescue dog will not be classified as such by another. The ability of owners to tolerate, or not tolerate, many different kinds of dog behaviour can vary considerably, and is often the key to why one household can rehome a particular dog so successfully when another could not.

As long as people continue to give dogs' needs and future welfare such little regard before acquiring them, or letting them breed, or are able to see owning a dog as a simple 'right' rather than a privilege carrying set responsibilities, it's hard to imagine an era when rescue dogs won't be around in large numbers. The ability of human irresponsibility to cause upheaval and suffering in many forms, and to many different creatures - including our own kind - is a sad but seemingly inescapable fact of life.

Ultimately, I think that people who rescue dogs know they cannot change the world, but what they can do is make a difference to just one unwanted animal, stripped of any power to determine its own fate. This in itself is all the justification they need for doing it. I hope that you can make a difference to one abandoned dog's future and that, with enough patience, persistence and understanding, you will subsequently find it one of best things you have ever done in your life.

Further Advice and Useful Contacts

Rescue centres

The following rescue organisations include those belonging to The Association of British Dogs' (& Cats') Homes. Many have different adoption centres across the country:

BATTERSEA DOGS' HOME
4 Battersea Park Road
London
SW8 4AA
Tel: 0207 622 3626

THE BIRMINGHAM DOGS HOME
New Bartholomew Street
Digbeth
Birmingham
B5 5QS
Tel: 0121 643 5211

THE BLUE CROSS
Shilton Road,
Burford
Oxon
OX18 4PF
Tel: 01993 822651

CHELTENHAM ANIMAL CENTRE
Gordner's Lane
Off Swindon Road
Cheltenham
Glos
GL51 9JW
Tel: 01242 523521

EDINBURGH DOG & CAT HOME
26 Seafield Road East
Portobello
Edinburgh
EH15 1EH
Tel: 0131 669 5331

MANCHESTER DOGS HOME
Crofters House
Moss Brook Road
Off Church Lane
Harpurhey
Manchester
M9 5PG
Tel: 0161 205 2874

NATIONAL ANIMAL WELFARE TRUST
Tylers Way
Watford By Pass
Watford
Herts
WD2 8HQ
Tel: 0208 950 0177

NATIONAL CANINE DEFENCE LEAGUE
17 Wakley Street
London EC1V 7LT
Tel: 0207 837 0006

NEWCASTLE UPON TYNE DOG & CAT SHELTER
Benton North Farm
Benton Lane
Benton
Newcastle
0191 2322878 / 215 0435

PLYMOUTH DISTRICT DOG & CAT HOME
Gables Farm
204 Merafield Road
Plymouth
PL7 1UQ
Tel: 01752 331602

RSPCA
The Causeway
Horsham
West Sussex
RH12 1HQ
01403 264181

SCOTTISH SPCA
Braehead Mains
603 Queensferry Road
Edinburgh
EH4 6EA
Tel: 0131 339 0222

WOOD GREEN ANIMAL SHELTERS
Heydon
Royston
Herts
SG8 8PN
Tel: 01763 838329

For details of **rescue agencies dealing with specific pedigree breeds** contact:

THE KENNEL CLUB
1-5 Clarges Street
London W1 8AB
Tel: 0870 6066750

Training & Behavioural Advice

ASSOCIATION OF PET BEHAVIOUR COUNSELLORS
PO Box 46
Worcester
WR8 9YS
Tel: 01386 751151

THE UK REGISTRY OF CANINE BEHAVIOURISTS
53A Oxford Gardens
London W10 5UJ
Enquiries: 0207 243 0359 day
          0208 969 5670 evening

(Note: your vet can refer you to members of the above organisations. If in doubt about advice sources, it is highly recommended that whomever you choose for training or behavioural guidance belongs to an *established professional body* recognised by other canine professionals - e.g. vets, rescue centre managers - for the competence and experience of their members).

THE ASSOCIATION OF PET DOG TRAINERS
Peacocks Farm
North Chapel
Petworth
W. Sussex
GU28 9JB
(Send a sae for details of APDT trainers / training clubs in your area)

More Training & Competitive Events

For details of more local training clubs and how to get involved in:

- Agility
- Flyball
- Obedience
- Working Trials
- Showing
- The Good Citizen Dog Test Scheme

Contact: **The Kennel Club**, details under **Rescue**. For **Exemption Shows** see **Dog Publications**. Also be aware that The Kennel Club produce a very helpful book, *Dog Days Out!*, outlining all you need to know about different kinds of competition with your dog. Details as above. Or you can visit their website: **www.the-kennel-club.org.uk**

Veterinary Advice

THE BRITISH VETERINARY ASSOCIATION
7 Mansfield Street
London
W1M OAT
Tel: 0207 636 6541

BRITISH SMALL ANIMAL VETERINARY ASSOCIATION
Woodrow House
1 Telford Way
Waterwells Business Park
Quedgeley
Glos
GL2 4AB
Tel: 01452 726700

Homeopathic Remedies

THE BRITISH HOMEOPATHIC ASSOCIATION
27A Devonshire Street
London W1N 1RJ
Tel: 0207 935 2163

THE BRITISH ASSOCIATION OF HOMEOPATHIC VETERINARY SURGEONS
Tel: 01367 718115

THE DR. BACH CENTRE
Mount Vernon
Sotwell
Wallingford
Oxon
OX10 OPZ
Tel: 01491 834678

Older Pet Owners

Should you be an older pet owner, or one suffering from a serious illness, and have concerns about the future welfare of your animals contact:

THE CINNAMON TRUST
Foundry House
Foundry Square
Hayle
Cornwall
TR27 4HH
Tel: 01736 757900
(See end of **Chapter four** for more details on this charity)

Dog Publications & News

DOGS TODAY (MONTHLY)
Pet Subjects Ltd
Pankhurst Farm
Bagshot Road
West End
Nr. Woking
Surrey
GU24 9QR
Tel: 01276 858880

YOUR DOG (MONTHLY)
Roebuck House
33 Broad Street
Stamford
Lincs
PE9 1RB
Tel: 01780 766199

DOG WORLD (WEEKLY)
Somerfield House
Wotton Road
Ashford
Kent
TN23 6LW
Tel: 01233 621877

OUR DOGS (WEEKLY)
5 Oxford Road
Station Approach
Manchester
M60 1SX
Tel: 0161 2281984

The above can keep you up-to-date with canine news and events, and also give details of local **Exemption Shows** in your area.

Index

Index

Index

Index

Index